# Rest Areas & Welcome Centers

## Along US Interstates

Published by:
Roundabout Publications
PO Box 19235
Lenexa, KS 66285

800-455-2207

www.TravelBooksUSA.com

## Please Note

Every effort has been made to make this book as complete and as accurate as possible. However, there may be mistakes both typographical and in content. Therefore, this text should be used as a general guide to Rest Areas and Welcome Centers. Although we regret any inconvenience caused by inaccurate information, the author and Roundabout Publications shall have neither liability nor responsibility to any person or entity with respect to any loss or damage caused, or alleged to be caused, directly or indirectly by the information contained in this book.

 Published by: Roundabout Publications, P.O. Box 19235, Lenexa, Kansas 66285. Phone: 800-455-2207. Internet: www.travelbooksusa.com

**Library of Congress Control Number:** 2002094434

**ISBN:** 1-885464-05-3

**Publisher's Cataloging-in-Publications**
*(Provided by Quality Books, Inc.)*

Herow, William C.
Rest areas & welcome centers along US interstates / [William C. Herow]. -- 2nd ed.
p. cm.
LCCN: 2002094434
ISBN: 1-885464-05-3

1. Roadside rest areas--United States--Guidebooks.
2. Automobile travel--United States--Guidebooks.
I. Title

GV1024.H47 2003 388.3'12
QBI02-200712

# Contents

# Introduction

Each year millions of travelers take to America's Interstate highways to get them where they want to go. Some are on vacation, others are traveling on business, and some are full-time RVers enjoying retirement on the road. Whatever the reason, it is nice to know in advance where the services available to travelers are. That's what this book is about.

### Rest Areas

Rest areas not only provide relief when nature calls but are also places for weary travelers to rest a while. They also provide the opportunity for walking the family pet or purchasing a soft drink and snack from a vending machine. Some rest areas, particularly along toll highways, sell gasoline or fast food. These are usually referred to as service areas.

In addition to rest areas and welcome centers (where a traveler can obtain information about the state they are entering), this book also identifies the location of discount stores and travel centers.

### Discount Stores

Discount stores like Wal-Mart or K-Mart are, obviously, a good place to buy items that were forgotten and not packed or to restock your supplies. Some of the larger stores sell groceries or have a fast food restaurant inside. And for RVers, some stores allow free overnight parking. Check with the management before assuming overnight parking is allowed, some RVers have been asked to leave in the middle of the night!

### Travel Centers

Travel centers are usually large establishments that provide a host of services. It used to be that these areas catered to truck drivers. Now they offer services not only to truckers but to all travelers. Most have fast food restaurants or home-style restaurants. They offer gasoline and diesel fuel, LP gas, and dump stations for RVers. Travelers can also shop for convenience items, soft drinks, and snacks. And some also allow free overnight parking.

### About this Book

*Rest Areas and Welcome Centers* contains a lot of useful information. Knowing how to read this book will enhance the value of the information it contains.

The book is arranged alphabetically by state with Interstates listed from lowest to highest. Each state begins with information about the rules for using a rest area, road condition and emergency phone numbers, and tourism contacts. Each Interstate is introduced with a brief description, including its length and general direction of travel within the state. That is followed by the **Rest Areas and Welcome Centers Chart** (*see Figure 1*). Next is the **Discount Stores and Travel Centers Chart** (*see Figure 2*).

Often you will find in the *rest area usage rules* that there is no limit to length of stay but that overnight parking or camping is not permitted. What this means, generally, is that although there is no time limit to your stay, you should not intentionally set up camp for the night. That is to say that RVers should not put out their awning and set up lawn chairs. Travelers in automobiles should not pitch a tent. Rest areas are not places for free overnight camping but rather a place for weary travelers to rest.

The **Rest Areas and Welcome Centers Chart** (*Figure 1*) identifies the location of each area by their mile marker and the facilities available. Among the facilities are restrooms, phones, picnic tables, vending machines, RV dump stations, and pet walk areas. The chart also indicates

**Figure 1**

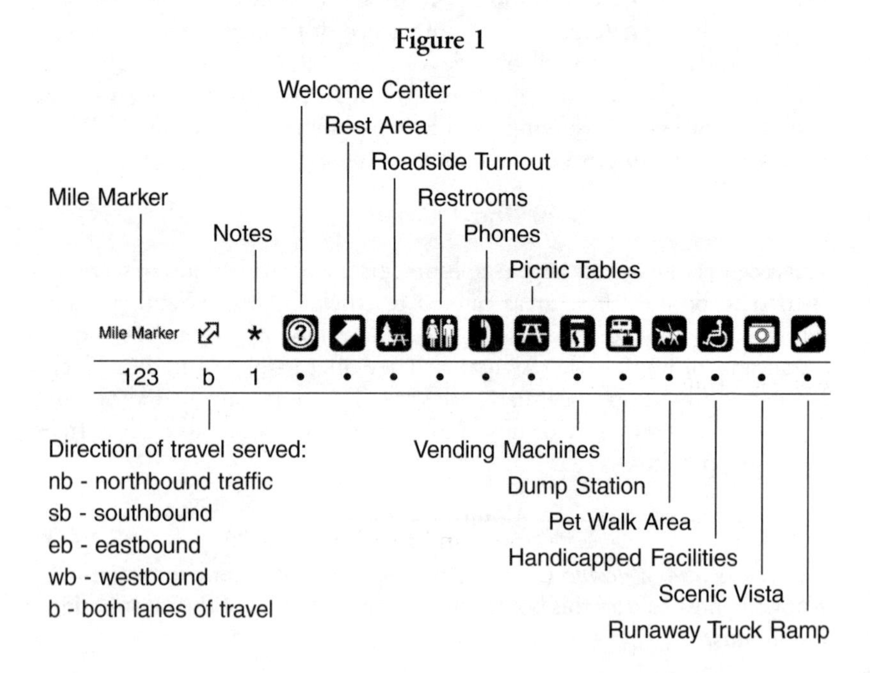

whether some facilities are handicapped accessible. It also shows scenic vista areas and the location of runaway truck ramps.

The **Discount Stores and Travel Centers Chart** (*Figure 2*) identifies the location of these establishments that are along the Interstate. Included are Wal-Mart, Sam's Club, K-Mart, and Target stores. Selected travel centers include AmBest, Flying J, Love's, Petro, Pilot, Speedway, Travel Centers of America, and Williams.

**Figure 2**

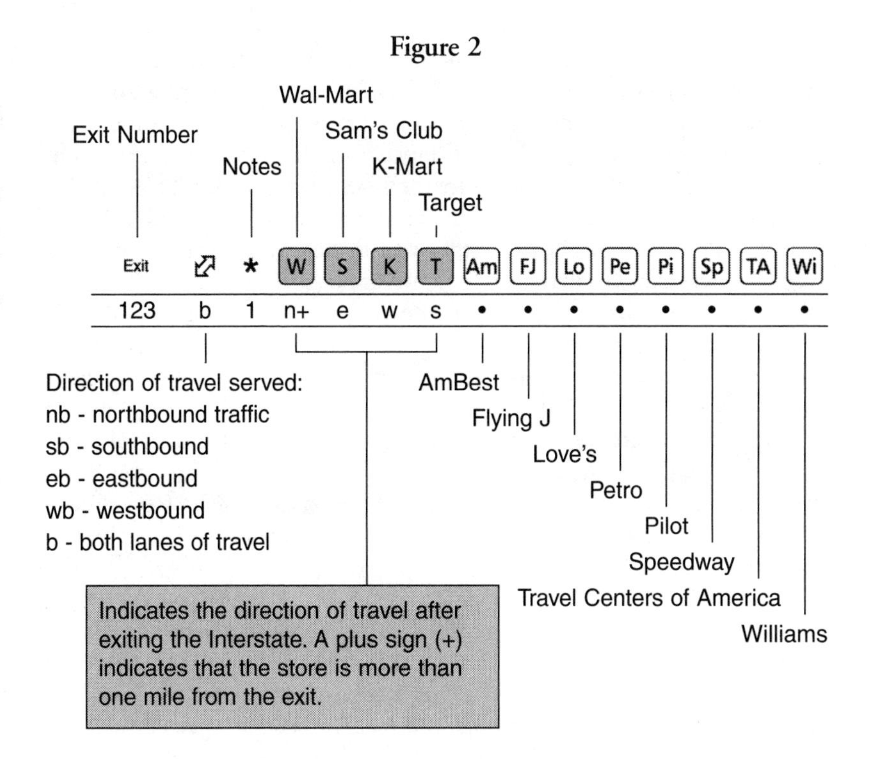


It is important to note that your direction of travel determines how you read the charts. If you are traveling south or west, read down the chart. If you are traveling north or east, read up the chart. As a reminder of this, you'll find directional arrows to the left of the charts.

## Mile Markers and Exit Numbers

Having a basic understanding of mile markers and exit numbers will help you better use this book.

Mile markers, or mileposts as they are also known, are the little vertical green signs on the edge of highways. They are placed at one-mile intervals. Mile marker numbering begins at the most southerly or westerly point in a state. For example, if you enter Colorado from New Mexico, mile markers will increase as you travel north through Colorado. Likewise if you were to enter Colorado from Utah, mile markers would increase as you traveled east through Colorado. California is the only state that does not use mile markers. Instead they use a Post Mile system with numbering beginning and ending at county lines.

Interstate exit numbers are determined by one of two methods. The first, and most widely used, is based on the *mile marker system*. Using this method, the first exit number on an Interstate as you travel south to north or west to east is determined by its distance from the state line. For example, if an exit is located between mile markers 4 and 5, it is numbered as Exit #4. The next exit, if located at mile marker 8.7, would be numbered as Exit #8. Thus you would know that you must travel another 4 miles to reach the next exit. Using this method of exit numbering helps to determine the location and distance to a desired exit.

The second method of numbering Interstate exits is the *consecutive numbering system*, which means Interstate exit numbers begin at the most southerly or westerly point and increase consecutively as you travel north or east. Using this method, the first exit on an Interstate as you travel south to north or west to east is Exit #1. Each exit thereafter increases consecutively as #2, #3, #4, and so on. Few states use this method of numbering Interstate exits.

As mentioned above, California does not use mile markers nor does it indicate exits with a number. This is changing, however. In January of 2002, California began erecting signs displaying exit numbers based on the mile marker system. Completion of this project is expected in 2005. The exit numbers and mile marker numbers used in this book for California are based on the new proposed numbers that California has assigned. Notes at the bottom of each chart will help you identify Interstate exits in California until the re-numbering project is completed.

**Notes**

It is our hope that you find this book an invaluable aid as you travel along America's Interstate highways. If you discover errors or additions that need to be made to this book, please let us know. We always welcome comments or suggestions for improvement.

## Clear Channel Radio Stations

Following is a list of Clear Channel Radio Stations, some of the most powerful (50 kilowatt power) stations in the United States. The stations are designated to operate over an extended area and frequently can be heard for hundreds of miles. The station's signals are generally protected for a distance of up to 750 miles at night.

**Alaska**

Anchorage .............. KENI 650
Anchorage ............ KFQD 750
Fairbanks ............. KCBF 820

**Arizona**

Window Rock ....... KTNN 660

**Arkansas**

Little Rock ............. KAAY 1090

**California**

Fresno .................. KFRE 940
Los Angeles ............. KFI 640
Los Angeles ......... KTNQ 1020
Los Angeles ............ KNX 1070
Sacramento .......... KHTK 1140
Sacramento ........... KFBK 1530
San Francisco ...... KNBR 680
San Francisco ....... KFAX 1100

**Colorado**

Denver ..................... KOA 850

**Connecticut**

Hartford ................. WTIC 1080

**District of Columbia**

Washington ......... WTOP 1500

**Florida**

Miami ..................... WAQI 710
Orlando ............... WQTM 540

**Georgia**

Atlanta .................... WSB 750

**Idaho**

Boise ...................... KBOI 670

**Illinois**

Chicago ............... WSCR 670
Chicago ................. WGN 720
Chicago ............... WBBM 780
Chicago .................. WLS 890
Chicago ............... WMVP 1000

**Indiana**

Fort Wayne ......... WOWO 1190

**Iowa**

Des Moines ........... WHO 1040
Waterloo ................ KXEL 1540

**Kentucky**

Louisville ............. WHAS 840

**Louisiana**

Shreveport .......... KWKH 1130

**Maryland**

Baltimore .............. WBAL 1090

**Massachusetts**

Boston ................. WRKO 680
Boston ..................... WBZ 1030

**Michigan**

Detroit .................... WJR 760

**Minnesota**

Minneapolis ......... WCCO 830
St. Paul ................... KSTP 1500

**Missouri**

Kansas City ............ WHB 810
St. Louis ............... KMOX 1120

**Nebraska**

Lexington .............. KRVN 880
Omaha .................. KFAB 1110

**New Mexico**

Albuquerque ......... KKOB 770

**New York**

Buffalo ................ WWKB 1520
New York .............. WFAN 660
New York ............... WOR 710
New York ............. WABC 770
New York ............. WCBS 880
New York ............. WEVD 1050
New York ............. WBBR 1130
New York ............ WQEW 1560
Rochester ............ WHAM 1180
Schenectady ......... WGY 810

**North Carolina**

Charlotte ................ WBT 1110
Raleigh ................. WPTF 680

**Ohio**

Cincinnati .............. WLW 700
Cincinnati .............. WSAI 1530
Cleveland ............ WTAM 1100
Cleveland ............ WKNR 1220

**Oklahoma**

Oklahoma City .... KOMA 1520
Tulsa ..................... KVOO 1170

**Oregon**

Eugene ................ KPNW 1120
Portland ................... KEX 1190

**Pennsylvania**

Philadelphia ....... WKYW 1060
Philadelphia ........ WPHT 1210
Pittsburgh ............. KDKA 1020

**Tennessee**

Nashville ............... WSM 650
Nashville .............. WLAC 1510

**Texas**

Dallas ................... KRLD 1080
Fort Worth ........... WBAP 820
San Antonio ......... WOAI 1200

**Utah**

Salt Lake City .......... KSL 1160

**Virginia**

Richmond ............. WRVA 1140

**Washington**

Seattle ................... KIRO 710
Seattle ................. KOMO 1000
Seattle .................. KRPM 1090
Spokane ................. KGA 1510

**West Virginia**

Wheeling ............. WWVA 1170

**Wyoming**

Casper ................ KTWO 1030

## Hotel / Motel Toll-free Numbers

Below is a convenient list of toll-free telephone numbers and web sites for selected hotels and motels across the United States.

| Name | Phone | Web Site |
|---|---|---|
| Adams Mark Hotels & Resorts | 800-444-2326 | www.adamsmark.com |
| AmericInn | 800-634-3444 | www.americinn.com |
| AmeriHost Inn | 800-434-5800 | www.amerihostinn.com |
| Baymont Inn & Suites | 877-229-6668 | www.baymontinn.com |
| Best Inn, Suites & Hotels | 800-237-8466 | www.bestinn.com |
| Best Western Hotels | 800-780-7234 | www.bestwestern.com |
| Budget Host | 800-283-4678 | www.budgethost.com |
| Choice International Hotels | 800-424-6423 | www.choicehotels.com |
| Clarion Inn | 800-424-6423 | www.choicehotels.com |
| Comfort Inn & Suites | 800-424-6423 | www.choicehotels.com |
| Country Hearth Inn | 800-848-5767 | www.countryhearth.com |
| Country Inn & Suites | 800-456-4000 | www.countryinns.com |
| Courtyard by Marriott | 800-236-2427 | www.marriott.com |
| Crowne Plaza Hotels & Resorts | 800-227-6963 | www.crowneplaza.com |
| Days Inn | 800-329-7466 | www.daysinn.com |
| DoubleTree Hotel, Suites & Resorts | 800-222-8733 | www.doubletreehotels.com |
| Drury Inn | 800-378-7946 | www.drury-inn.com |
| Econo Lodge | 800-424-6423 | www.choicehotels.com |
| Embassy Suites | 800-362-2779 | www.embassysuites.com |
| Exel Inns | 800-367-3935 | www.exelinns.com |
| Extended StayAmerica | 800-398-7829 | www.extstay.com |
| Fairfield Inn by Marriott | 800-236-2427 | www.marriott.com |
| Fairmont Hotels & Resorts | 800-257-7544 | www.fairmont.com |
| Flag Inn | 800-424-6423 | www.choicehotels.com |
| Great Western Hotels | 800-634-6635 | www.greatwesternhotels.com |
| GuestHouse Inn & Suites | 800-214-8378 | www.guesthouseintl.com |
| Hampton Inn & Suites | 800-426-7866 | www.hamptoninn.com |
| Hawthorne Suites | 800-527-1133 | www.hawthorn.com |
| Hilton Hotels | 800-445-8667 | www.hilton.com |
| Holiday Inn | 800-465-4329 | www.holiday-inn.com |
| Holiday Inn Express | 800-465-4329 | www.hiexpress.com |
| Homewood Suites | 800-445-8667 | www.homewood-suites.com |
| Howard Johnson | 800-446-4656 | www.hojo.com |
| Hyatt Hotels & Resorts | 800-233-1234 | www.hyatt.com |
| Inter-Continental Hotels & Resorts | 800-327-0200 | www.interconti.com |

| Name | Phone | Web Site |
|---|---|---|
| Jameson Inn | 800-525-3766 | www.jamesoninns.com |
| Key West Inn & Suites | 866-253-9937 | www.keywestinn.net |
| LaQuinta Inn | 800-642-4241 | www.laquinta.com |
| Lees Inn & Suites | 800-733-5337 | www.leesinn.com |
| MainStay Suites | 800-424-6423 | www.choicehotels.com |
| Marriott Hotels & Resorts | 800-236-2427 | www.marriott.com |
| Microtel Inn & Suites | 888-771-7171 | www.microtelinn.com |
| Motel 6 | 800-466-8356 | www.motel6.com |
| Omni Hotels | 800-843-6664 | www.omnihotels.com |
| Park Plaza / Inns | 888-201-1801 | www.parkhtls.com |
| Passport Inn | 800-874-7798 | www.bookroomsnow.com |
| Preferred Hotels & Resorts | 800-323-7500 | www.preferredhotels.com |
| Quality Inn, Hotels & Suites | 800-424-6423 | www.choicehotels.com |
| Radisson Hotels | 888-201-1718 | www.radisson.com |
| Ramada Inn | 800-272-6232 | www.ramada.com |
| Red Carpet Inn | 800-874-7798 | www.bookroomsnow.com |
| Red Lion Hotel & Inns | 800-733-5466 | www.redlion.com |
| Red Roof Inn | 800-733-7663 | www.redroof.com |
| Renaissance Hotel | 800-236-2427 | www.marriott.com |
| Residence Inn by Marriott | 800-236-2427 | www.marriott.com |
| Ritz-Carlton Hotel | 800-241-3333 | www.ritzcarlton.com |
| Rodeway Inn | 800-424-6423 | www.choicehotels.com |
| Scottish Inn | 800-874-7798 | www.bookroomsnow.com |
| Sheraton Hotels & Resorts | 888-625-5144 | www.sheraton.com |
| Shilo Inn | 800-222-2244 | www.shiloinns.com |
| Shoney's Inn | 800-552-4667 | www.shoneysinn.com |
| Signature Inn | 800-822-5252 | www.signature-inns.com |
| Silver Cloud Inn & Hotels | 800-551-7207 | www.scinns.com |
| Sleep Inn | 800-424-6423 | www.choicehotels.com |
| Staybridge Suites | 800-238-8000 | www.staybridge.com |
| Super 8 Motel | 800-800-8000 | www.super8.com |
| Swissotels | 800-637-9477 | www.swissotel.com |
| Travelodge | 800-578-7878 | www.travelodge.com |
| Vagabond Inn | 800-522-1555 | www.vagabondinns.com |
| Wellesley Inn | 800-444-8888 | www.wellesleyinnandsuites.com |
| West Coast Hotels | 800-325-4000 | www.westcoasthotels.com |
| Westin Hotels & Resorts | 800-937-8461 | www.westin.com |
| Westmark Hotel | 800-544-0970 | www.westmarkhotels.com |
| Wingate Inn | 800-228-1000 | www.wingateinns.com |
| Wyndham Hotels & Resorts | 877-999-3223 | www.wyndham.com |

## Alabama

**Rest Area Usage:** There is no limit to length of stay, however, no camping or overnight parking is permitted. **Road Conditions:** No central phone number. *Internet*: www.dot.state.al.us **State Police:** *General*, 334-242-4371; *Emergency*, 911 or *47 on cell phone **Tourism Contact:** Alabama Bureau of Tourism & Travel, 401 Adams Ave, Suite 126, Montgomery AL 36104. *Phone*: 800-252-2262 or 334-242-4169. *Internet*: www.touralabama.org

**10** Interstate 10 runs east to west for 67 miles from the Florida state line to the Mississippi state line.

| Mile Marker | | * | | | | | | | | | | | | |
|---|---|---|---|---|---|---|---|---|---|---|---|---|---|---|
| 66 | wb | | • | | | • | • | • | • | • | • | • | | |
| 1 | eb | | • | | | • | • | • | • | • | • | • | | |

E ↕ W

| Exit | | * | W | S | K | T | Am | FJ | Lo | Pe | Pi | Sp | TA | Wi |
|---|---|---|---|---|---|---|---|---|---|---|---|---|---|---|
| 53 | b | | | | | | • | | | | | | | |
| 44 | b | | | | | | | | • | | | | | |
| 35 | b | | s+ | | | | | | | | | | | |
| 17 | b | | n | | | | | | | | | | | |
| 15ab | b | | | | n | | | | | | | | | |
| 13 | b | | | | | | | | | | • | | | |
| 4 | b | | | | | | | | | | | | • | |

**20** Interstate 20 runs east to west for approximately 215 miles from the Georgia state line to the Mississippi state line. A portion of the highway from Birmingham to Mississippi is also I-59.

E ↕ W

| Mile Marker | | * | | | | | | | | | | | | |
|---|---|---|---|---|---|---|---|---|---|---|---|---|---|---|
| 213 | wb | | • | | | • | • | • | • | • | • | • | | |
| 85 | b | 1 | | • | | • | • | • | • | • | • | • | | |
| 39 | wb | 1 | | • | | • | • | • | • | • | • | • | | |
| 38 | eb | 1 | | • | | • | • | • | • | • | • | • | | |
| 0.5 | eb | 1 | • | | | • | • | • | • | • | • | • | | |

Notes: 1) Shared with I-59

| Exit | ↗ | * | W | S | K | T | Am | FJ | Lo | Pe | Pi | Sp | TA | Wi |
|---|---|---|---|---|---|---|---|---|---|---|---|---|---|---|
| 185 | b | | s | | | | | | | | | | | |
| 144 | b | | s | | | | | | | | | | | |
| 133 | b | | s | s | s | | | | | | | | | |
| 132ab | b | | | | s | | | | | | | | | |
| 123 | b | 1 | | | | | | | | | • | | | |
| 118 | b | 2 | s+ | | | | | | | | | | | |
| 108 | b | 1 | s | | | | | | | | | | | |
| 104 | b | 1 | | | | | | • | | | | | | |
| 100 | b | 1 | | | | | | | | • | | | | |
| 77 | b | 1 | | | | | | | | | | | • | |
| 76 | b | 1 | | | | | | | | | • | | | |
| 73 | b | 1 | s | s | | | | | | | | | | |
| 71a | b | 1 | | | s | | | | | | | | | |

E ↕ W

Notes: 1) Shared with I-59; 2) Shared with I-59 / Wal-mart is on Aaron Aronov Dr

**59**

Interstate 59 runs north to south for 242 miles from the Georgia state line to the Mississippi state line. A portion of the highway from Birmingham to Mississippi is also I-20.

| Mile Marker | ↗ | * | ? | | | | | | | | | | | |
|---|---|---|---|---|---|---|---|---|---|---|---|---|---|---|
| 241 | sb | | • | | | • | • | • | • | • | • | • | | |
| 168 | sb | | | • | | • | • | • | • | • | • | • | | |
| 165 | nb | | | • | | • | • | • | • | • | • | • | | |
| 85 | b | 1 | | • | | • | • | • | • | • | • | • | | |
| 39 | sb | 1 | | • | | • | • | • | • | • | • | • | | |
| 38 | nb | 1 | | • | | • | • | • | • | • | • | • | | |
| 0.5 | nb | 1 | • | | | • | • | • | • | • | • | • | | |

N ↕ S

Notes: 1) Shared with I-20

| Exit | ↗ | * | W | S | K | T | Am | FJ | Lo | Pe | Pi | Sp | TA | Wi |
|---|---|---|---|---|---|---|---|---|---|---|---|---|---|---|
| 218 | b | | w | | w | | | | | | | | | |
| 141 | b | | | | w | | | | | | | | | |
| 134 | b | | w | | | | | | | | | | | |
| 123 | b | 1 | | | | | | | | | • | | | |
| 118 | b | 2 | e+ | | | | | | | | | | | |
| 108 | b | 1 | e | | | | | | | | | | | |
| 104 | b | 1 | | | | | | • | | | | | | |
| 100 | b | 1 | | | | | | | | • | | | | |
| 77 | b | 1 | | | | | | | | | | | • | |

N ↕ S

| Exit |  | * | W | S | K | T | Am | FJ | Lo | Pe | Pi | Sp | TA | Wi |
|---|---|---|---|---|---|---|---|---|---|---|---|---|---|---|
| 76 | b | 1 |  |  |  |  |  |  |  |  | • |  |  |  |
| 73 | b | 1 | e | e |  |  |  |  |  |  |  |  |  |  |
| 71a | b | 1 |  |  | e |  |  |  |  |  |  |  |  |  |

Notes: 1) Shared with I-20; 2) Shared with I-20 / Wal-mart is on Aaron Aronov Dr

65

Interstate 65 runs north to south for 367 miles from the Tennessee state line to Interstate 10.

| Mile Marker |  | * |  |  |  |  |  |  |  |  |  |  |  |  |
|---|---|---|---|---|---|---|---|---|---|---|---|---|---|---|
| 364 | sb |  | • |  |  | • | • | • | • | • | • | • |  |  |
| 302 | b |  |  | • |  | • | • | • | • | • | • | • |  |  |
| 213 | b |  |  | • |  | • | • | • | • | • | • | • |  |  |
| 134 | b |  |  | • |  | • | • | • | • | • | • | • |  |  |
| 89 | sb |  |  | • |  | • | • | • | • | • | • | • |  |  |
| 85 | nb |  |  | • |  | • | • | • | • | • | • | • |  |  |

N
S

| Exit |  | * | W | S | K | T | Am | FJ | Lo | Pe | Pi | Sp | TA | Wi |
|---|---|---|---|---|---|---|---|---|---|---|---|---|---|---|
| 351 | b |  | w |  |  |  |  |  |  |  |  |  |  |  |
| 334 | b |  |  |  |  |  |  |  |  |  |  |  |  | • |
| 271 | b |  | e |  |  |  |  |  |  |  |  |  |  |  |
| 264 | b |  |  |  |  |  |  | • |  |  |  |  |  |  |
| 256ab | b |  |  |  | e |  |  |  |  |  |  |  |  |  |
| 255 | b |  | w | w |  |  |  |  |  |  |  |  |  |  |
| 246 | b |  |  |  |  |  |  |  |  |  | • |  |  |  |
| 242 | b |  | w |  |  |  |  |  |  |  |  |  |  |  |
| 231 | b |  | w |  |  |  |  |  |  |  |  |  |  |  |
| 179 | b |  | w |  |  |  |  |  |  |  |  |  |  |  |
| 168 | b |  |  |  |  |  |  |  |  |  |  |  | • |  |
| 130 | b |  | w |  |  |  |  |  |  |  |  |  |  |  |
| 19 | b |  |  |  |  |  |  |  |  |  | • |  |  |  |
| 13 | b |  | e |  |  |  |  |  |  |  |  |  |  |  |
| 3 | b |  | w | w | w |  |  |  |  |  |  |  |  |  |

N
S

85

Interstate 85 runs north to south for 80 miles from the Georgia state line to I-65 in Montgomery.

| Mile Marker |  | * |  |  |  |  |  |  |  |  |  |  |  |  |
|---|---|---|---|---|---|---|---|---|---|---|---|---|---|---|
| 78 | sb |  | • |  |  | • | • | • | • | • | • | • |  |  |

| Mile Marker | Dir | * | Info | Arrow | Trees | Restrooms | Phone | Picnic | Vending | RV | Pets | Handicap | Camera | Truck |
|---|---|---|---|---|---|---|---|---|---|---|---|---|---|---|
| 44 | b | | | • | | • | • | • | • | • | • | • | | |

N ↕ S

| Exit | Dir | * | W | S | K | T | Am | FJ | Lo | Pe | Pi | Sp | TA | Wi |
|---|---|---|---|---|---|---|---|---|---|---|---|---|---|---|
| 79 | b | | e | | | | | | | | | | | |
| 70 | b | | | | | | • | | | | | | | |
| 51 | b | | w | | | | | | | | | | | |
| 22 | b | | | | | | | | | • | | | | |
| 6 | b | | | e | | | | | | | | | | |

# Arizona

**Rest Area Usage:** There is no limit to length of stay. Camping is not allowed but overnight parking is permitted. **Road Conditions:** 888-411-7623 (general) **State Police:** *General*, 602-223-2000; *Emergency*, 911 **Tourism Contact:** Arizona Office of Tourism, 2702 N Third St, Ste 4015, Phoenix AZ 85004. *Phone*: 888-520-3434 or 602-230-7733. *Internet*: www.arizonaguide.com

Interstate 8 runs east to west for about 178 miles from Interstate 10 to the California state line.

| Mile Marker | Dir | * | Info | Arrow | Trees | Restrooms | Phone | Picnic | Vending | RV | Pets | Handicap | Camera | Truck |
|---|---|---|---|---|---|---|---|---|---|---|---|---|---|---|
| 150 | wb | | | | • | | | • | | | | | | |
| 149 | eb | | | | • | | | • | | | | | | |
| 85 | wb | | | • | | • | • | • | • | | • | • | | |
| 84 | eb | | | • | | • | • | • | • | | • | • | | |
| 56 | b | | | • | | • | • | • | • | | • | • | | |
| 22 | b | | | | • | | | | | | | | | |

E ↕ W

| Exit | Dir | * | W | S | K | T | Am | FJ | Lo | Pe | Pi | Sp | TA | Wi |
|---|---|---|---|---|---|---|---|---|---|---|---|---|---|---|
| 115 | b | | | | | | | | • | | | | | |
| 2 | b | | n | n | | | | | | | | | | |

Interstate 10 runs east to west for about 391 miles from the New Mexico state line to the California state line.

E ↕ W

| Mile Marker | ⤢ | * | Info | Arrow | Trees | Restrooms | Phone | Picnic | Vending | Food | Pets | Handicap | Camera | RV |
|---|---|---|---|---|---|---|---|---|---|---|---|---|---|---|
| 389 | b | | | • | | • | • | • | • | | • | • | | |
| 320 | b | | | • | | • | • | • | • | | • | • | | |
| 183 | wb | | | • | | • | • | • | • | | • | • | | |
| 181 | eb | | | • | | • | • | • | • | | • | • | | |
| 86 | b | | | • | | • | • | • | • | | • | | | |
| 52 | b | | | • | | • | • | • | • | | • | • | | |
| 4 | b | | | • | | • | • | • | • | | • | • | | |

E ↕ W

| Exit | ⤢ | * | W | S | K | T | Am | FJ | Lo | Pe | Pi | Sp | TA | Wi |
|---|---|---|---|---|---|---|---|---|---|---|---|---|---|---|
| 340 | b | | | | | | • | | | | | | | |
| 248 | b | | | | n | | | | | | | | | |
| 208 | b | | | | | | | • | | | | | | • |
| 203 | b | | | | | | | | | | | | • | |
| 200 | b | | | | | | | | • | • | • | | | |
| 194 | b | | s+ | | s+ | | | | | | | | | |
| 159 | b | | | n | | s | | | | | | | | |
| 157 | b | | n | | | | | | | | | | | |
| 155 | b | | | | n | | | | | | | | | |
| 146 | b | | | | s | | | | | | | | | |
| 138 | b | | | | | | | | | | • | | | |
| 137 | b | | | | | | | • | | | | | | |
| 136 | b | | n | | | | | | | | | | | |
| 135 | b | | | n | n | | | | | | | | | |
| 133 | b | | | | | | | | | | | | | • |
| 129 | b | | n | | | | | | | | | | | |
| 128 | b | | | | | n | | | | | | | | |
| 114 | b | | | | | | | | • | | | | | |
| 103 | b | | | | | | • | | | | | | | |
| 17 | b | | | | | | | | • | | • | | | |
| 1 | b | | | | | | | • | | | | | | |

15

Interstate 15 runs north to south for about 30 miles from the Utah state line to the Nevada state line.

| Mile Marker | ⤢ | * | Info | Arrow | Trees | Restrooms | Phone | Picnic | Vending | Food | Pets | Handicap | Camera | RV |
|---|---|---|---|---|---|---|---|---|---|---|---|---|---|---|
| 21 | sb | | | | • | | | | | | | | | |

| Mile Marker | | * | | | | | | | | | | | | |
|---|---|---|---|---|---|---|---|---|---|---|---|---|---|---|
| 16 | b | 1 | | | • | | | | | | | | | |
| 15 | nb | 1 | | | • | | | | | | | | | |
| 14 | nb | 1 | | | • | | | | | | | | | |
| 10 | nb | 1 | | | • | | | | | | | | | |

N ↕ S

Notes: 1) Truck parking

17

Interstate 17 runs north to south for about 147 miles from I-40 in Flagstaff to I-10 in Phoenix.

| Mile Marker | | * | | | | | | | | | | | | |
|---|---|---|---|---|---|---|---|---|---|---|---|---|---|---|
| 312 | sb | | | | • | | | | | | | | • | |
| 300 | sb | | | | | | | | | | | | | • |
| 297 | b | | | • | | • | • | • | • | | • | • | | |
| 283 | nb | | | | | | | | | | | | | • |
| 252 | b | | | • | | • | • | • | • | | | • | • | |

| Exit | | * | W | S | K | T | Am | FJ | Lo | Pe | Pi | Sp | TA | Wi |
|---|---|---|---|---|---|---|---|---|---|---|---|---|---|---|
| 214ab | b | | | | | w | | | | | | | | |
| 212ab | b | | | w | | | | | | | | | | |
| 206 | b | | | | w | | | | | | | | | |

N ↕ S

19

Interstate 19 runs north to south for approximately 64 miles (103 kilometers) from Interstate 10 in Tucson to the Mexico border. Instead of the mile marker system, Interstate 19 uses kilometers.

| Mile Marker | | * | | | | | | | | | | | | |
|---|---|---|---|---|---|---|---|---|---|---|---|---|---|---|
| 54 | b | 1 | | • | | • | • | • | • | | • | • | | |

| Exit | | * | W | S | K | T | Am | FJ | Lo | Pe | Pi | Sp | TA | Wi |
|---|---|---|---|---|---|---|---|---|---|---|---|---|---|---|
| 95 | b | 1 | w | | w | | | | | | | | | |
| 69 | b | 1 | e | | | | | | | | | | | |
| 12 | b | 1 | | | | | | | | | • | | | |
| 4 | b | 1 | e | | e | | | | | | | | | |

N ↕ S

Notes: 1) I-19 uses kilometers instead of miles

Interstate 40 runs east to west for 360 miles from the New Mexico state line to the California state line.

| | Mile Marker | ⇗ | * | | | | | | | | | | | | |
|---|---|---|---|---|---|---|---|---|---|---|---|---|---|---|---|
| | 359 | b | | • | | | • | • | • | • | | • | • | | |
| E | 316 | b | | | | • | | | • | | | | | | |
| ↑ | 235 | b | 1 | | • | | • | • | • | • | | • | • | | |
| ↓ | 183 | wb | | | • | | • | • | • | • | | • | • | | |
| W | 182 | eb | | | • | | • | • | • | • | | • | • | | |
| | 155 | wb | | | | • | | | | | | | | | |
| | 23 | b | | | • | | • | • | • | • | | • | • | | |

Notes: 1) Vending wb only

| | Exit | ⇗ | * | W | S | K | T | Am | FJ | Lo | Pe | Pi | Sp | TA | Wi |
|---|---|---|---|---|---|---|---|---|---|---|---|---|---|---|---|
| | 283 | b | | | | | | • | | | | | | | |
| | 277 | b | | | | | | | | • | | | | | |
| | 255 | b | | | | | | | • | | | | | | |
| | 253 | b | | n | | | | | | | | • | | | |
| E | 198 | b | | | n | | | | | | | | | | |
| ↕ | 195b | b | | n | | | n | | | | | | | | |
| W | 66 | b | | | | | | | | | • | | | | |
| | 59 | b | | | | | | | | • | | | | | |
| | 53 | b | | | | n | | | • | | | | | | |
| | 51 | b | | n | | | | | | | | | | | |
| | 48 | b | | | | | | | | | | • | | • | |
| | 9 | b | | | | | | | | | | • | | | |

## Arkansas

**Rest Area Usage:** There is no limit to length of stay. Camping is not permitted, however, overnight parking for safety reasons only is allowed. **Road Conditions:** 800-245-1672 or 501-569-2374 (weather), 501-569-2227 (construction) **State Police:** *General*, 501-618-8000; *Emergency*, 911 **Tourism Contact:** Arkansas Tourism Office, 1 Capitol Mall, Dept 7701, Little Rock AR 72201. *Phone*: 800-628-8725. *Internet*: www.arkansas.com

Interstate 30 runs east to west from Interstate 40 in North Little Rock to the Texas state line. The highway is approximately 143 miles long.

| Mile Marker | ⤢ | * | [info] | [arrow] | [trees] | [restrooms] | [phone] | [picnic table] | [drink] | [vending] | [pets] | [handicap] | [camera] | [RV] |
|---|---|---|---|---|---|---|---|---|---|---|---|---|---|---|
| 140 | b | | • | | | • | • | | • | | • | | | |
| 93 | b | | | • | | • | • | • | • | | • | • | | |
| 56 | b | | | • | | • | | • | • | | • | • | | |
| 1 | eb | | • | | | • | • | • | • | | • | • | | |

E ↕ W

| Exit | ⤢ | * | W | S | K | T | Am | FJ | Lo | Pe | Pi | Sp | TA | Wi |
|---|---|---|---|---|---|---|---|---|---|---|---|---|---|---|
| 131 | b | | s | | | | | | | | | | | |
| 130 | b | | s | | | | | | | | | | | |
| 121 | b | | | | | | | | | | • | | | |
| 118 | b | | s | | | | | | | | | | | |
| 98ab | b | | s | | | | | | | | | | | |
| 73 | b | | n | | | | | | | | | | | |
| 46 | b | | | | | | | | • | | | | | |
| 44 | b | | | | | | • | | | | | | | |
| 30 | b | | s | | | | | | | | | | | |
| 7 | b | | | | | | | • | | | | | | |

E ↕ W

Interstate 40 is about 285 miles long. It runs east to west from the Tennessee state line to the Oklahoma state line.

| Mile Marker | ⤢ | * | [info] | [arrow] | [trees] | [restrooms] | [phone] | [picnic table] | [drink] | [vending] | [pets] | [handicap] | [camera] | [RV] |
|---|---|---|---|---|---|---|---|---|---|---|---|---|---|---|
| 274 | wb | | • | | | • | • | • | | | • | • | | |
| 243 | wb | | | • | | • | • | • | • | | • | • | | |
| 235 | eb | | | • | | • | • | • | • | | • | • | | |
| 199 | b | | | • | | • | | • | • | | | • | | |
| 109 | b | | | • | | • | • | • | | | • | • | | |
| 72 | wb | | | • | | • | • | • | • | | • | • | | |
| 70 | wb | | | | • | | | | | | | | • | |
| 68 | eb | | | • | | • | • | • | • | | • | • | | |
| 36 | b | | | • | | • | • | • | | | • | • | | |
| 2 | eb | | • | | | • | • | • | • | | • | • | | |

E ↕ W

| Exit | ⤢ | * | W | S | K | T | Am | FJ | Lo | Pe | Pi | Sp | TA | Wi |
|---|---|---|---|---|---|---|---|---|---|---|---|---|---|---|
| 280 | b | | | | | | | • | | • | • | | | • |
| 278 | b | 1 | s | | | | | | | | | | | |

| Exit | ↗ | * | W | S | K | T | Am | FJ | Lo | Pe | Pi | Sp | TA | Wi |
|---|---|---|---|---|---|---|---|---|---|---|---|---|---|---|
| 276 | b | | s | | | | | | | | | | | |
| 260 | b | | | | | | | | | | | | • | |
| 241ab | b | | s | | | | | | | | | | | |
| 233 | b | | | | | | | | • | | | | | |
| 216 | b | | s | | | | | | | | | | | |
| 161 | b | | | | | | • | | • | • | • | | | |
| 155 | b | 2 | | | | n | | | | | | | | |
| 152 | b | | n | | | | | | | | | | | |
| 125 | b | | s | | | | | | | | | | | |
| 108 | b | | s | | | | | | | | | | | |
| 107 | b | | | | | | | | • | | | | | |
| 84 | b | | s | | | | | • | | | | | | • |
| 58 | b | | n | | | | | | | | | | | |
| 37 | b | | | | | | | | • | | | | | |
| 13 | b | | s | | | | | | | | | | | |
| 5 | b | | n | | | | | | | | | | | |

Notes: 1) shared with I-55; 2) store is one mile north of exit off US 167

Interstate 55 runs north to south for 72 miles from the Missouri state line to the Tennessee state line. A small stretch of I-55 in West Memphis is also I-40.

| Mile Marker | ↗ | * | | | | | | | | | | | | |
|---|---|---|---|---|---|---|---|---|---|---|---|---|---|---|
| 68 | sb | | • | | | • | • | • | | | | • | | |
| 45 | nb | | | • | | • | | • | | | • | • | | |
| 35 | sb | | | • | | • | • | • | | | • | • | | |

| Exit | ↗ | * | W | S | K | T | Am | FJ | Lo | Pe | Pi | Sp | TA | Wi |
|---|---|---|---|---|---|---|---|---|---|---|---|---|---|---|
| 67 | b | | e | | w | | | | | | | | | |
| 278 | b | 1 | w | | | | | | | | | | | |
| 4 | b | | | | | | | • | | • | • | | | • |

Notes: 1) shared with I-40

Interstate 430 is 13 miles long and runs between I-30 and I-40.

| Exit | ↗ | * | W | S | K | T | Am | FJ | Lo | Pe | Pi | Sp | TA | Wi |
|---|---|---|---|---|---|---|---|---|---|---|---|---|---|---|
| 8 | b | | | | w | | | | | | | | | |
| 6 | b | | w | | | | | | | | | | | |

# California

**Rest Area Usage:** There is an 8 hour stay limit. No camping or overnight parking is permitted. **Road Conditions:** 916-445-1534 (weather), 916-445-7623 or 800-427-7623 (construction) **State Police:** *General*, 916-657-7261; *Emergency*, 911 **Tourism Contact:** California Division of Tourism, PO Box 1499, Sacramento CA 95812. *Phone*: 800-862-2543. *Internet*: www.visitcalifornia.com

Interstate 5 runs north to south for approximately 797 miles from the Oregon state line to the Mexico border. Since California does not use an exit numbering system, use the notes at the end of each chart to help identify the following areas.

| Mile Marker | | * | | | | | | | | | | | | |
|---|---|---|---|---|---|---|---|---|---|---|---|---|---|---|
| 788 | b | 1 | | • | | • | • | • | • | | • | • | | |
| 780 | sb | | | | • | | | | | | | | • | |
| 753 | b | 2 | | • | | • | • | • | • | | • | • | | |
| 723 | nb | | | | • | | | | | | | | • | |
| 705 | sb | 3 | | • | | • | • | • | • | | | • | | |
| 694 | nb | 4 | | • | | • | • | • | | | • | • | | |
| 667 | b | 5 | • | | | • | • | | | | | • | | |
| 656 | sb | 6 | | • | | • | • | • | • | | • | • | | |
| 655 | nb | 7 | | • | | • | • | • | • | | • | • | | |
| 633 | b | 8 | | • | | • | • | • | • | | • | • | | |
| 608 | b | 9 | | • | | • | • | • | • | • | • | • | | |
| 583 | b | 10 | | • | | • | • | • | | | • | • | | |
| 557 | b | 11 | | • | | • | • | • | • | | • | • | | |
| 529 | sb | 12 | | • | | • | • | • | | | • | • | | |
| 445 | b | 13 | | • | | • | • | • | • | • | • | • | | |
| 430 | nb | | | | • | | | | | | | | • | |
| 423 | sb | | | | • | | | | | | | | • | |
| 386 | b | 14 | | • | | • | • | • | • | | • | • | | |
| 320 | b | 15 | | • | | • | • | • | • | | • | • | | |
| 259 | b | 16 | | • | | • | • | • | | | • | • | | |
| 211 | nb | 17 | | | | | | | | | | | | • |
| 204 | b | 18 | | • | | • | • | • | • | • | • | • | | |
| 105 | b | 19 | • | | | • | • | | | | | • | | |
| 63 | sb | | | | • | | | | | | | | • | |
| 60 | b | 20 | | • | | • | • | • | • | • | • | • | | |

| Mile Marker | ↗ | * | Information | Sign | Picnic Area | Restrooms | Phone | Picnic Tables | Vending | Facilities | Pet Area | Handicapped | Camera | Trucks |
|---|---|---|---|---|---|---|---|---|---|---|---|---|---|---|
| 51 | b | 21 | • | | | • | • | | | | | • | | |
| 44 | b | | | | • | | | | | | | | • | |
| 39 | sb | | | | • | | | | | | | | • | |

Notes: 1) Randolph C Collier Rest Area, 2.5 miles north of Route 96.
2) Weed Airport Rest Area, 6 miles north of Weed.
3) Lakehead Rest Area, 0.9 miles north of Lakehead.
4) O'Brien Rest Area, 9 miles north of Project City.
5) Welcome Center is ten miles south of Redding, exit Deschutes Rd.
6) Herbert S Miles Rest Area, 5 miles north of Red Bluff.
7) Herbert S Miles Rest Area, 4.4 miles north of Red Bluff.
8) Helmick Rest Area, 1.3 miles north of Corning Rd.
9) Willows Rest Area, 2 miles south of Artois.
10) Maxwell Rest Area, 2 miles south of Maxwell.
11) Dunnigan Rest Area, 0.5 miles north of Dunnigan.
12) Elkhorn Rest Area, at Sacramento International Airport.
13) Westley Rest Area, 0.9 miles south of the San Joaquin County line in Stanislaus County.
14) John "Chuck" Erreca Rest Area, 0.7 miles north of the Fresno County line in Merced County.
15) Coaling/Avenal Rest Area, 1.2 miles north of Lassen Ave.
16) Buttonwillow Rest Area, 2 miles north of Route 58 Interchange.
17) Ramp is about 9 miles from summit.
18) Tejon Pass Rest Area, 3.5 miles north of Gorman.
19) Welcome Center is at the intersection of I-5 and CA 22 at Main St exit
20) Aliso Creek Rest Area, 5.8 miles north of Oceanside.
21) Welcome Center is 35 miles north of San Diego in Oceanside. Take the Coast Highway exit and follow the Traveling Bear signs.

N ↕ S

| Exit | ↗ | * | W | S | K | T | Am | FJ | Lo | Pe | Pi | Sp | TA | Wi |
|---|---|---|---|---|---|---|---|---|---|---|---|---|---|---|
| 773 | b | 1 | w | | | | | | | | | | | |
| 678 | b | 2 | e | | | e | | | | | | | | |
| 677 | b | 3 | | | e | | | | | | | | | |
| 673 | b | 4 | | | | | | | | | | | • | |
| 649 | b | 5 | w | | w | | | | | | | | | |
| 630 | b | 6 | | | | | | | | • | | | • | |
| 603 | b | 7 | w | | | | | | | | | | | |
| 554 | b | 8 | | | | | | | | | • | | | |
| 537 | b | 9 | e | | | | | | | | | | | |
| 536 | b | 10 | | | | e | | | | | | | | |
| 485 | b | 11 | | | | | | • | | | | | | |
| 471 | b | 12 | | | | | • | | | | | | | |
| 407 | b | 13 | | | | | | | | | • | | • | |

| Exit | ↗ | * | W | S | K | T | Am | FJ | Lo | Pe | Pi | Sp | TA | Wi |
|---|---|---|---|---|---|---|---|---|---|---|---|---|---|---|
| 403 | b | 14 | | | | | | | | • | | | | |
| 278 | b | 15 | | | | | | | | | • | | • | |
| 257 | b | 16 | | | | | • | | | | | | • | |
| 219 | b | 17 | | | | | | | | • | | | • | |
| 205 | b | 18 | | | | | | • | | | | | | |
| 167 | b | 19 | w | | | | | | | | | | | |
| 154 | b | 20 | | | | e | | | | | | | | |
| 146b | b | 21 | | | e | | | | | | | | | |
| 112 | b | 22 | e | | | w | | | | | | | | |
| 104 | b | 23 | | | | e | | | | | | | | |
| 101a | b | 24 | | | e | | | | | | | | | |
| 100 | b | 25 | | | | e | | | | | | | | |
| 91 | b | 26 | | | e | | | | | | | | | |
| 90 | b | 27 | | | | e | | | | | | | | |
| 78 | b | 28 | | | w | | | | | | | | | |
| 76 | b | 29 | e | | | | | | | | | | | |
| 51b | b | 30 | e | | | e | | | | | | | | |
| 8b | b | 31 | e | | | | | | | | | | | |
| 6 | b | 32 | | | | e | | | | | | | | |

Notes:
1) CA 3 (South of Yreka)
2) CA 299 E, CA 44 (in Redding)
3) Hilltop Dr, Cypress Ave (in Redding)
4) Knighton Rd (near Redding)
5) CA 99, Main St (in Red Bluff)
6) South Ave (in Corning)
7) CA 162, Willows (in Willows)
8) County Road 8 (near Dunnigan)
9) CA 113 S, Main St (in Woodland)
10) County Road 102 (in Woodland)
11) CA 12 (near Lodi)
12) CA 4, Charter Way (in Stockton)
13) CA 33 (near Santa Nella Village)
14) CA 152 (near Los Banos)
15) CA 46 (near Lost Hills)
16) CA 58 (near Buttonwillow)
17) Laval Rd (near Wheeler Ridge)
18) Frazier Park Rd (near Frazier Park)
19) Lyons Ave, Pico Canyon Rd (in Valencia)
20) Osborne St (in Pacoima)
21) Burbank Blvd (in Burbank)
22) Euclid St (in Anaheim)
23) Santa Ana Blvd, Grand Ave (in Santa Ana)
24) Tustin Ranch Rd (in Tustin)

25) Jamboree Rd (in Tustin)
26) El Toro Road (in Lake Forest)
27) Alicia Parkway (in Mission Viejo)
28) Camino de Estrella (in San Clemente)
29) Avenida Pico (in San Clemente)
30) CA 78, Vista Way (in Oceanside)
31) E St (in Chula Vista), Wal-mart is north of E St on N Broadway
32) Palomar St (in Castle Park)

Interstate 8 runs east to west for 172 miles from the Arizona state line to Sunset Cliffs Blvd in San Diego. Since California does not use an exit numbering system, use the notes at the end of each chart to help identify the following areas.

| Mile Marker | | * | ? | | | | | | | | | | | |
|---|---|---|---|---|---|---|---|---|---|---|---|---|---|---|
| 155 | b | 1 | | • | | • | | | | | | | | |
| 108 | b | 2 | | • | | • | • | • | | • | • | • | | |
| 81 | eb | | | | | | | | | | | | | • |
| 75 | eb | | | | • | | • | | | | | | | |
| 51 | b | 3 | | • | | • | • | • | | • | • | • | | |
| 37 | eb | | | | • | | | | | | | | • | |
| 24 | wb | | | | • | | • | | | | | | | |

Notes: 1) Sand Hills Rest Area, 20 miles west of Arizona State Line.
2) Sunbeam Rest Area, 6 miles west of El Centro.
3) Buckman Springs Rest Area, 3.3 miles east of Pine Valley.

| Exit | | * | W | S | K | T | Am | FJ | Lo | Pe | Pi | Sp | TA | Wi |
|---|---|---|---|---|---|---|---|---|---|---|---|---|---|---|
| 114 | b | 1 | n+ | | n+ | | | | | | | | | |
| 22 | b | 2 | s | | | | | | | | | | | |
| 17 | b | 3 | | | n | | | | | | | | | |
| 13b | b | 4 | | | | n | | | | | | | | |

Notes: 1) Imperial Ave (in El Centro)
2) Los Coches Rd (in El Cajon)
3) Magnolia Ave (in El Cajon)
4) Jackson Dr, Grossmont Blvd (in La Mesa)

Interstate 10 runs east to west for approximately 244 miles from the Arizona state line to CA 1 in Santa Monica. Since California does not use an exit numbering system, use the notes at the end of each chart to help identify the following areas.

| | Mile Marker | | * | | | | | | | | | | | | |
|---|---|---|---|---|---|---|---|---|---|---|---|---|---|---|---|
| E | 222 | b | 1 | | • | | • | • | • | | • | • | • | | |
| ↕ | 159 | b | 2 | | • | | • | • | • | • | • | • | • | | |
| | 113 | b | 3 | | • | | • | • | • | • | | | • | | |
| W | 91 | wb | 4 | | • | | • | • | • | | | • | • | | |
| | 86 | eb | 5 | | • | | • | • | • | | | • | • | | |

Notes: 1) Wiley's Well Rest Area, 15 miles west of Blythe.
2) Cactus City Rest Area, 15 miles east of Indio.
3) Whitewater Rest Area, 1 mile west of Whitewater.
4) Brookside Rest Area, 3 miles west of Beaumont.
5) Wildwood Rest Area, 1 mile west of Calimesa.

| | Exit | | * | W | S | K | T | Am | FJ | Lo | Pe | Pi | Sp | TA | Wi |
|---|---|---|---|---|---|---|---|---|---|---|---|---|---|---|---|
| | 239 | b | 1 | | | n | | | | | | | | | |
| | 146 | b | 2 | | | | | | | • | | | | • | |
| | 142 | b | 3 | | | | s | | | | | | | | |
| | 130 | b | 4 | | | | | | • | | | | | | |
| E | 120 | b | 5 | | | | | | | | | • | | | |
| ↕ | 96 | b | 6 | | | s | | | | | | | | | |
| W | 77 | b | 7 | | | s | | | | | | | | | |
| | 76 | b | 8 | s | | | | | | | | | | | |
| | 73 | b | 9 | | n | | | | | | | | | | |
| | 71 | b | 10 | s | | | | | | | | | | | |
| | 68 | b | 11 | n | | | | | | | | | | | |
| | 64 | b | 12 | | | n | s | | | | | | | | |
| | 57 | b | 13 | | n | | | | | | | | | • | |
| E | 53 | b | 14 | | | n | | | | | | | | | |
| ↕ | 50 | b | 15 | | | | s | | | | | | | | |
| | 49 | b | 16 | | | s | | | | | | | | | |
| W | 48 | b | 17 | | n | | | | | | | | | | |
| | 37 | b | 18 | | | | n | | | | | | | | |
| | 34 | b | 19 | | | s | | | | | | | | | |
| | 32 | b | 20 | | | | n | | | | | | | | |
| | 29 | b | 21 | | | n | | | | | | | | | |

Notes: 1) Lovekin Blvd (in Blythe)
2) Dillon Rd (east of Indio)
3) Monroe St (in Indio)
4) Ramon Rd (in Thousand Palms)
5) Indian Ave (near North Palm Springs)
6) Highland Springs Ave (in Banning)
7) Alabama St (in Redlands)

8) California Ave (in Redlands)
9) Waterman Ave (in San Bernardino)
10) Mount Vernon Ave (in Colton)
11) Riverside Ave (East of Bloomington)
12) Sierra Ave (in Fontana)
13) Milliken Ave (near Ontario)
14) San Bernardino Ave, 4th St (in Ontario)
15) Mountain Ave (in Ontario)
16) Central Ave (in Montclair)
17) Monte Vista Ave (in Montclair)
18) Citrus Ave (in West Covina)
19) Pacific Ave (in West Covina)
20) Francisquito Ave (in Baldwin Park)
21) Peck Road North (in El Monte)

15

Interstate 15 runs north to south for about 292 miles from the Nevada state line to San Diego. Since California does not use an exit numbering system, use the notes at the end of each chart to help identify the following areas.

| Mile Marker | ↗ | * | (?) | (arrow) | (tree/picnic) | (restrooms) | (phone) | (picnic table) | (drinking) | (vending) | (pet) | (handicap) | (camera) | (truck ramp) |
|---|---|---|---|---|---|---|---|---|---|---|---|---|---|---|
| 279 | nb | 1 | | | | | | | | | | | | • |
| 270 | b | 2 | | • | | • | • | • | | | • | • | | |
| 217 | b | 3 | | • | | • | • | • | | | • | • | | |
| 178 | b | 4 | • | | | • | • | | | | | • | | |
| 130 | sb | 5 | | | | | | | | | | | | • |

Notes: 1) Ramp is about 5 miles from the summit.
2) Valley Wells Rest Area, 26 miles west of Nevada State Line.
3) Clyde V Kane Rest Area, 30 miles east of Barstow.
4) Take the Lenwood Road exit and follow the Traveling Bear signs. Welcome Center is located in Barstow at the Tanger Outlet Shopping Center.
5) Ramp is about 2 1/2 miles from the summit.

| Exit | ↗ | * | W | S | K | T | Am | FJ | Lo | Pe | Pi | Sp | TA | Wi |
|---|---|---|---|---|---|---|---|---|---|---|---|---|---|---|
| 181 | b | 1 | | | | | | | | | | | • | |
| 178 | b | 2 | | | | | • | • | | | • | | | |
| 150 | b | 3 | | | | w | | | | | | | | |
| 147 | b | 4 | e | | | | | | | | | | | |
| 141 | b | 5 | | | | | | | | | • | | | |
| 112 | b | 6 | e | | | e | | | | | | | | |
| 110 | b | 7 | | w | | | | | | | | | | |
| 98 | b | 8 | | | | w | | | | | | | | |

| Exit | ↗ | * | W | S | K | T | Am | FJ | Lo | Pe | Pi | Sp | TA | Wi |
|---|---|---|---|---|---|---|---|---|---|---|---|---|---|---|
| 93 | b | 9 | w | w | | | | | | | | | | |
| 73 | b | 10 | e | | | | | | | | | | | |
| 65 | b | 11 | | | | e | | | | | | | | |
| 64 | b | 12 | w | | | | | | | | | | | |
| 61 | b | 13 | | | e | | | | | | | | | |
| 59 | b | 14 | | | | e | | | | | | | | |
| 32 | b | 15 | | | e+ | | | | | | | | | |
| 31 | b | 16 | | | | w | | | | | | | | |
| 21 | b | 17 | | | e | | | | | | | | | |
| 8 | b | 18 | w | | | | | | | | | | | |

N ↕ S

Notes: 1) West Main St (in Barstow)
2) Lenwood Rd (near Barstow)
3) CA 18, Palmdale Rd (near Victorville)
4) Bear Valley Rd (south of Victorville)
5) US 395 (near Hesperia)
6) CA 66, Foothill Blvd (near Rancho Cucamonga)
7) 4th St (in Ontario)
8) 2nd St (north of Corona)
9) Ontario Ave (near El Cerrito)
10) Railroad Canyon Rd (1 mile south of Lake Elsinore)
11) California Oaks Rd, Kalmia St (in Murrieta)
12) Murrieta Hot Springs Rd (in Murrieta)
13) CA 79 N, Winchester Rd (2 miles north of Temecula)
14) Rancho California Rd (in Temecula)
15) CA 78 (in Escondido) / off CA 78 on W Mission Ave
16) Valley Pkwy (in Escondido)
17) Carmel Mtn Rd (in San Diego)
18) Aero Dr (in San Diego)

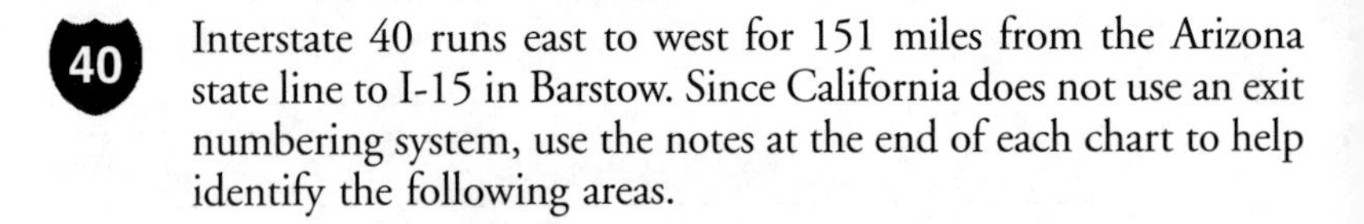


Interstate 40 runs east to west for 151 miles from the Arizona state line to I-15 in Barstow. Since California does not use an exit numbering system, use the notes at the end of each chart to help identify the following areas.

| Mile Marker | ↗ | * | ? | | | | | | | | | | | |
|---|---|---|---|---|---|---|---|---|---|---|---|---|---|---|
| 106 | b | 1 | | • | | • | • | • | | | • | • | | |
| 28 | b | 2 | | • | | • | • | • | | | • | • | | |

Notes: 1) John Wilkie Rest Area, 45 miles west of Needles.
2) Desert Oasis Rest Area, 9 miles east of Newberry.

| Exit | ↗ | * | W | S | K | T | Am | FJ | Lo | Pe | Pi | Sp | TA | Wi |
|---|---|---|---|---|---|---|---|---|---|---|---|---|---|---|
| 1 | b | 1 | s | | | | | | | | | | | |

Notes: 1) Montara Rd (in Barstow)

Interstate 80 runs east to west for 208 miles from the Nevada state line to 7th Street in San Francisco. Since California does not use an exit numbering system, use the notes at the end of each chart to help identify the following areas.

| Mile Marker | ↗ | * | | | | | | | | | | | | |
|---|---|---|---|---|---|---|---|---|---|---|---|---|---|---|
| 180 | b | | | | • | | | | | | | | • | |
| 177 | b | 1 | | • | | • | • | • | | | • | • | • | |
| 157 | wb | | | | • | | | | | | | | • | |
| 152 | wb | 2 | | | | | | | | | | | | • |
| 148 | wb | 3 | | | | | | | | | | | | • |
| 143 | b | 4 | | • | | • | • | • | | | • | • | | |
| 34 | wb | 5 | | • | | • | • | • | | | • | • | • | |

E ↕ W

Notes: 1) Donner Summit Rest Area, on Donner Pass.
2) Ramp is about 25 miles from the summit.
3) Ramp is about 29 miles from the summit.
4) Gold Run Rest Area, between Sawmill and Gold Run.
5) Hunter Hill Rest Area, 7 miles east of Vallejo.

| Exit | ↗ | * | W | S | K | T | Am | FJ | Lo | Pe | Pi | Sp | TA | Wi |
|---|---|---|---|---|---|---|---|---|---|---|---|---|---|---|
| 106 | b | 1 | n+ | | | | | | | | | | | |
| 105b | b | 2 | | | n+ | | | | | | | | | |
| 105a | b | 3 | | s | | | | | | | | | | |
| 102 | b | 4 | | | s | | | | | | | | | |
| 96 | b | 5 | | | | s | | | | | | | | |
| 89 | b | 6 | | | s | | | | | | | | | |
| 88 | b | 7 | n | | | | | | | | | | | |
| 55 | b | 8 | s | s | | s | | | | | | | | |
| 48 | b | 9 | | | s | | | | | | | | | |
| 44 | b | 10 | | | | s | | | | | | | | |
| 43 | b | 11 | s | | | | | | | | | | | |
| 32 | b | 12 | | | | s | | | | | | | | |
| 21 | b | 13 | | | s | | | | | | | | | |
| 20 | b | 14 | | | | s | | | | | | | | |
| 18 | b | 15 | | | n | | | | | | | | | |
| 15 | b | 16 | | | | s | | | | | | | | |

E ↕ W

Notes: 1) CA 65 (near Roseville ) off CA 65 on Stanford Ranch Rd
2) Taylor Rd (in Roseville)
3) Atlantic St, Eureka Rd (in Roseville)
4) Riverside Ave (in Citrus Heights)
5) Madison Ave (in North Highlands)
6) Northgate Blvd (in Sacramento)
7) Truxel Rd (in Sacramento)
8) Monte Vista Ave (in Vacaville)
9) N Texas St (in Fairfield)
10) W Texas St, Rockville Rd (in Fairfield)
11) CA 12 E, Abernathy Rd (Near Fairfield)
12) Redwood St (in Vallejo)
13) Appian Way (in Pinole)
14) Richmond Pkwy (in Pinole)
15) San Pablo Dam Rd (East of San Pablo)
16) Cutting Blvd, Potrero St (in Richmond)

Interstate 110 is a spur route that begins on I-10 in Los Angeles and runs south to CA Hwy 47. It is approximately 25 miles long. Since California does not use an exit numbering system, use the notes at the end of the chart to help identify the following areas.

| Exit | ↗ | * | W | S | K | T | Am | FJ | Lo | Pe | Pi | Sp | TA | Wi |
|---|---|---|---|---|---|---|---|---|---|---|---|---|---|---|
| 8 | b | 1 | | | e | | | | | | | | | |
| 5 | b | 2 | | | w | e | | | | | | | | |

Notes: 1) Torrance Blvd (in Carson)
2) Sepulveda Blvd (in Carson)

Interstate 205 begins on I-5 near Tracy and runs west to I-508. It is approximately 13 miles long. Since California does not use an exit numbering system, use the notes at the end of the chart to help identify the following areas.

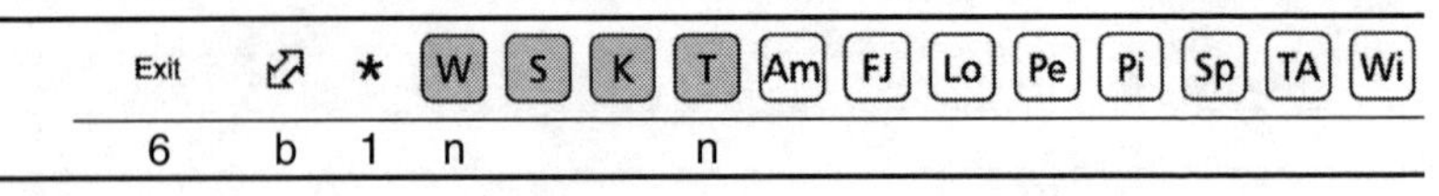

| Exit | ↗ | * | W | S | K | T | Am | FJ | Lo | Pe | Pi | Sp | TA | Wi |
|---|---|---|---|---|---|---|---|---|---|---|---|---|---|---|
| 6 | b | 1 | n | | | n | | | | | | | | |

Notes: 1) Grant Line Rd (in Tracy)

Interstate 210 begins on I-10 near San Dimas and runs west to I-5 in San Fernando. It is approximately 49 miles long. Since California does not use an exit numbering system, use the notes at the end of the chart to help identify the following areas.

| | Exit | ⇗ | * | W | S | K | T | Am | FJ | Lo | Pe | Pi | Sp | TA | Wi |
|---|---|---|---|---|---|---|---|---|---|---|---|---|---|---|---|
| E | 45 | b | 1 | | | | s | | | | | | | | |
| | 44 | b | 2 | s | | | | | | | | | | | |
| | 35 | b | 3 | s | | | n | | | | | | | | |
| W | 5 | b | 4 | | s | | | | | | | | | | |

Notes: 1) Arrow Hwy (in San Dimas)
2) CA 30 E, Lone Hill Ave (in Glendora)
3) Mountain Ave (in Duarte)
4) Maclay St (in San Fernando)

Interstate 215 begins on I-15 near San Bernardino and runs south to I-15 near Murrieta. Since California does not use an exit numbering system, use the notes at the end of the chart to help identify the following areas.

| | Exit | ⇗ | * | W | S | K | T | Am | FJ | Lo | Pe | Pi | Sp | TA | Wi |
|---|---|---|---|---|---|---|---|---|---|---|---|---|---|---|---|
| | 41 | b | 1 | | | | e | | | | | | | | |
| N | 39 | b | 2 | w | | | | | | | | | | | |
| | 33 | b | 3 | | | e | | | | | | | | | |
| S | 28 | b | 4 | e | e | | | | | | | | | | |
| | 22 | b | 5 | e+ | | | | | | | | | | | |
| | 10 | b | 6 | | | | e | | | | | | | | |

Notes: 1) Orange Show Rd (in San Bernardino)
2) Washington St (in Colton)
3) Blaine St, 3rd St (in Riverside)
4) Eucalyptus Ave (in Moreno Valley)
5) Ramona Expy (south of Moreno Valley) on Perris Blvd
6) Newport Rd (2 miles south of Sun City)

Interstate 280 runs north to south for about 60 miles from Fourth Street in downtown San Francisco to US 101 in San Jose. Since California does not use an exit numbering system, use the notes at the end of the chart to help identify the following areas.

| Mile Marker | ⇗ | * | ? | | | | | | | | | | | |
|---|---|---|---|---|---|---|---|---|---|---|---|---|---|---|
| 37 | b | | | | • | | | | | | | | • | |
| 36 | nb | 1 | | • | | • | • | • | • | • | | • | | |
| 31 | b | | | | • | | | | | | | | • | |

Notes: 1) Crystal Springs Rest Area, near San Francisco Reservoir in San Mateo County.

| Exit | ↗ | ★ | W | S | K | T | Am | FJ | Lo | Pe | Pi | Sp | TA | Wi |
|---|---|---|---|---|---|---|---|---|---|---|---|---|---|---|
| 47 | b | 1 | | | | e | | | | | | | | |
| 7 | b | 2 | | | | w | | | | | | | | |
| 4 | sb | 3 | | | w | | | | | | | | | |

Notes: 1) CA 1, Mission St (in Colma)
2) Saratoga-Sunnyvale Rd (in Cupertino)
3) Meridian St (in San Jose)

Interstate 405 runs north to south for about 56 miles. It begins at I-5 in Irvine and ends at I-5 in Sylmar. Since California does not use an exit numbering system, use the notes at the end of the chart to help identify the following areas.

| Exit | ↗ | ★ | W | S | K | T | Am | FJ | Lo | Pe | Pi | Sp | TA | Wi |
|---|---|---|---|---|---|---|---|---|---|---|---|---|---|---|
| 47 | b | 1 | | | w | | | | | | | | | |
| 38a | b | 2 | | e+ | | | | | | | | | | |
| 30a | b | 3 | | | | e | | | | | | | | |
| 26 | b | 4 | | | e | w | | | | | | | | |
| 22 | b | 5 | | | | e | | | | | | | | |
| 16 | b | 6 | | | e | w | | | | | | | | |
| 14 | b | 7 | | e | | | | | | | | | | |
| 11 | b | 8 | | | | w | | | | | | | | |
| 9b | b | 9 | | | | e | | | | | | | | |

Notes: 1) CA 42, Manchester Blvd (in Inglewood)
2) Normandie Ave (in Gardena)
3) Atlantic Blvd (in Long Beach)
4) Bellflower Blvd (in Long Beach)
5) Seal Beach Blvd (in Long Beach)
6) CA 39, Beach Blvd (in Westminster)
7) Brookhurst St (in Fountain Valley)
8) Harbor Blvd (in Fountain Valley)
9) Bristol St (in Costa Mesa)

Interstate 580 runs east to west for 82 miles. It begins on I-5 south of Tracy and ends at US 101 in San Rafael. Since California does not use an exit numbering system, use the notes at the end of the chart to help identify the following areas.

| Exit | ↗ | ★ | W | S | K | T | Am | FJ | Lo | Pe | Pi | Sp | TA | Wi |
|---|---|---|---|---|---|---|---|---|---|---|---|---|---|---|
| 54 | b | 1 | | | | s | | | | | | | | |

E ↕ W

| Exit | ⇗ | * | W | S | K | T | Am | FJ | Lo | Pe | Pi | Sp | TA | Wi |
|---|---|---|---|---|---|---|---|---|---|---|---|---|---|---|
| 52 | b | 2 | s | | | | | | | | | | | |
| 46 | b | 3 | s | | | | | | | | | | | |
| 44a | b | 4 | | | | n | | | | | | | | |

Notes: 1) CA 84, 1st St, Springtown Blvd (in Livermore)
2) N Livermore Ave (in Livermore)
3) Hacienda Dr (in Pleasanton)
4) Foothills Rd, San Ramon Rd (in Dublin)

Interstate 605 runs north to south for 25 miles from Huntington Drive in Duarte to I-405 in Los Alamitos. Since California does not use an exit numbering system, use the notes at the end of the chart to help identify the following areas.

| Exit | ⇗ | * | W | S | K | T | Am | FJ | Lo | Pe | Pi | Sp | TA | Wi |
|---|---|---|---|---|---|---|---|---|---|---|---|---|---|---|
| 11 | b | 1 | | e | | | | | | | | | | |
| 3 | b | 2 | | w | | | | | | | | | | |

Notes: 1) Florence Ave (in Downey)
2) Carson St (in Long Beach)

Interstate 680 runs north to south for 71 miles from I-80 near Fairfield to US 101 in San Jose. Since California does not use an exit numbering system, use the notes at the end of the chart to help identify the following areas.

| Mile Marker | ⇗ | * | ? | | | | | | | | | | | |
|---|---|---|---|---|---|---|---|---|---|---|---|---|---|---|
| 61 | b | | | | • | | | | | | | | • | |

N ↕ S

| Exit | ⇗ | * | W | S | K | T | Am | FJ | Lo | Pe | Pi | Sp | TA | Wi |
|---|---|---|---|---|---|---|---|---|---|---|---|---|---|---|
| 53 | b | 1 | | | w | w | | | | | | | | |
| 52 | b | 2 | | e | | | | | | | | | | |
| 47 | b | 3 | | | | e | | | | | | | | |
| 34 | b | 4 | | | | e | | | | | | | | |
| 6 | b | 5 | | | | e | | | | | | | | |
| 2b | b | 6 | | | w | | | | | | | | | |

Notes: 1) CA 4 E, Concord Ave, Pacheco Blvd (in Pacheco)
2) Concord Ave (in Concord)
3) N Main St, to Walnut Creek (in Walnut Creek)
4) Bollinger Canyon Rd (in San Ramon)

5) Landess Ave, Montague Expressway (in Malpitas)
6) McKee Rd (in San Jose)

Interstate 710 runs north to south for 29 miles between Valley Boulevard in Alhambra and East Shoreline Drive in Long Beach. Since California does not use an exit numbering system, use the notes at the end of the chart to help identify the following area.

| Exit | | * | W | S | K | T | Am | FJ | Lo | Pe | Pi | Sp | TA | Wi |
|---|---|---|---|---|---|---|---|---|---|---|---|---|---|---|
| 13 | b | 1 | | | | e | | | | | | | | |

Notes: 1) CA 42, Firestone Blvd (in Bell Gardens)

Interstate 805 runs north to south for 31 miles between I-5 near Del Mar and I-5 near the Mexico border. Since California does not use an exit numbering system, use the notes at the end of the chart to help identify the following areas.

| Exit | | * | W | S | K | T | Am | FJ | Lo | Pe | Pi | Sp | TA | Wi |
|---|---|---|---|---|---|---|---|---|---|---|---|---|---|---|
| 22 | b | 1 | | | e | | | | | | | | | |
| 2 | b | 2 | e | | | | | | | | | | | |

Notes: 1) Clairemont Mesa Blvd (1 mile south of CA 52)
2) Palm Ave (in San Ysidro)

Interstate 880 runs north to south for about 46 miles between Seventh Street in downtown San Francisco and I-280 in San Jose. Since California does not use an exit numbering system, use the notes at the bottom of the chart to help identify the following areas.

| Exit | | * | W | S | K | T | Am | FJ | Lo | Pe | Pi | Sp | TA | Wi |
|---|---|---|---|---|---|---|---|---|---|---|---|---|---|---|
| 38 | b | 1 | | | w | | | | | | | | | |
| 34 | b | 2 | w | | | | | | | | | | | |
| 30 | b | 3 | | | | e | | | | | | | | |
| 24 | b | 4 | w | | | | | | | | | | | |
| 23 | b | 5 | w | | | | | | | | | | | |
| 19 | b | 6 | | | w | | | | | | | | | |
| 17 | b | 7 | | | | e | | | | | | | | |
| 8b | b | 8 | w | | | | | | | | | | | |

Notes: 1) High St (in Oakland)
2) Davis St (in San Leandro)

3) Hesperian Blvd (in San Lorenzo)
4) Whipple Rd, Dyer St (in Union City)
5) Alvarado-Niles Rd (in Union City)
6) CA 84 E, Thornton Ave (in Fremont)
7) Mowry Ave (in Fremont)
8) CA 237, Alviso Rd, Calaveras Rd (in Milpitas)

# Colorado

**Rest Area Usage:** There is no limit to length of stay, however, no camping or overnight parking is permitted. **Road Conditions:** 877-315-7623 or 303-639-1111 (general) **State Police:** *General*, 303-239-4500; *Emergency*, 911 **Tourism Contact:** Colorado Travel & Tourism Authority, 1127 Pennsylvania St, Denver CO 80203. *Phone*: 800-265-6723 or 303-892-3885. *Internet*: www.colorado.com

25

Interstate 25 runs north to south for about 300 miles from the Wyoming state line to the New Mexico state line.

| Mile Marker | | * | [Info] | [Arrow] | [Trees/Picnic] | [Restrooms] | [Phone] | [Picnic Table] | [Vending] | [Map/Kiosk] | [Pet Area] | [Handicap] | [Laundry] | [Other] |
|---|---|---|---|---|---|---|---|---|---|---|---|---|---|---|
| 296 | b | | | | • | | | | | | | | | |
| 268 | b | | • | | | • | • | • | | | | • | | |
| 266 | b | | | • | | • | • | • | | | • | • | | |
| 171 | b | | | • | | • | • | • | • | | • | • | | |
| 115 | nb | | | • | | • | • | • | • | • | • | • | | |
| 112 | sb | | | • | | • | • | • | • | • | • | • | | |
| 74 | b | | | • | | • | • | • | • | | • | • | | |
| 18 | b | | | • | | • | • | • | | | | • | | |
| 14 | b | | • | | | • | • | • | | | | • | | |
| 1 | nb | | | | • | | | | | | | | • | |

| Exit | | * | W | S | K | T | Am | FJ | Lo | Pe | Pi | Sp | TA | Wi |
|---|---|---|---|---|---|---|---|---|---|---|---|---|---|---|
| 257ab | b | | | | | w | | | | | | | | |
| 254 | b | | | | | | • | | | | | | | |
| 221 | b | | e | | e | e | | | | | | | | |
| 207 | b | | | e | | | | | | | | | | |
| 197 | b | | | | e | e | | | | | | | | |
| 194 | b | 1 | w+ | w+ | | | | | | | | | | |

| Exit | ↗ | * | W | S | K | T | Am | FJ | Lo | Pe | Pi | Sp | TA | Wi |
|---|---|---|---|---|---|---|---|---|---|---|---|---|---|---|
| 184 | b | | e | | | | | | | | | | | |
| 150 | b | | e | e | | | | | | | | | | |
| 141 | b | | w | | | | | | | | | | | |
| 138 | b | | | | | w | | | | | | | | |
| 132 | b | 2 | e+ | | | | | | | | | | | |
| 110 | b | | | | | | • | | | | | | | |
| 102 | b | | | e | | | | | | | | | | |
| 101 | b | | e | | w | | | | | | | | | |
| 11 | b | | w | | | | | | | | | | | |

Notes: 1) on Quebec St off CO 470; 2) on US 85

**70** Interstate 70 runs east to west for 447 miles from the Kansas state line to the Utah state line.

| Mile Marker | ↗ | * | Info | Scenic | Trees | Restrooms | Phone | Picnic | Vending | Map | Pets | Handicap | Camera | RV |
|---|---|---|---|---|---|---|---|---|---|---|---|---|---|---|
| 437 | wb | | • | | | • | • | • | • | • | • | • | | |
| 383 | b | | | • | | • | • | • | | • | • | • | | |
| 332 | wb | | | • | | • | • | • | • | | • | • | | |
| 306 | b | | | • | | • | • | • | | | • | • | | |
| 257 | eb | | | | | | | | | | | | | • |
| 254 | eb | | | | • | | | | | | | | • | |
| 226 | eb | | | | • | | | | | | | | • | |
| 213 | eb | | | | • | | | | | | | | | |
| 212 | wb | | | | | | | | | | | | | • |
| 209 | wb | | | | | | | | | | | | | • |
| 203 | b | | | | • | | • | | | | | | • | |
| 190 | b | | | • | | • | • | • | | | | • | | |
| 189 | b | | | | • | | | | | | | | | |
| 186 | wb | | | | | | | | | | | | | • |
| 183 | wb | | | | | | | | | | | | | • |
| 163 | b | | | • | | • | • | • | | • | | • | | |
| 162 | b | | | | • | | | | | | | | • | |
| 128 | b | | | • | | • | • | • | | | • | • | | |
| 121 | b | | | • | | • | • | • | | | | • | | |
| 119 | b | | | • | | • | • | • | | | | • | | |
| 115 | eb | | | • | | • | • | • | | | | • | | |
| 108 | b | | | | • | | | | | | | | | |
| 50 | eb | | | | • | | | | | | | | | |
| 19 | b | | • | | | • | • | • | | • | • | • | | |

| Exit | ↗ | * | W | S | K | T | Am | FJ | Lo | Pe | Pi | Sp | TA | Wi |
|---|---|---|---|---|---|---|---|---|---|---|---|---|---|---|
| 361 | b | | | | | | | • | | | | | | |
| 359 | b | | | | | | • | | | | | | | |
| 285 | b | | | | | | | • | | | | | | |
| 278 | b | | | | | | | | | | | | • | |
| 276 | b | | | | | | | | | | • | | | |
| 272 | b | | | | n | | | | | | | | | |
| 270 | b | | | | | s | | | | | | | | |
| 269a | b | | | n | | | | | | | | | | |
| 266 | b | | | | | | | | | | | | • | |
| 264 | b | | s | | | | | | | | | | | |
| 252 | b | | s | | | | | | | | | | | |
| 203 | b | | s | | | | | | | | | | | |
| 167 | b | | s | | | | | | | | | | | |
| 116 | b | | s+ | | | | | | | | | | | |
| 114 | b | | | | n | | | | | | | | | |
| 37 | b | | s+ | | s+ | | | | | | | | | |

76

Interstate 76 runs east to west from the Nebraska state line to I-70 in Denver. It is about 184 miles long.

| Mile Marker | ↗ | * | ? | | | | | | | | | | | |
|---|---|---|---|---|---|---|---|---|---|---|---|---|---|---|
| 180 | b | | • | | | • | • | • | • | • | • | • | | |
| 125 | b | | | • | | • | • | • | | • | • | • | | |
| 66 | b | | | • | | • | • | • | | | | • | | |

| Exit | ↗ | * | W | S | K | T | Am | FJ | Lo | Pe | Pi | Sp | TA | Wi |
|---|---|---|---|---|---|---|---|---|---|---|---|---|---|---|
| 180 | b | | | | | | | • | | | | | | |
| 80 | b | | | | s | | | | | | | | | |
| 1a | b | | | n | | | | | | | | | | |

Interstate 225 is about 12 miles long and runs between I-25 in Denver and I-70 in Aurora.

| Exit | ↗ | * | W | S | K | T | Am | FJ | Lo | Pe | Pi | Sp | TA | Wi |
|---|---|---|---|---|---|---|---|---|---|---|---|---|---|---|
| 7 | b | | e | e | | e | | | | | | | | |

## Connecticut

**Rest Area Usage:** There is no limit to length of stay, however, no camping or overnight parking is permitted. **Road Conditions:** 800-443-6817 (weather) **State Police:** *General*, 860-685-8000; *Emergency*, 911 **Tourism Contact:** Connecticut Department of Economic Development, Tourism Division, 505 Hudson St, Hartford CT 06106. *Phone*: 800-282-6863 or 860-270-8080. *Internet*: www.ctbound.org

Interstate 84 runs east to west for 98 miles from the Massachusetts state line to the New York state line. Exit numbers are based on the consecutive numbering system rather than the mile marker system.

| Mile Marker | ↗ | * | Info (?) | Arrow | Trees | Restrooms | Phone | Picnic Table | Vending | Building | Pet Area | Handicap | Camera | Truck |
|---|---|---|---|---|---|---|---|---|---|---|---|---|---|---|
| 85 | b | 1 | • | • | | • | • | • | • | • | • | • | | |
| 42 | eb | | | • | | • | • | • | • | • | • | • | | |
| 2 | eb | | • | | | • | • | • | • | • | • | • | | |

Notes: 1) Rest area eastbound, Welcome Center westbound

| Exit | ↗ | * | W | S | K | T | Am | FJ | Lo | Pe | Pi | Sp | TA | Wi |
|---|---|---|---|---|---|---|---|---|---|---|---|---|---|---|
| 71 | b | | | | | | | | | | | | • | |
| 64 | b | | | | n | | | | | | | | | |
| 63 | b | | n | | | | | | | | | | | |
| 62 | b | | | n | | | | | | | | | | |
| 36 | b | | s | | | | | | | | | | | |
| 32 | b | | s | | | | | | | | | | | |
| 28 | b | | | | | | | | | | | | • | |
| 15 | b | | | | n | | | | | | | | | |

Interstate 91 runs north to south for 58 miles from the Massachusetts state line to I-95 in New Haven. Exit numbers are based on the consecutive numbering system rather than the mile marker system.

| Mile Marker | ↗ | * | Info (?) | Arrow | Trees | Restrooms | Phone | Picnic Table | Vending | Building | Pet Area | Handicap | Camera | Truck |
|---|---|---|---|---|---|---|---|---|---|---|---|---|---|---|
| 22 | nb | | | • | | • | • | • | • | • | • | • | | |
| 15 | sb | | | • | | • | • | • | • | • | • | • | | |

| Exit | ↗ | * | W | S | K | T | Am | FJ | Lo | Pe | Pi | Sp | TA | Wi |
|---|---|---|---|---|---|---|---|---|---|---|---|---|---|---|
| 48 | b | | | | | e | | | | | | | | |
| 44 | b | | e | | | | | | | | | | | |
| 39 | b | | | | w | | | | | | | | | |
| 24 | b | | w | | | | | | | | | | | |
| 21 | b | | w | | | | | | | | | | | |
| 8 | b | | | | e | | | | | | | | | |

Interstate 95 runs north to south for 112 miles from the Rhode Island state line to the New York state line. Exit numbers are based on the consecutive numbering system rather than the mile marker system.

| Mile Marker | ↗ | * | ? | ↗ | Trees | Restrooms | Phone | Picnic | Vending | Food | Pets | Handicapped | Camera | RV |
|---|---|---|---|---|---|---|---|---|---|---|---|---|---|---|
| 110 | sb | | • | | | • | • | • | | | | • | | |
| 100 | nb | | | | • | | | | | | | | • | |
| 74 | nb | | • | | | • | • | • | | | | • | | |
| 66 | b | 1 | | • | | • | • | | • | | • | • | | |
| 53 | b | 1 | | • | | • | • | | • | | • | • | | |
| 41 | b | 1 | | • | | • | • | • | • | | • | • | | |
| 25 | b | 1 | | • | | • | • | • | • | | • | • | | |
| 12 | nb | 1 | | • | | • | • | • | • | | • | • | | |
| 11 | sb | 1 | | • | | • | • | • | • | | • | • | | |

Notes: 1) Service Area, Gas, Food

| Exit | ↗ | * | W | S | K | T | Am | FJ | Lo | Pe | Pi | Sp | TA | Wi |
|---|---|---|---|---|---|---|---|---|---|---|---|---|---|---|
| 86 | b | | w | | | | | | | | | | | |
| 82 | b | | | | | w | | | | | | | | |
| 81 | b | | w | | | | | | | | | | | |
| 67 | b | | e | | | | | | | | | | | |
| 56 | b | | | | | | | | | | | | • | |
| 54 | b | | e | | | | | | | | | | | |
| 42 | b | 1 | | w | | | | | | | | | | |
| 40 | b | | | | | | | | | | • | | | |
| 34 | b | | | | e | | | | | | | | | |
| 33 | b | | e | | | | | | | | | | | |

Notes: 1) on US 1

I-395 is about 56 miles long and runs north to south from the Massachusetts state line to I-95, west of New London. Exit numbers are based on the consecutive numbering system rather than the mile marker system.

| Mile Marker | | * | ? | | | | | | | | | | | |
|---|---|---|---|---|---|---|---|---|---|---|---|---|---|---|
| 35 | b | | | • | | • | | | | | | • | | |
| 8 | sb | | | • | | • | • | • | • | | | • | | |

N ↕ S

| Exit | | * | W | S | K | T | Am | FJ | Lo | Pe | Pi | Sp | TA | Wi |
|---|---|---|---|---|---|---|---|---|---|---|---|---|---|---|
| 97 | b | | w | | e | | | | | | | | | |
| 84 | b | | e | | | | | | | | | | | |
| 80 | b | | w | | | | | | | | | | | |

## Delaware

**Rest Area Usage:** There is a 4 hour stay limit, no camping or overnight parking is allowed. **Road Conditions:** 800-652-5600 or 302-760-2080 (general) **State Police:** *General*, 302-739-5901; *Emergency*, 911 **Tourism Contact:** Delaware Tourism Office, 99 Kings Hwy, Dover DE 19901. *Phone*: 800-441-8846 or 302-739-4271. *Internet*: www.visitdelaware.com

Interstate 95 runs north to south for 23 miles from the Pennsylvania state line to the Maryland state line.

| Mile Marker | | * | ? | | | | | | | | | | | |
|---|---|---|---|---|---|---|---|---|---|---|---|---|---|---|
| 5 | b | 1 | | • | | • | • | • | • | | | • | | |

Notes: 1) Delaware House Service Area, Gas, Food, ATM

| Exit | | * | W | S | K | T | Am | FJ | Lo | Pe | Pi | Sp | TA | Wi |
|---|---|---|---|---|---|---|---|---|---|---|---|---|---|---|
| 11 | b | | | | e | | | | | | | | | |

# Florida

**Rest Area Usage:** There is a 3 hour stay limit, no camping or overnight parking allowed. **Road Conditions:** No central phone number. *Internet*: www11.myflorida.com **State Police:** *General*, 850-487-3139; *Emergency*, 911 **Tourism Contact:** Visit Florida, 661 E Jefferson St, Ste 300, Tallahassee FL 32301. *Phone*: 888-735-2872 or 850-488-5607. *Internet*: www.flausa.com **Notes:** In 2002 the Florida Department of Transportation began changing exit numbers along their Interstates. The exit numbers are being changed from the consecutive system to the mile marker system. References to the old exit numbers are given at the end of the charts.

Interstate 4 runs east to west for 134 miles from I-95 in Daytona Beach to I-275 in Tampa.

| Mile Marker | | * | | | | | | | | | | | | |
|---|---|---|---|---|---|---|---|---|---|---|---|---|---|---|
| 126 | eb | | | | • | | | | | | | | | |
| 95 | b | | | • | | • | • | • | • | | • | • | | |
| 46 | b | | | • | | • | • | • | • | | • | • | | |

E ↕ W

| Exit | | * | W | S | K | T | Am | FJ | Lo | Pe | Pi | Sp | TA | Wi |
|---|---|---|---|---|---|---|---|---|---|---|---|---|---|---|
| 98 | b | 1 | | | s | s | | | | | | | | |
| 74a | b | 2 | | | n | | | | | | | | | |
| 55 | b | 3 | | | | | | | | | | • | | |
| 32 | b | 4 | n | n | n | | | | | | | | | |
| 10 | b | 5 | | | | | | • | | | | | • | |
| 3 | b | 6 | | | | | | | | | | • | | |

Notes: 1) Old Exit 50; 2) Old Exit 29; 3) Old Exit 23; 4) Old Exit 18; 5) Old Exit 8; 6) Old Exit 3

Interstate 10 runs east to west for 370 miles from I-95 in Jacksonville to the Alabama state line.

| Mile Marker | | * | | | | | | | | | | | | |
|---|---|---|---|---|---|---|---|---|---|---|---|---|---|---|
| 352 | eb | | | • | | • | • | • | • | | | • | | |
| 351 | wb | | | • | | • | • | • | • | | | • | | |
| 318 | b | | | • | | • | • | • | • | | • | • | | |

| Mile Marker |  | * |  |  |  |  |  |  |  |  |  |  |  |  |
|---|---|---|---|---|---|---|---|---|---|---|---|---|---|---|
| 295 | wb |  |  | • |  | • | • | • | • |  | • | • |  |  |
| 294 | eb |  |  | • |  | • | • | • | • |  | • | • |  |  |
| 265 | b |  |  | • |  | • | • | • | • |  | • | • |  |  |
| 234 | b |  |  | • |  | • | • | • |  |  | • | • |  |  |
| 194 | b |  |  | • |  | • | • | • | • |  | • | • |  |  |
| 161 | b |  |  | • |  | • | • | • | • |  | • | • |  |  |
| 133 | b |  |  | • |  | • | • | • |  |  | • | • |  |  |
| 96 | b | 1 |  | • |  | • | • | • |  |  | • | • |  |  |
| 60 | wb |  |  | • |  | • | • | • | • |  | • | • |  |  |
| 58 | eb |  |  | • |  | • | • | • | • |  | • | • |  |  |
| 31 | b |  |  | • |  | • | • | • |  |  | • | • |  |  |
| 4 | eb |  | • |  |  | • | • | • | • |  | • | • |  |  |

E ↕ W

Notes: 1) South at exit 96 to Rest Area

| Exit |  | * | W | S | K | T | Am | FJ | Lo | Pe | Pi | Sp | TA | Wi |
|---|---|---|---|---|---|---|---|---|---|---|---|---|---|---|
| 357 | b | 1 | s |  |  |  |  |  |  |  |  |  |  |  |
| 343 | b | 2 |  |  |  |  |  |  |  |  | • |  | • |  |
| 335 | b | 3 | n |  |  |  |  |  |  |  |  |  |  |  |
| 283 | b | 4 | s |  |  |  |  |  |  |  |  |  |  |  |
| 203 | b | 5 | n |  |  |  |  |  |  |  |  |  |  |  |
| 199 | b | 6 |  | n |  |  |  |  |  |  |  |  |  |  |
| 192 | b | 7 |  |  |  |  |  | • |  |  |  |  |  | • |
| 142 | b | 8 |  |  |  |  |  |  |  |  | • | • | • |  |
| 120 | b | 9 | n |  |  |  |  |  |  |  |  |  |  |  |
| 83 | b | 10 | n |  |  |  |  |  |  |  |  |  |  |  |
| 56 | b | 11 | n |  |  |  |  |  |  |  |  |  |  |  |
| 22 | b | 12 | n+ |  | n+ |  |  |  |  |  |  |  |  |  |
| 13 | b | 13 |  |  |  |  |  |  |  |  | • |  |  |  |
| 10b | b | 14 | n |  |  |  |  |  |  |  |  |  |  |  |

E ↕ W

Notes: 1) Old Exit 54; 2) Old Exit 50; 3) Old Exit 48; 4) Old Exit 40; 5) Old Exit 30; 6) Old Exit 29; 7) Old Exit 27; 8) Old Exit 21; 9) Old Exit 18; 10) Old Exit 14; 11) Old Exit 12; 12) Old Exit 7; 13) Old Exit 5; 14) Old Exit 3ab

75

Interstate 75 runs north to south for 472 miles from the Georgia state line to the junction with FL 826 in Miami.

| Mile Marker |  | * |  |  |  |  |  |  |  |  |  |  |  |  |
|---|---|---|---|---|---|---|---|---|---|---|---|---|---|---|
| 470 | sb |  | • |  |  | • | • | • | • |  | • | • |  |  |

| Mile Marker | | * | | | | | | | | | | | | |
|---|---|---|---|---|---|---|---|---|---|---|---|---|---|---|
| 413 | b | | | • | | • | • | • | • | | • | • | | |
| 383 | b | | | • | | • | • | • | • | | • | • | | |
| 346 | b | | | • | | • | • | • | • | | • | • | | |
| 307 | b | | | • | | • | • | • | • | | • | • | | |
| 278 | b | | | • | | • | • | • | • | | • | • | | |
| 238 | b | | | • | | • | • | • | • | | • | • | | |
| 161 | b | 1 | | • | | • | • | • | • | | • | • | | |
| 131 | b | 2 | | • | | • | • | • | • | | • | • | | |
| 63 | b | | | • | | • | • | • | • | | • | • | | |
| 41 | sb | | | | • | | | • | | | | | | |
| 38 | nb | | | | • | | | • | | | | | | |
| 35 | b | | | • | | • | • | • | • | | • | • | | |
| 32 | b | | | | • | | | • | | | | | | |

Notes: 1) East at exit 161 to Rest Area; 2) East at exit 131 to Rest Area

| Exit | | * | W | S | K | T | Am | FJ | Lo | Pe | Pi | Sp | TA | Wi |
|---|---|---|---|---|---|---|---|---|---|---|---|---|---|---|
| 427 | b | 1 | e | | e | | | | | | | | | |
| 387 | b | 2 | | | w | | | | | | | | | |
| 384 | b | 3 | e | | | e | | | | | | | | |
| 368 | b | 4 | | | | | | | | • | | | | |
| 358 | b | 5 | | | | | | | | | • | | | • |
| 350 | b | 6 | e | w | e | e | | | | | | | | |
| 341 | b | 7 | | | | | | | | | • | | | |
| 329 | b | 8 | | | | | | | | | • | | • | |
| 285 | b | 9 | | | | | | • | | | | | | |
| 257 | b | 10 | | e | e | | | | | | | | | |
| 240 | b | 11 | e | | | | | | | | | | | |
| 224 | b | 12 | | | e | | | | | | • | | | |
| 217 | b | 13 | | | e | | | | | | | | | |
| 210 | b | 14 | | | | w | | | | | | | | |
| 207 | b | 15 | w | | | | | | | | | | | |
| 161 | b | 16 | | | | | | | | | • | | | |
| 139 | b | 17 | | | | | | | | | • | | | |
| 9ab | b | 18 | | | w | | | | | | | | | |

Notes: 1) Old Exit 82; 2) Old Exit 76; 3) Old Exit 75; 4) Old Exit 72; 5) Old Exit 71; 6) Old Exit 68; 7) Old Exit 67; 8) Old Exit 66; 9) Old Exit 59; 10) Old Exit 51; 11) Old Exit 46; 12) Old Exit 43; 13) Old Exit 41; 14) Old Exit 39; 15) Old Exit 38; 16) Old Exit 28; 17) Old Exit 24; 18) Old Exit 5

Interstate 95 runs north to south for 382 miles from the Georgia state line to US 1 in Miami.

| Mile Marker | | * | | | | | | | | | | | | |
|---|---|---|---|---|---|---|---|---|---|---|---|---|---|---|
| 378 | sb | | • | | | • | • | • | • | | • | • | | |
| 331 | b | | | • | | • | • | • | • | | • | • | | |
| 302 | b | | | • | | • | • | • | • | | • | • | | |
| 255 | sb | | | • | | • | • | • | • | | • | • | | |
| 253 | nb | | | • | | • | • | • | • | | • | • | | |
| 227 | sb | | | • | | • | • | • | • | | • | • | | |
| 225 | nb | | | • | | • | • | • | • | | • | • | | |
| 209 | b | | | | • | | | • | | | | | | |
| 189 | b | | | | • | | | • | | | | | | |
| 168 | b | | | • | | • | • | • | • | | • | • | | |
| 133 | b | | | • | | • | • | • | • | | • | • | | |
| 106 | b | | | • | | • | • | • | • | | • | • | | |

| Exit | | * | W | S | K | T | Am | FJ | Lo | Pe | Pi | Sp | TA | Wi |
|---|---|---|---|---|---|---|---|---|---|---|---|---|---|---|
| 360 | b | 1 | | e | | | | | | | | | | |
| 329 | b | 2 | | | | | | | | | • | | • | |
| 305 | b | 3 | | | | | | • | | | | | | |
| 289 | b | 4 | w | | w | | | | | | | | | |
| 268 | b | 5 | e | | e | | | | | | | | | |
| 261 | b | 6 | | | | e | | | | | | | | |
| 256 | b | 7 | e | | | | | | | | | | | |
| 249 | b | 8 | e | | | | | | | | | | | |
| 215 | b | 9 | e | | | | | | | | | | | |
| 201 | b | 10 | | | | | | | | | • | | | |
| 180 | b | 11 | | e | | | | | | | | | | |
| 176 | b | 12 | e | | | | | | | | | | | |
| 173 | b | 13 | | | | | | | | | | • | | |
| 147 | b | 14 | | | | | | | | | | | • | |
| 131b | b | 15 | | | | | | • | | | | | | |
| 129 | b | 16 | e | | | | | | | | • | | | |
| 87ab | b | 17 | e | | | | | | | | | | | |
| 77 | b | 18 | | | e | | | | | | | | | |
| 71 | b | 19 | | | | e | | | | | | | | |
| 60 | b | 20 | | e | | | | | | | | | | |
| 59 | b | 21 | | | | w | | | | | | | | |
| 57 | b | 22 | w | | | | | | | | | | | |

| | Exit | | * | W | S | K | T | Am | FJ | Lo | Pe | Pi | Sp | TA | Wi |
|---|---|---|---|---|---|---|---|---|---|---|---|---|---|---|---|
| N | 51 | b | 23 | | | | e | | | | | | | | |
| | 44 | b | 24 | | | e | | | | | | | | | |
| | 38 | b | 25 | e | | | | | | | | | | | |
| S | 22 | b | 26 | | | e | | | | | | | | | |

Notes: 1) Old Exit 125; 2) Old Exit 96; 3) Old Exit 93; 4) Old Exit 91c; 5) Old Exit 88; 6) Old Exit 87; 7) Old Exit 85; 8) Old Exit 84; 9) Old Exit 79; 10) Old Edit 75; 11) Old Exit 71; 12) Old Exit 70a; 13) Old Exit 70; 14) Old Exit 68; 15) Old Exit 66b; 16) Old Exit 65; 17) Old Exit 59ab; 18) Old Exit 56; 19) Old Exit 53; 20) Old Exit 45; 21) Old Exit 44c; 22) Old Exit 44; 23) Old Exit 41; 24) Old Exit 38; 25) Old Exit 35ab; 26) Old Exit 25

Interstate 275 runs north to south for about 60 miles from I-75 north of Tampa to I-75 north of Bradenton.

| | Mile Marker | | * | ? | | | | | | | | | | | |
|---|---|---|---|---|---|---|---|---|---|---|---|---|---|---|---|
| N | 13 | b | | | • | | • | • | • | • | | • | • | | |
| S | 7 | b | | | • | | • | • | • | • | | • | • | | |

| Exit | | * | W | S | K | T | Am | FJ | Lo | Pe | Pi | Sp | TA | Wi |
|---|---|---|---|---|---|---|---|---|---|---|---|---|---|---|
| 49 | b | 1 | | | w | | | | | | | | | |
| 41ab | b | 2 | w | w+ | | | | | | | | | | |

Notes: 1) Old Exit 32; 2) Old Exit 23ab

I-295 forms a partial loop around Jacksonville that is 35 miles long.

| Exit | | * | W | S | K | T | Am | FJ | Lo | Pe | Pi | Sp | TA | Wi |
|---|---|---|---|---|---|---|---|---|---|---|---|---|---|---|
| 32 | b | 1 | e | | | | | | | | | | | |
| 19 | b | 2 | e | | w | | | | | | | | | |
| 16 | b | 3 | e | | | | | | | | | | | |
| 12 | b | 4 | | w | | w | | | | | | | | |
| 5ab | b | 5 | w | | | | | | | | | | | |

Notes: 1) Old Exit 13a; 2) Old Exit 7; 3) Old Exit 5; 4) Old Exit 4; 5) Old Exit 2ab

Interstate 595 is about 12 miles long and runs east to west between US 1 in Fort Lauderdale and I-75 in Weston.

| Exit | ⤢ | * | W | S | K | T | Am | FJ | Lo | Pe | Pi | Sp | TA | Wi |
|---|---|---|---|---|---|---|---|---|---|---|---|---|---|---|
| 5 | b | 1 | | | s | | | | | | | | | |

Notes: 1) Old Exit 6

Florida's Turnpike is a system of 443 miles of limited-access toll highways. The charts below cover 312 miles of the system from I-75 in northern Florida to Homestead in southern Florida.

| Mile Marker | ⤢ | * | ? | ⬈ | 🌲 | 🚻 | ☎ | ⛱ | ▯ | ▤ | 🐕 | ♿ | ◙ | ✎ |
|---|---|---|---|---|---|---|---|---|---|---|---|---|---|---|
| 299 | b | 1 | | • | | • | • | • | | | | • | | |
| 263 | b | 1 | | • | | • | • | • | | | | • | | |
| 229 | b | 1 | | • | | • | • | • | | | | • | | |
| 184 | b | 1 | | • | | • | • | • | | | | • | | |
| 144 | b | 1 | | • | | • | • | • | | | | • | | |
| 94 | b | 1 | | • | | • | • | • | | | | • | | |
| 65 | b | 1 | | • | | • | • | • | | | | • | | |
| 19 | b | 1 | | • | | • | • | • | | | | • | | |

N ↕ S

Notes: 1) Service Area, Gas, Food

| Exit | ⤢ | * | W | S | K | T | Am | FJ | Lo | Pe | Pi | Sp | TA | Wi |
|---|---|---|---|---|---|---|---|---|---|---|---|---|---|---|
| 193 | b | | | | | | | | | | • | | | |

## Georgia

**Rest Area Usage:** There is no limit to length of stay, however, no camping or overnight parking is permitted. **Road Conditions:** 404-635-8000 (construction) **State Police:** *General*, 404-657-9300; *Emergency*, 911 **Tourism Contact:** Georgia Department of Industry, Trade & Tourism, 285 Peachtree Center Ave NE, Suite 1000, Atlanta GA 30303. *Phone*: 800-847-4842 or 404-656-3590. *Internet*: www.georgia.org

I-16 runs east to west for 167 miles from Savannah to I-75 in Macon.

| Mile Marker | ⤢ | * | ? | ⬈ | 🌲 | 🚻 | ☎ | ⛱ | ▯ | ▤ | 🐕 | ♿ | ◙ | ✎ |
|---|---|---|---|---|---|---|---|---|---|---|---|---|---|---|
| 46 | wb | | | • | | • | • | • | • | • | • | • | | |

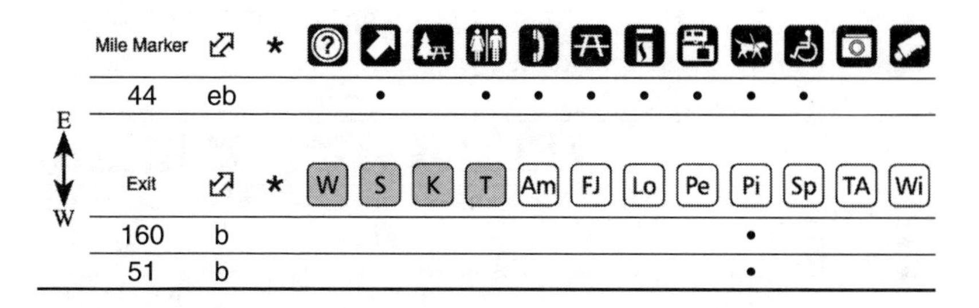

| Mile Marker | ⤢ | * | Info | Arrow | Trees/Picnic | Restrooms | Phone | Picnic Table | Vending | RV | Pet | Handicapped | Camera | Truck |
|---|---|---|---|---|---|---|---|---|---|---|---|---|---|---|
| 44 | eb | | | • | | • | • | • | • | • | • | • | | |

E ↕ W

| Exit | ⤢ | * | W | S | K | T | Am | FJ | Lo | Pe | Pi | Sp | TA | Wi |
|---|---|---|---|---|---|---|---|---|---|---|---|---|---|---|
| 160 | b | | | | | | | | | | • | | | |
| 51 | b | | | | | | | | | | • | | | |

**20**

Interstate 20 runs east to west for 202 miles from the South Carolina state line to the Alabama state line.

| Mile Marker | ⤢ | * | Info | Arrow | Trees/Picnic | Restrooms | Phone | Picnic Table | Vending | RV | Pet | Handicapped | Camera | Truck |
|---|---|---|---|---|---|---|---|---|---|---|---|---|---|---|
| 201 | wb | | • | | | • | • | • | • | • | • | • | | |
| 182 | b | | | • | | • | • | • | • | • | • | • | | |
| 108 | wb | | | • | | • | • | • | • | • | • | • | | |
| 103 | eb | | | • | | • | • | • | • | • | • | • | | |
| 79 | eb | | | | • | | • | | | | | | | |
| 1 | eb | | • | | | • | • | • | • | | • | • | | |

E ↕ W

| Exit | ⤢ | * | W | S | K | T | Am | FJ | Lo | Pe | Pi | Sp | TA | Wi |
|---|---|---|---|---|---|---|---|---|---|---|---|---|---|---|
| 200 | b | | | | | | | | | | • | | | |
| 196b | b | | n | n | | | | | | | | | | |
| 196a | b | | | | | s | | | | | | | | |
| 172 | b | | s+ | | s | | | | | | | | | |
| 114 | b | | n | | | | | | | | | | • | • |
| 90 | b | | | | s | | | | | | | | | |
| 82 | b | | n | | | s | | | | | | | | |
| 74 | b | | | | | | | | | | | • | | |
| 68 | b | | n | | | | | | | | | | | |
| 46ab | b | | | | | | | | | | | | | |
| 44 | b | | s | | | | | | | | | | | |
| 41 | b | | | | | | | | | | | • | | |
| 37 | b | | | | | | | | | | | | | |
| 36 | b | | | | | s | | | | | | | | |
| 34 | b | | n | n | s | | | | | | | | | |
| 24 | b | | s | | | | | | | | | | | |
| 19 | b | | | | | | | • | | | | | | • |
| 11 | b | | n | | | | | | | | | | | |
| 5 | b | | | | | | | | | | • | | | |

Interstate 59 runs north to south for 20 miles from I-24 near the Tennessee state line to the Alabama state line.

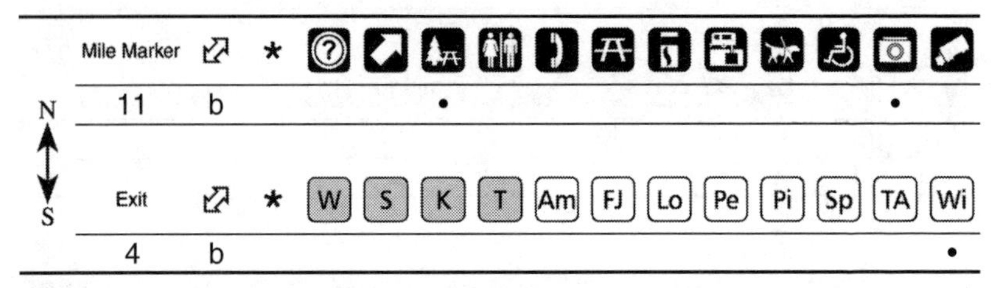

| Mile Marker | ↗ | * | ? | | | | | | | | | | | |
|---|---|---|---|---|---|---|---|---|---|---|---|---|---|---|
| 11 | b | | | | • | | | | | | | | • | |

| Exit | ↗ | * | W | S | K | T | Am | FJ | Lo | Pe | Pi | Sp | TA | Wi |
|---|---|---|---|---|---|---|---|---|---|---|---|---|---|---|
| 4 | b | | | | | | | | | | | | | • |

Interstate 75 runs north to south for 355 miles from the Tennessee state line to the Florida state line.

| Mile Marker | ↗ | * | ? | | | | | | | | | | | |
|---|---|---|---|---|---|---|---|---|---|---|---|---|---|---|
| 352 | sb | | • | | | • | • | • | • | • | • | • | | |
| 319 | sb | | | • | | • | • | • | • | • | • | • | | |
| 308 | nb | | | • | | • | • | • | • | • | • | • | | |
| 179 | sb | | | • | | • | • | • | • | | • | • | | |
| 118 | sb | | | • | | • | • | • | • | • | • | • | | |
| 108 | nb | | | • | | • | • | • | • | • | • | • | | |
| 85 | nb | | | • | | • | • | • | • | • | • | • | | |
| 76 | sb | | | • | | • | • | • | • | • | • | • | | |
| 48 | sb | | | • | | • | • | • | • | • | • | • | | |
| 47 | nb | | | • | | • | • | • | • | • | • | • | | |
| 3 | nb | | • | | | • | • | • | • | | • | • | | |

| Exit | ↗ | * | W | S | K | T | Am | FJ | Lo | Pe | Pi | Sp | TA | Wi |
|---|---|---|---|---|---|---|---|---|---|---|---|---|---|---|
| 350 | b | | w+ | | | | | | | | | | | |
| 345 | b | | | | | | • | | | | | | | |
| 333 | b | | | | e | | | | | | | | | |
| 328 | b | | | | | | | | | | • | | | |
| 326 | b | | | | | | | | | | | | | • |
| 320 | b | | | | | | | • | | | | | | |
| 312 | b | | w | | | | | | | | | | | |
| 296 | b | | | | | | | | | | • | | • | |
| 290 | b | | | | | | | | | | | • | | |
| 278 | b | | | | w | | | | | | | | | |
| 271 | b | | e | | | | | | | | | | | |
| 269 | b | | | | | w | | | | | | | | |
| 263 | b | | | w+ | w+ | | | | | | | | | |

| Exit | ↗ | * | W | S | K | T | Am | FJ | Lo | Pe | Pi | Sp | TA | Wi |
|---|---|---|---|---|---|---|---|---|---|---|---|---|---|---|
| 260 | b | | | | | w | | | | | | | | |
| 241 | b | | | | e | | | | | | | | | |
| 235 | b | | | | e | | | | | | | | | |
| 233 | b | | w | | | | | | | | | | | |
| 231 | b | | | | | w | | | | | | | | |
| 218 | b | | e | | | | | | | | | • | | |
| 201 | b | | | | | | | • | | | | | • | |
| 187 | b | | w | | | | | | | | | | | |
| 169 | b | | | | w | | | | | | | | | |
| 162 | b | | w | | w | | | | | | | | | |
| 149 | b | | | | | | | | | | • | • | | |
| 136 | b | | e | | | | | | | | | • | | |
| 101 | b | | w | | | | | | | | | | | • |
| 97 | b | | | | | | | | | | | | • | |
| 63a | b | | e | | e | | | | | | | | | |
| 60 | b | | | | | | | | | | • | | | |
| 18 | b | | e | | | e | | | | | | | | |
| 16 | b | | | e | | | | | | | | | | |
| 11 | b | | | | | | | | | | • | | | |
| 2 | b | | | | | | | • | | | | | • | |

**85** Interstate 85 runs north to south for 179 miles from the South Carolina state line to the Alabama state line.

| Mile Marker | ↗ | * | Info | Welcome | Picnic area | Restrooms | Phone | Picnic tables | Vending | Map | Pets | Handicap | Camera | Security |
|---|---|---|---|---|---|---|---|---|---|---|---|---|---|---|
| 176 | sb | | • | | | • | • | • | • | • | • | • | | |
| 160 | nb | | | • | | • | • | • | • | | • | • | | |
| 114 | sb | | | • | | • | • | • | • | | • | • | | |
| 112 | nb | | | • | | • | • | • | • | | • | • | | |
| 0.5 | nb | | • | | | • | • | • | • | • | • | • | | |

| Exit | ↗ | * | W | S | K | T | Am | FJ | Lo | Pe | Pi | Sp | TA | Wi |
|---|---|---|---|---|---|---|---|---|---|---|---|---|---|---|
| 160 | b | | | | | | | • | | • | | | | |
| 149 | b | | e | | | | | | | | | | • | |
| 147 | b | | | | | | | | | | | | | • |
| 129 | b | | | | | | | | | | • | | | |
| 115 | b | | w+ | | | w | | | | | | | | |
| 104 | b | | e | | e | | | | | | | | | |
| 103 | b | | | w | | | | | | | | | | |

| | Exit | ↗ | * | W | S | K | T | Am | FJ | Lo | Pe | Pi | Sp | TA | Wi |
|---|---|---|---|---|---|---|---|---|---|---|---|---|---|---|---|
| N ↕ S | 99 | b | | | | e+ | | | | | | | | | |
| | 91 | b | | | w | | | | | | | | | | |
| | 89 | b | | | | | e | | | | | | | | |
| | 69 | b | | | | | w | | | | | | | | |
| | 66 | b | | | | | | | | | | | • | | |
| | 64 | b | | w | | | | | | | | | | | |
| | 47 | b | | e | | | | | | | | | | | |
| | 41 | b | | | | | | | | | | | | | • |
| | 13 | b | | | | | | | | | | • | | | |

## 95

Interstate 95 runs north to south for 113 miles from the South Carolina state line to the Florida state line.

| Mile Marker | ↗ | * | ? | ↗ | 🌲 | 🚻 | ☎ | ⛱ | Vending | 🚌 | 🐕 | ♿ | 📷 | 🚛 |
|---|---|---|---|---|---|---|---|---|---|---|---|---|---|---|
| 111 | sb | | • | | | • | • | • | • | | • | • | | |
| 41 | sb | | | • | | • | • | • | • | • | • | • | | |
| 1 | nb | 1 | • | | | • | • | • | • | • | • | • | | |

Notes: 1) East at exit to Welcome Center

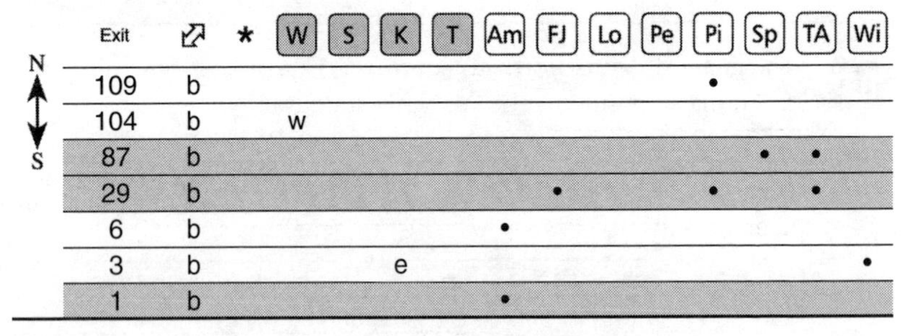

| | Exit | ↗ | * | W | S | K | T | Am | FJ | Lo | Pe | Pi | Sp | TA | Wi |
|---|---|---|---|---|---|---|---|---|---|---|---|---|---|---|---|
| N ↕ S | 109 | b | | | | | | | | | | • | | | |
| | 104 | b | | w | | | | | | | | | | | |
| | 87 | b | | | | | | | | | | | • | • | |
| | 29 | b | | | | | | | • | | | • | | • | |
| | 6 | b | | | | | | • | | | | | | | |
| | 3 | b | | | | e | | | | | | | | | • |
| | 1 | b | | | | | | • | | | | | | | |

## 185

Interstate 185 is about 48 miles long. It runs north to south between I-85 near La Grange and US 27 south of Columbus.

| Mile Marker | ↗ | * | ? | ↗ | 🌲 | 🚻 | ☎ | ⛱ | Vending | 🚌 | 🐕 | ♿ | 📷 | 🚛 |
|---|---|---|---|---|---|---|---|---|---|---|---|---|---|---|
| 12 | b | 1 | • | | | • | • | • | • | • | • | • | | |

Notes: 1) West at exit to Welcome Center

| Exit | ↗ | * | W | S | K | T | Am | FJ | Lo | Pe | Pi | Sp | TA | Wi |
|---|---|---|---|---|---|---|---|---|---|---|---|---|---|---|
| 8 | b | | e | e | w | | | | | | | | | |
| 4 | b | | e | | | | | | | | | | | |

Interstate 285 is a 62-mile loop around Atlanta. Exit numbering begins at Washington Road and increases in a clockwise direction.

| Exit | | * | W | S | K | T | Am | FJ | Lo | Pe | Pi | Sp | TA | Wi |
|---|---|---|---|---|---|---|---|---|---|---|---|---|---|---|
| 53 | b | | | | | | | | | | | • | • | |
| 51 | b | | | | | | | | | | • | | | |
| 43 | b | | | | | w | | | | | | | | |
| 32 | b | | | | e | e | | | | | | | | |
| 29 | b | | n | | | | | | | | | | | |
| 25 | b | | | | n | | | | | | | | | |
| 19 | b | | | | | n | | | | | | | | |
| 16 | b | | | | | | | | | | • | | | |
| 12 | b | | | | | | | | | • | | | | |

Interstate 475 runs north to south for 16 miles. It begins on I-75 at exit 177 and ends at I-75 exit 156, bypassing Macon.

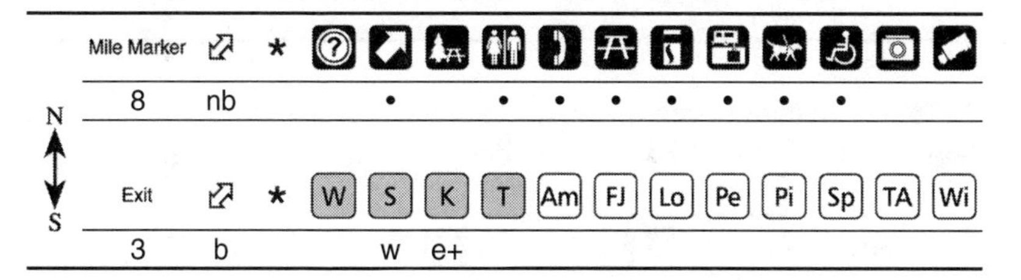

| Mile Marker | | * | | | | | | | | | | | | |
|---|---|---|---|---|---|---|---|---|---|---|---|---|---|---|
| 8 | nb | | | • | | • | • | • | • | • | • | • | | |

N ↕ S

| Exit | | * | W | S | K | T | Am | FJ | Lo | Pe | Pi | Sp | TA | Wi |
|---|---|---|---|---|---|---|---|---|---|---|---|---|---|---|
| 3 | b | | | w | e+ | | | | | | | | | |

Interstate 575 is 27 miles long. It runs north to south from GA 5 near Nelson to I-75 exit 268, north of Atlanta.

| Exit | | * | W | S | K | T | Am | FJ | Lo | Pe | Pi | Sp | TA | Wi |
|---|---|---|---|---|---|---|---|---|---|---|---|---|---|---|
| 20 | b | | e | | | | | | | | | | | |
| 8 | b | | e | | | | | | | | | | | |
| 7 | b | | | | w | | | | | | | | | |

Interstate 675 runs north to south for 10 miles between I-285 and I-75 near Atlanta.

| Exit | | * | W | S | K | T | Am | FJ | Lo | Pe | Pi | Sp | TA | Wi |
|---|---|---|---|---|---|---|---|---|---|---|---|---|---|---|
| 2 | b | | | | | | | | | | | • | | |
| 1 | b | | e | | e | | | | | | | | | |

Interstate 985 is 25 miles long. It runs north to south from US 23 near Gainesville to I-85 exit 113.

| Exit | ↗ | * | W | S | K | T | Am | FJ | Lo | Pe | Pi | Sp | TA | Wi |
|---|---|---|---|---|---|---|---|---|---|---|---|---|---|---|
| 16 | b | | | n | | | | | | | | | | |
| 4 | b | | s | | | | | | | | | | | |

## Idaho

**Rest Area Usage:** There is an 8 hour stay limit, overnight parking permitted. No camping or sleeping outside of vehicle is allowed. **Road Conditions:** 888-432-7623 or 208-336-6600 (general) **State Police:** *General*, 208-846-7512; *Emergency*, *477 on cell phone or 208-772-8585 (north) or 208-846-7500 (west) or 208-236-6066(east) **Tourism Contact:** Idaho Travel Council, PO Box 83720, Boise ID 83720. *Phone*: 800-847-4843. *Internet*: www.visitid.org

Interstate 15 runs north to south for 196 miles from the Montana state line to the Utah state line.

N ↕ S

| Mile Marker | ↗ | * | (?) | ↗ | 🌲 | 🚻 | ☎ | 🛋 | 🥤 | 🖽 | 🐕 | ♿ | 🗖 | 🚛 |
|---|---|---|---|---|---|---|---|---|---|---|---|---|---|---|
| 167 | b | 1 | | • | | • | • | • | | | • | • | | |
| 142 | b | | | | • | | | | | | | | | |
| 101 | b | | | • | | • | • | • | | | • | • | | |
| 59 | b | | | • | | • | • | • | • | | • | • | | |
| 25 | sb | | | • | | • | • | • | • | | • | • | | |
| 7 | nb | | • | | | • | • | • | • | | • | • | | |

Notes: 1) East at exit to Rest Area

N ↕ S

| Exit | ↗ | * | W | S | K | T | Am | FJ | Lo | Pe | Pi | Sp | TA | Wi |
|---|---|---|---|---|---|---|---|---|---|---|---|---|---|---|
| 119 | b | | | | | | • | | | | | | | |
| 93 | b | | e | | | | | • | | | | | | |
| 47 | b | | | | | | | • | | | | | | |

Interstate 84 runs east to west for approximately 276 miles from the Utah state line to the Oregon state line.

| Mile Marker | ↗ | * | Info | Arrow | Trees | Restrooms | Phone | Picnic | Vending | RV | Pets | Handicap | Camera | Truck |
|---|---|---|---|---|---|---|---|---|---|---|---|---|---|---|
| 269 | b | | | • | | • | • | • | | | • | • | | |
| 229 | b | | | • | | • | • | • | • | | • | • | | |
| 171 | eb | | | • | | • | • | • | • | | • | • | | |
| 133 | b | 1 | | • | | • | • | • | • | | • | • | | |
| 62 | b | | | • | | • | • | • | • | | • | • | | |
| 1 | eb | | • | | | • | • | • | • | | • | • | | |

Notes: 1) Phones at wb Rest Area only

| Exit | ↗ | * | W | S | K | T | Am | FJ | Lo | Pe | Pi | Sp | TA | Wi |
|---|---|---|---|---|---|---|---|---|---|---|---|---|---|---|
| 208 | b | | s | | | | | | | | | | | |
| 182 | b | | | | | | • | | | | | | | |
| 173 | b | | | | | s+ | | • | | | | | | |
| 168 | b | | n | | | | | | | | | | | |
| 95 | b | | s | | | | | | | | • | | | |
| 54 | b | | | | | | | • | | | | | • | |
| 50 | b | | s | | | | | | | | | | | |
| 29 | b | | | | | | | • | | | | | | |

86

Interstate 86 runs east to west for about 63 miles from I-15 in Pocatello to I-84 exit 222, east of Heyburn.

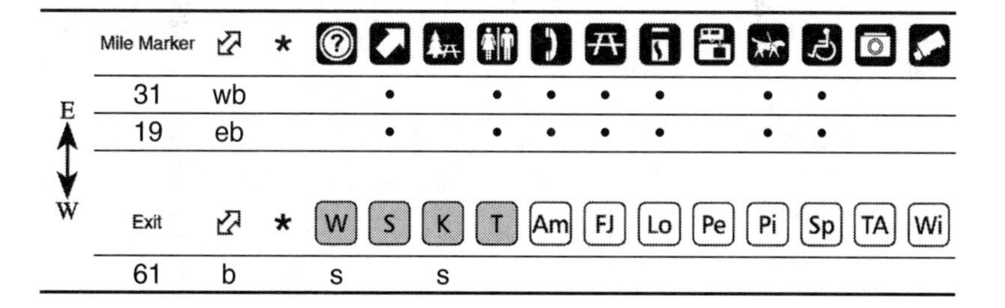

| Mile Marker | ↗ | * | Info | Arrow | Trees | Restrooms | Phone | Picnic | Vending | RV | Pets | Handicap | Camera | Truck |
|---|---|---|---|---|---|---|---|---|---|---|---|---|---|---|
| 31 | wb | | | • | | • | • | • | • | | • | • | | |
| 19 | eb | | | • | | • | • | • | • | | • | • | | |

| Exit | ↗ | * | W | S | K | T | Am | FJ | Lo | Pe | Pi | Sp | TA | Wi |
|---|---|---|---|---|---|---|---|---|---|---|---|---|---|---|
| 61 | b | | s | | s | | | | | | | | | |

90

Interstate 90 runs east to west for 74 miles from the Montana state line to the Washington state line.

| Mile Marker | ↗ | * | Info | Arrow | Trees | Restrooms | Phone | Picnic | Vending | RV | Pets | Handicap | Camera | Truck |
|---|---|---|---|---|---|---|---|---|---|---|---|---|---|---|
| 73 | wb | | | | • | | | | | | | | • | |
| 72 | eb | | | | • | | | | | | | | • | |
| 71 | wb | | | | | | | | | | | | | • |
| 70 | wb | | | | | | | | | | | | | • |

| Mile Marker | ↗ | * | | | | | | | | | | | | |
|---|---|---|---|---|---|---|---|---|---|---|---|---|---|---|
| 28 | b | | | | • | | | | | | | | | |
| 8 | b | 1 | • | • | | • | • | • | • | | • | • | | |

Notes: 1) Welcome Center eb, Rest Area wb

| E↕W Exit | ↗ | * | W | S | K | T | Am | FJ | Lo | Pe | Pi | Sp | TA | Wi |
|---|---|---|---|---|---|---|---|---|---|---|---|---|---|---|
| 12 | b | | | | n | | | | | | | | | |
| 7 | b | | n | | | | | | | | | | | |
| 2 | b | | | | | | | • | | | | | | |

**184** Interstate 184 is a 6-mile spur off I-84 that ends at 13th Street in downtown Boise.

| Exit | ↗ | * | W | S | K | T | Am | FJ | Lo | Pe | Pi | Sp | TA | Wi |
|---|---|---|---|---|---|---|---|---|---|---|---|---|---|---|
| 1 | b | | | | | w | | | | | | | | |

# Illinois

**Rest Area Usage:** There is a 3 hour stay limit, however, the length of stay may be limited further when capacities of the facilities are approached or exceeded. Camping or overnight parking is not permitted. **Road Conditions:** 800-452-4368 or 312-368-4636 (general) **State Police:** *General*, 217-786-7103; *Emergency*, 911 **Tourism Contact:** Illinois Bureau of Tourism, 620 E Adams St, Springfield IL 62701. *Phone*: 800-226-6632. *Internet*: www.enjoyillinois.com

**24** Interstate 24 runs east to west for 38 miles from the Kentucky state line to Interstate 57 exit 44.

| Mile Marker | ↗ | * | | | | | | | | | | | | |
|---|---|---|---|---|---|---|---|---|---|---|---|---|---|---|
| 37 | b | 1 | • | | | • | • | • | • | | • | • | | |

Notes: 1) North at exit to Welcome Center

Interstate 39 runs north to south for about 140 miles from the Wisconsin state line to I-55 exit 164. From Rockford to the Wisconsin state line, the Interstate is also I-90.

| Mile Marker | [direction] | * | (?) | [arrow] | [trees] | [restrooms] | [phone] | [picnic] | [vending] | [icon] | [pet] | [wheelchair] | [icon] | [icon] |
|---|---|---|---|---|---|---|---|---|---|---|---|---|---|---|
| 2 | nb | 1 | • | | | • | • | • | • | • | • | • | | |
| 85 | b | | | • | | • | • | • | • | • | • | • | | |

Notes: 1) Shared with I-90 / Follows I-90 numbering

| Exit | [direction] | * | W | S | K | T | Am | FJ | Lo | Pe | Pi | Sp | TA | Wi |
|---|---|---|---|---|---|---|---|---|---|---|---|---|---|---|
| 99 | b | | | | | | | | | • | | | | |

55

I-55 runs north to south for 295 miles from Chicago to the Missouri state line. Portions of the Interstate are shared with I-70, I-72, and I-74.

| Mile Marker | [direction] | * | (?) | [arrow] | [trees] | [restrooms] | [phone] | [picnic] | [vending] | [icon] | [pet] | [wheelchair] | [icon] | [icon] |
|---|---|---|---|---|---|---|---|---|---|---|---|---|---|---|
| 194 | b | | | • | | • | • | • | • | | • | • | | |
| 149 | b | | | • | | • | • | • | • | | • | • | | |
| 103 | sb | | | • | | • | • | • | • | | • | • | | |
| 102 | nb | | | • | | • | • | • | • | | • | • | | |
| 64 | b | | | • | | • | • | • | • | | • | • | | |
| 27 | b | 1 | • | • | | • | • | • | • | | | • | | |

Notes: 1) Welcome Center nb, Rest Area sb

| Exit | [direction] | * | W | S | K | T | Am | FJ | Lo | Pe | Pi | Sp | TA | Wi |
|---|---|---|---|---|---|---|---|---|---|---|---|---|---|---|
| 289 | nb | | | | | | | | | | | • | | |
| 279b | b | | w+ | w+ | | w+ | | | | | | | | |
| 267 | b | | w | | | | | | | | | | | |
| 257 | b | | | | e | | | | | | | | | |
| 197 | b | | e | | e | | | | | | | | | |
| 160 | b | 1 | | | | | | | | | • | • | • | |
| 126 | b | | e+ | | | | | | | | | | | |
| 98b | b | 2 | | | w | | | | | | | | | |
| 52 | b | | e | | | | | | | | | | | |
| 18 | b | 3 | | | | | | | | | • | | | |
| 4 | b | 3 | | | | | • | | | | | | | |

Notes: 1) Shared with I-74; 2) Shared with I-72; 3) Shared with I-70

Interstate 57 runs north to south for 358 miles from Chicago to the Missouri state line. Portions of the Interstate are shared with I-64 and I-70.

| Mile Marker | | * | | | | | | | | | | | | |
|---|---|---|---|---|---|---|---|---|---|---|---|---|---|---|
| 332 | b | | • | | | • | • | • | • | • | • | • | | |
| 268 | b | | | • | | • | • | • | • | • | • | • | | |
| 222 | b | | | • | | • | • | • | • | | • | • | | |
| 165 | b | | | • | | • | • | • | • | • | • | • | | |
| 114 | b | | | • | | • | • | • | • | | • | • | | |
| 79 | sb | | | • | | • | • | • | • | | • | • | | |
| 74 | nb | | | • | | • | • | • | • | | • | • | | |
| 40 | b | | | | • | | | | | | | | • | |
| 32 | b | | • | | | • | • | • | • | | • | • | | |

| Exit | | * | W | S | K | T | Am | FJ | Lo | Pe | Pi | Sp | TA | Wi |
|---|---|---|---|---|---|---|---|---|---|---|---|---|---|---|
| 340ab | b | | e | e | e | e | | | | | | | | |
| 335 | b | | | | | | | | | • | • | | | |
| 315 | b | | w | | w | e | | | | | | | | |
| 229 | b | | | | | | | | | | | • | | |
| 212 | b | | | | | | | | | | • | | | |
| 190ab | b | | w | | | | | | | | | | | |
| 162 | b | 1 | | | | | | | | | • | | | |
| 160 | b | 1 | w | | e | | | • | | • | | | • | |
| 116 | b | | | | e | | | | | | | | | |
| 95 | b | 2 | w | | e | | | | | | | | • | |
| 71 | b | | w | | | | | | | | | | | |
| 65 | b | | | | w | | | | | | | | | |
| 54ab | b | | w | w | | | | | | | | | | |

Notes: 1) Shared with I-70; 2) Shared with I-64

I-64 runs east to west for approximately 132 miles from the Indiana state line to the Missouri state line. A portion of the Interstate is also I-57.

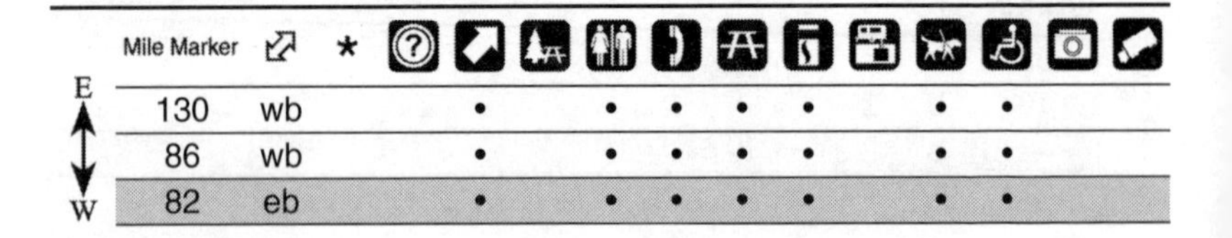

| Mile Marker | | * | | | | | | | | | | | | |
|---|---|---|---|---|---|---|---|---|---|---|---|---|---|---|
| 130 | wb | | | • | | • | • | • | • | | • | • | | |
| 86 | wb | | | • | | • | • | • | • | | • | • | | |
| 82 | eb | | | • | | • | • | • | • | | • | • | | |

| Mile Marker | ⇗ | * | | | | | | | | | | | | |
|---|---|---|---|---|---|---|---|---|---|---|---|---|---|---|
| 25 | b | 1 | • | • | | • | • | • | • | | • | • | | |

Notes: 1) Welcome Center eb, Rest Area wb

E ↕ W

| Exit | ⇗ | * | W | S | K | T | Am | FJ | Lo | Pe | Pi | Sp | TA | Wi |
|---|---|---|---|---|---|---|---|---|---|---|---|---|---|---|
| 95 | b | 1 | s | | n | | | | | | | | • | |
| 14 | b | | s | s | | | | | | | | | | |
| 12 | b | | | | s | s | | | | | | | | |

Notes: 1) Shared with I-57 / Follows I-57 numbering

**70** I-70 runs east to west for 156 miles from the Indiana state line to the Missouri state line. Portions of the Interstate are also I-55 and I-57.

| Mile Marker | ⇗ | * | | | | | | | | | | | | |
|---|---|---|---|---|---|---|---|---|---|---|---|---|---|---|
| 149 | wb | | • | | | • | • | • | • | | • | • | | |
| 86 | b | | | • | | • | • | • | • | • | • | • | | |
| 27 | b | 1 | • | • | | • | • | • | • | | • | • | | |

Notes: 1) Welcome Center eb, Rest Area wb

E ↕ W

| Exit | ⇗ | * | W | S | K | T | Am | FJ | Lo | Pe | Pi | Sp | TA | Wi |
|---|---|---|---|---|---|---|---|---|---|---|---|---|---|---|
| 162 | b | 1 | | | | | | | | | • | | | |
| 160 | b | 1 | n | | s | | | • | | • | | | • | |
| 61 | b | | s | | | | | | | | | | | |
| 18 | b | 2 | | | | | | | | | • | | | |
| 4 | b | 2 | | | | | • | | | | | | | |

Notes: 1) Shared with I-57 / Follows I-57 numbering; 2) Shared with I-55

**72** Interstate 72 runs east to west for about 182 miles from I-57 in Champaign to US 36 near the Missouri state line. A portion of the Interstate is shared with Interstate 55.

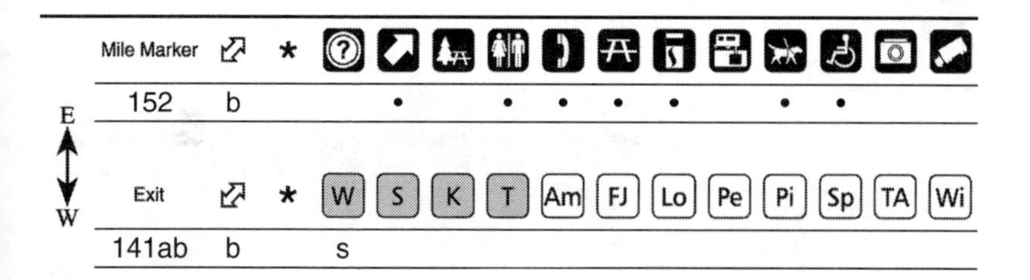

E ↕ W

| Mile Marker | ⇗ | * | | | | | | | | | | | | |
|---|---|---|---|---|---|---|---|---|---|---|---|---|---|---|
| 152 | b | | | • | | • | • | • | • | | • | • | | |

| Exit | ⇗ | * | W | S | K | T | Am | FJ | Lo | Pe | Pi | Sp | TA | Wi |
|---|---|---|---|---|---|---|---|---|---|---|---|---|---|---|
| 141ab | b | | s | | | | | | | | | | | |

| Exit | ↗ | * | W | S | K | T | Am | FJ | Lo | Pe | Pi | Sp | TA | Wi |
|---|---|---|---|---|---|---|---|---|---|---|---|---|---|---|
| 98b | b | 1 | | | n | | | | | | | | | |
| 93 | b | | n | n | n | n | | | | | | | | |

Notes: 1) Shared with I-55 / Follows I-55 numbering

**74**

Interstate 74 runs east to west for 221 miles from the Indiana state line to the Iowa state line. An additional four-mile stretch is in Iowa. Portions of the Interstate are also I-55.

E ↕ W

| Mile Marker | ↗ | * | ? | | | | | | | | | | | |
|---|---|---|---|---|---|---|---|---|---|---|---|---|---|---|
| 208 | wb | | • | | | • | • | • | • | | • | • | | |
| 156 | b | | | • | | • | • | • | • | | • | • | | |
| 114 | b | | | • | | • | • | • | • | • | • | • | | |
| 62 | b | | | • | | • | • | • | • | | • | • | | |
| 30 | wb | | | • | | • | • | • | • | • | • | • | | |
| 28 | eb | | | • | | • | • | • | • | • | • | • | | |

E ↕ W

| Exit | ↗ | * | W | S | K | T | Am | FJ | Lo | Pe | Pi | Sp | TA | Wi |
|---|---|---|---|---|---|---|---|---|---|---|---|---|---|---|
| 181 | b | | n | n | s | n | | | | | | | | |
| 160 | b | 1 | | | | | | | | | • | • | • | |
| 102 | b | | | | s | | | | | | | | | |
| 95a | b | | s | | | | | | | | | | | |
| 90 | b | 2 | n+ | | | | | | | | | | | |
| 89 | b | | | | | n | | | | | | | | |
| 32 | b | | | | | | • | | | | | | | |
| 4ab | b | | n | | | | | | | | | | | |
| 3 | b | 3 | | | s | | | | | | | | | |
| 2 | b | 3 | s | s | | | | | | | | | | |
| 1 | b | 3 | | | | s | | | | | | | | |

Notes: 1) Shared with I-55 / Follows I-55 numbering; 2) On University St; 3) In Iowa

**80**

Interstate 80 runs east to west for 163 miles from the Indiana state line to the Iowa state line. A small segment is shared with I-94 and I-294.

| Mile Marker | ↗ | * | ? | | | | | | | | | | | |
|---|---|---|---|---|---|---|---|---|---|---|---|---|---|---|
| 159 | b | 1 | | • | | • | • | • | | | | • | | |
| 119 | wb | | | • | | • | • | • | • | | • | • | | |

| Mile Marker | Direction | * | Info | Sign | Trees | Restrooms | Phone | Picnic | Vending | RV | Pets | Handicap | Camera | Other |
|---|---|---|---|---|---|---|---|---|---|---|---|---|---|---|
| 117 | eb | | | • | | • | • | • | • | | • | • | | |
| 51 | b | | | • | | • | • | • | • | • | • | • | | |
| 1 | eb | | • | | | • | • | • | | | • | • | • | |

Notes: 1) Service Area, Gas, Food

| Exit | Direction | * | W | S | K | T | Am | FJ | Lo | Pe | Pi | Sp | TA | Wi |
|---|---|---|---|---|---|---|---|---|---|---|---|---|---|---|
| 161 | b | 1 | n | s | n | | | | | | | | | |
| 157 | b | 2 | | | s | | | | | | | | | |
| 137 | b | | | | n | | | | | | | | | |
| 130ab | b | | n | n | n | | | | | | | | | |
| 122 | b | | | | | | | | | | • | | | |
| 112 | b | | s | | | | • | | | | | | | |
| 90 | b | | s | | s | | | | | | | | | |
| 77 | b | | | | | | | • | | | | | | |
| 75 | b | | s | | s | s | | | | | | | | |
| 56 | b | | s | | | | | | | | • | | | |
| 19 | b | | n | | | | | | | | | | | |

Notes: 1) Shared with I-94; 2) Shared with I-294

I-88 runs east to west for 156 miles from I-290 in Chicago to I-80 near Moline. A portion of the Interstate is also the East-West Tollway.

| Mile Marker | Direction | * | Info | Sign | Trees | Restrooms | Phone | Picnic | Vending | RV | Pets | Handicap | Camera | Other |
|---|---|---|---|---|---|---|---|---|---|---|---|---|---|---|
| 108 | b | 1 | | • | | • | • | • | | | | • | | |

Notes: 1) Service Area, Gas, Food

| Exit | Direction | * | W | S | K | T | Am | FJ | Lo | Pe | Pi | Sp | TA | Wi |
|---|---|---|---|---|---|---|---|---|---|---|---|---|---|---|
| 131 | b | | | | s | | | | | | | | | |
| 41 | b | | n | | | | | | | | | | | |

Interstate 90 runs east to west for 108 miles from the Indiana state line to the Wisconsin state line. Portions of the Interstate are also I-39, I-94, and the Northwest Tollway. Mile markers on the Northwest Tollway *decrease* from west to east, the opposite of the normal numbering system.

| Mile Marker | ⤢ | * | [?] | [arrow] | [trees] | [restrooms] | [phone] | [picnic table] | [vending] | [RV] | [pet] | [handicap] | [other] | [other] |
|---|---|---|---|---|---|---|---|---|---|---|---|---|---|---|
| 5 | b | 1 | | • | | • | • | • | | | | • | | |
| 55 | b | 1 | | • | | • | • | • | | | | • | | |
| 2 | eb | 2 | • | | | • | • | • | • | • | • | • | | |

Notes: 1) Service Area, Gas, Food / Follows Northwest Tollway numbering; 2) Shared with I-39

| Exit | ⤢ | * | W | S | K | T | Am | FJ | Lo | Pe | Pi | Sp | TA | Wi |
|---|---|---|---|---|---|---|---|---|---|---|---|---|---|---|
| 45a | b | 1 | | | n | | | | | | | | | |
| 5 | b | 2 | | n | | | | | | | | | | |
| 7 | b | 2 | n | n | | | | | | | | | | |
| 22 | b | 2 | | | n | | | | | | | | | |
| 26 | b | 2 | s | | | | | | | | | | | |
| 36 | b | 2 | | | | | • | | | | | | • | |
| 53 | b | 2 | | | n+ | | | | | | | | | |
| 63 | b | 2 | s | s | s | s | | | | | | | | |
| 1 | b | | | | | | | • | | | | | | |

(E ↕ W)

Notes: 1) Shared with I-94 / Follows I-94 numbering; 2) Follows Northwest Tollway numbering

## 94

Interstate 94 runs east to west for 77 miles from the Indiana state line to the Wisconsin state line. Portions are also I-80, I-90 and the Tri-State Tollway. Mile markers on the Tri-State Tollway *decrease* from west to east, the opposite of the usual numbering system.

| Mile Marker | ⤢ | * | [?] | [arrow] | [trees] | [restrooms] | [phone] | [picnic table] | [vending] | [RV] | [pet] | [handicap] | [other] | [other] |
|---|---|---|---|---|---|---|---|---|---|---|---|---|---|---|
| 60 | b | 1 | | • | | • | • | • | | | | • | | |

Notes: 1) Service Area, Gas, Food / Follows Tri-State Tollway numbering

| Exit | ⤢ | * | W | S | K | T | Am | FJ | Lo | Pe | Pi | Sp | TA | Wi |
|---|---|---|---|---|---|---|---|---|---|---|---|---|---|---|
| 161 | b | 1 | n | s | n | | | | | | | | | |
| 73b | b | | | | | | • | | | | | | | |
| 45a | b | 2 | | | n | | | | | | | | | |
| 70 | b | 3 | s | s | | s | | | | | | | | |
| 1 | b | | | | | | | | | | | | • | |

(E ↕ W)

Notes: 1) Shared with I-80 / Follows I-80 numbering; 2) Shared with I-90; 3) Follows Tri-State Tollway numbering

Interstate 255 is a 30-mile route that runs between I-270 near Granite City, Illinois and I-55 in Missouri.

| Mile Marker | ↗ | * | ? | | | | | | | | | | | |
|---|---|---|---|---|---|---|---|---|---|---|---|---|---|---|
| 3 | b | 1 | | • | | • | • | • | | | | • | | |

Notes: 1) In Missouri, north at exit to Rest Area

N ↕ S

| Exit | ↗ | * | W | S | K | T | Am | FJ | Lo | Pe | Pi | Sp | TA | Wi |
|---|---|---|---|---|---|---|---|---|---|---|---|---|---|---|
| 13 | b | | w | | | | | | | | | | | |
| 2 | b | 1 | n | | | | | | | | | | | |
| 1a | b | 1 | | s | n | | | | | | | | | |

Notes: 1) In Missouri

I-270 forms an open loop around Saint Louis about 50 miles long. This portion in Illinois runs east to west from I-70/I-55 to the Missouri state line. See Missouri for that portion of the Interstate.

| Exit | ↗ | * | W | S | K | T | Am | FJ | Lo | Pe | Pi | Sp | TA | Wi |
|---|---|---|---|---|---|---|---|---|---|---|---|---|---|---|
| 12 | b | | n | | | | | | | | | | | |

Interstate 290 in the Chicago area is approximately 30 miles long. It begins on I-90 exit 8 and ends in downtown Chicago.

| Exit | ↗ | * | W | S | K | T | Am | FJ | Lo | Pe | Pi | Sp | TA | Wi |
|---|---|---|---|---|---|---|---|---|---|---|---|---|---|---|
| 20 | b | 1 | s+ | | | | | | | | | | | |

Notes: 1) On Des Plaines Ave

Interstate 294 in the Chicago area is 53 miles long. It connects I-94 in southern Chicago with I-94 in northern Chicago. Portions are also I-80 and the Tri-State Tollway. Mile markers on the Tri-State Tollway *decrease* from west to east, the opposite of the usual numbering system.

| Mile Marker | ↗ | * | ? | | | | | | | | | | | |
|---|---|---|---|---|---|---|---|---|---|---|---|---|---|---|
| 25 | b | 1 | | • | | • | • | • | | | | • | | |
| 38 | b | 1 | | • | | • | • | • | | | | • | | |

Notes: 1) Service Area, Gas, Food / Follows Tri-State Tollway numbering

| Exit | | * | W | S | K | T | Am | FJ | Lo | Pe | Pi | Sp | TA | Wi |
|---|---|---|---|---|---|---|---|---|---|---|---|---|---|---|
| 157 | b | 1 | | | s | | | | | | | | | |
| 18 | b | 2 | w | | | | | | | | | | | |
| 33 | b | 2 | e | e | | | | | | | | | | |

Notes: 1) Shared with I-80 / Follows I-80 numbering; 2) Follows Tri-State Tollway numbering

## Indiana

**Rest Area Usage:** There is no limit to length of stay, however, no camping or overnight parking is permitted. **Road Conditions:** 800-452-4368 (Winter-weather, Summer-construction) **State Police:** *General*, 317-899-8577 or 800-582-8440; *Emergency*, 911 **Tourism Contact:** Indiana Division of Tourism, 1 N Capitol Ave, Ste 700, Indianapolis IN 46204. *Phone*: 800-365-6946 or 317-232-8860. *Internet*: www.enjoyindiana.com

**64** Interstate 64 runs east to west for 124 miles from the Kentucky state line to the Illinois state line.

| Mile Marker | | * | | | | | | | | | | | | |
|---|---|---|---|---|---|---|---|---|---|---|---|---|---|---|
| 115 | wb | | • | | | • | • | • | • | | | • | | |
| 97 | b | | | | • | | | | | | | | | |
| 81 | wb | | | | • | | | | | | | | | |
| 80 | eb | | | | • | | | | | | | | | |
| 58 | b | | | • | | • | • | • | • | | • | • | | |
| 7 | eb | | • | | | • | • | • | | | • | • | | |

| Exit | | * | W | S | K | T | Am | FJ | Lo | Pe | Pi | Sp | TA | Wi |
|---|---|---|---|---|---|---|---|---|---|---|---|---|---|---|
| 105 | b | | s | | | | | | | | | | | |
| 57 | b | | | | | | • | | | | | | | |
| 25 | b | | | | | | | • | | | • | | | • |

**65** Interstate 65 runs north to south for 262 miles from US 12/20 in Gary to the Kentucky state line.

| Mile Marker | | * | | | | | | | | | | | | |
|---|---|---|---|---|---|---|---|---|---|---|---|---|---|---|
| 231 | b | | | • | | • | • | • | • | | • | • | | |

N ↕ S

| Mile Marker | | * | ? | | | | | | | | | | | |
|---|---|---|---|---|---|---|---|---|---|---|---|---|---|---|
| 196 | b | | | • | | • | • | • | • | | • | • | | |
| 150 | sb | | | • | | • | • | • | • | | • | • | | |
| 148 | nb | | | • | | • | • | • | • | | • | • | | |
| 73 | b | | | • | | • | • | • | • | | • | • | | |
| 22 | b | | | • | | • | • | • | • | | • | • | | |

N ↕ S

| Exit | | * | W | S | K | T | Am | FJ | Lo | Pe | Pi | Sp | TA | Wi |
|---|---|---|---|---|---|---|---|---|---|---|---|---|---|---|
| 255 | b | | | | | | | | | | | • | | |
| 253b | b | | | | w | | | | | | | | | |
| 253a | b | | e | e | | e | | | | | | | | |
| 240 | b | | | | | | | • | | | | | | • |
| 201 | b | | | | | | • | | | | • | | | |
| 172 | b | | w | w | | w | | | | | | | | |
| 139 | b | | | | | | | • | | | | | | |
| 130 | b | | | | | | | | | | | | • | |
| 99 | b | | | w | | | | | | | | | | • |
| 95 | b | | | | | | | | | | • | | | |
| 50ab | b | | w | | w | | | | | | | | • | |
| 29ab | b | | w | | | | | | | | | | | |
| 16 | b | | | | | | | | | | • | | | |
| 4 | b | | w | | w | w | | | | | | | | |

69

Interstate 69 runs north to south for 158 miles from the Michigan state line to I-465 exit 37 in Indianapolis.

N ↕ S

| Mile Marker | | * | ? | | | | | | | | | | | |
|---|---|---|---|---|---|---|---|---|---|---|---|---|---|---|
| 144 | sb | | | • | | • | • | • | • | | • | • | | |
| 93 | sb | | | • | | • | • | • | • | | • | • | | |
| 89 | nb | | | • | | • | • | • | • | | • | • | | |
| 50 | b | | | • | | • | • | • | • | | • | | | |

| Exit | | * | W | S | K | T | Am | FJ | Lo | Pe | Pi | Sp | TA | Wi |
|---|---|---|---|---|---|---|---|---|---|---|---|---|---|---|
| 157 | b | | | | | | | | | | • | | | |
| 148 | b | | | | | | | | | | | • | | |
| 129 | b | | e | | | | | | | | | | | |
| 112ab | b | | e | | | | | | | | | | | |
| 111ab | b | | | w | | | | | | | | | | |
| 45 | b | | | | | | • | | | | | | | |

| Exit | ⤢ | * | W | S | K | T | Am | FJ | Lo | Pe | Pi | Sp | TA | Wi |
|---|---|---|---|---|---|---|---|---|---|---|---|---|---|---|
| 34 | b | | | | | | | | | | • | | | • |
| 26 | b | | w | | | w | | | | | | | | |
| 14 | b | | | | | | | | | | • | | | |
| 3 | b | | e | e | | | | | | | | | | |

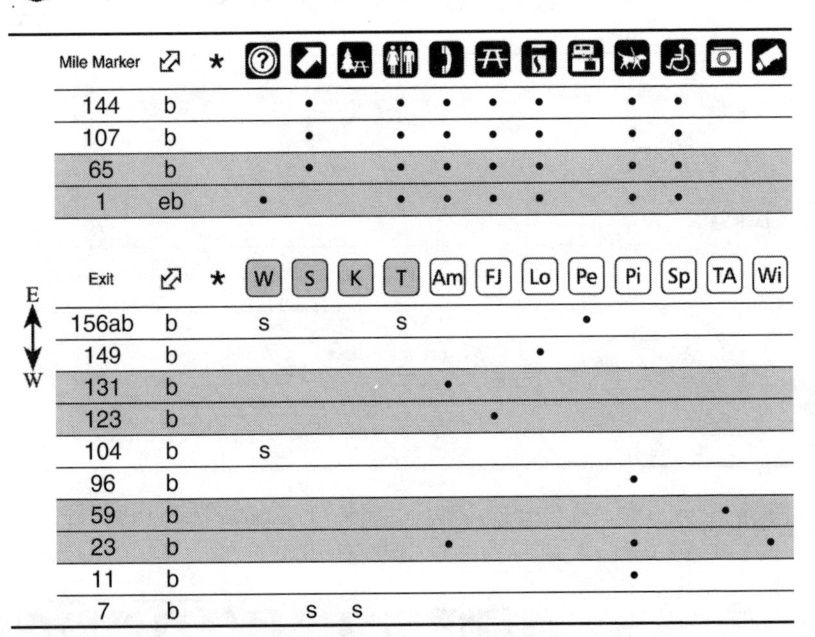

70

Interstate 70 runs east to west for 157 miles from the Ohio state line to the Illinois state line.

| Mile Marker | ⤢ | * | [?] | [arrow] | [trees] | [restrooms] | [phone] | [picnic table] | [vending] | [building] | [pet] | [handicap] | [icon] | [icon] |
|---|---|---|---|---|---|---|---|---|---|---|---|---|---|---|
| 144 | b | | | • | | • | • | • | • | | • | • | | |
| 107 | b | | | • | | • | • | • | • | | • | • | | |
| 65 | b | | | • | | • | • | • | • | | • | • | | |
| 1 | eb | | • | | | • | • | • | • | | • | • | | |

| Exit | ⤢ | * | W | S | K | T | Am | FJ | Lo | Pe | Pi | Sp | TA | Wi |
|---|---|---|---|---|---|---|---|---|---|---|---|---|---|---|
| 156ab | b | | s | | | s | | | | • | | | | |
| 149 | b | | | | | | | | • | | | | | |
| 131 | b | | | | | | • | | | | | | | |
| 123 | b | | | | | | | • | | | | | | |
| 104 | b | | s | | | | | | | | | | | |
| 96 | b | | | | | | | | | | • | | | |
| 59 | b | | | | | | | | | | | | • | |
| 23 | b | | | | | | • | | | | • | | | • |
| 11 | b | | | | | | | | | | • | | | |
| 7 | b | | | s | s | | | | | | | | | |

74

Interstate 74 runs east to west for 172 miles from the Ohio state line to the Illinois state line. A portion is also shared with I-465.

| Mile Marker | ⤢ | * | [?] | [arrow] | [trees] | [restrooms] | [phone] | [picnic table] | [vending] | [building] | [pet] | [handicap] | [icon] | [icon] |
|---|---|---|---|---|---|---|---|---|---|---|---|---|---|---|
| 152 | b | | | • | | • | • | • | • | | • | • | | |
| 57 | b | | | • | | • | • | • | • | | • | • | | |
| 23 | b | | | • | | • | • | • | • | | • | • | | |
| 1 | eb | | • | | | • | • | • | • | | • | • | | |

| Exit | ⤢ | * | W | S | K | T | Am | FJ | Lo | Pe | Pi | Sp | TA | Wi |
|---|---|---|---|---|---|---|---|---|---|---|---|---|---|---|
| 143 | b | | | | | | • | | | • | | | | |

| | Exit | ↗ | * | W | S | K | T | Am | FJ | Lo | Pe | Pi | Sp | TA | Wi |
|---|---|---|---|---|---|---|---|---|---|---|---|---|---|---|---|
| E | 134ab | b | | s | | s | | | | | | | | | |
| ↕ | 116 | b | | s | | | | | | | | | | | |
| W | 52 | b | 1 | | | s | | | | | | | | | |
| | 2ab | b | 1 | | | | n | | | | | | | | |
| | 4 | b | 1 | | | | | | • | | | • | | | |
| | 12ab | b | 1 | | | s | s | | | | | | | | |
| | 13ab | b | 1 | | n | | | | | | | | | | |
| | 66 | b | | s | | s | | | | | | | | | |
| | 4 | b | | | | | | | | | | • | | | |

Notes: 1) Follows I-465 numbering

**80** I-80 runs east to west for 152 miles from the Ohio state line to the Illinois state line. Portions are also I-90, I-94, and the Indiana Toll Road.

| | Mile Marker | ↗ | * | ? | ↗ | 🌲 | 🚻 | ☎ | Picnic | Vending | RV | Pets | ♿ | Camera | Dump |
|---|---|---|---|---|---|---|---|---|---|---|---|---|---|---|---|
| E | 146 | b | 1 | | • | | • | • | • | | | • | • | | |
| ↕ | 126 | b | 1 | | • | | • | • | • | | • | • | • | | |
| W | 90 | b | 1 | | • | | • | • | • | | • | • | • | | |
| | 56 | b | 1 | | • | | • | • | • | | • | • | • | | |
| | 22 | b | 1 | | • | | • | • | • | | | • | • | | |

Notes: 1) Shared with I-90 / Service Area, Gas, Food

| | Exit | ↗ | * | W | S | K | T | Am | FJ | Lo | Pe | Pi | Sp | TA | Wi |
|---|---|---|---|---|---|---|---|---|---|---|---|---|---|---|---|
| E | 92 | b | 1 | s | | n | | | | | | | | | |
| ↕ | 83 | b | 1 | | s+ | | | | | | | | | | |
| W | 72 | b | 1 | | | | | | | | | • | | | |
| | 15 | b | 2 | | | | | | • | | | • | | • | |
| | 9a | b | 2 | | | | | • | • | | | | | | |
| | 6 | b | 2 | | | | | | | | | • | | • | |
| | 5ab | b | 2 | | | s+ | | | | | | | | | |
| | 2ab | b | 2 | | | s | | | | | | • | | | |

Notes: 1) Shared with I-90; 2) Shared with I-94

**90** I-90 runs east to west for about 157 miles from the Ohio state line to the Illinois state line. Portions are also I-80 and the Indiana Toll Road.

| Mile Marker | ↗ | * | ? | ↗ | 🌲 | 🚻 | ☎ | Picnic | Vending | RV | Pets | ♿ | Camera | Dump |
|---|---|---|---|---|---|---|---|---|---|---|---|---|---|---|
| 146 | b | 1 | | • | | • | • | • | | | • | • | | |

| | Mile Marker | ↗ | * | Information | Arrow | Trees | Restrooms | Phone | Picnic Table | Vending | Icon 8 | Pet Area | Handicap | Icon 11 | Icon 12 |
|---|---|---|---|---|---|---|---|---|---|---|---|---|---|---|---|
| E | 126 | b | 1 | | • | | • | • | • | | • | • | • | | |
| ↕ | 90 | b | 1 | | • | | • | • | • | | • | • | • | | |
| | 56 | b | 1 | | • | | • | • | • | | • | • | • | | |
| W | 22 | b | 1 | | • | | • | • | • | | | • | • | | |

Notes: 1) Shared with I-80 / Service Area, Gas, Food

| | Exit | ↗ | * | W | S | K | T | Am | FJ | Lo | Pe | Pi | Sp | TA | Wi |
|---|---|---|---|---|---|---|---|---|---|---|---|---|---|---|---|
| E | 92 | b | 1 | s | | n | | | | | | | | | |
| ↕ | 83 | b | 1 | | s+ | | | | | | | | | | |
| | 72 | b | 1 | | | | | | | | | • | | | |
| W | 21 | b | | | | n | | | | | | | | | |

Notes: 1) Shared with I-80

**94** Interstate 94 runs east to west for 46 miles from the Michigan state line to the Illinois state line. A portion is also shared with I-80.

| Mile Marker | ↗ | * | Information | Arrow | Trees | Restrooms | Phone | Picnic Table | Vending | Icon 8 | Pet Area | Handicap | Icon 11 | Icon 12 |
|---|---|---|---|---|---|---|---|---|---|---|---|---|---|---|
| 43 | wb | | • | | | • | • | • | • | | • | • | | |

| | Exit | ↗ | * | W | S | K | T | Am | FJ | Lo | Pe | Pi | Sp | TA | Wi |
|---|---|---|---|---|---|---|---|---|---|---|---|---|---|---|---|
| E | 34ab | b | | n | | n | | | | | | | | | |
| ↕ | 26ab | b | | | | s | | | | | | | | | |
| | 22 | b | | | | | | • | | | | | | • | • |
| W | 15 | b | 1 | | | | | | • | | | • | | • | |
| | 9a | b | 1 | | | | | • | • | | | | | | |
| | 6 | b | 1 | | | | | | | | | • | | • | |
| | 5ab | b | 1 | | | s+ | | | | | | | | | |
| | 2ab | b | 1 | | | s | | | | | | • | | | |

Notes: 1) Shared with I-80

**265** Interstate 265 is a 7-mile route near New Albany. It connects I-64 exit 121 with I-65 exit 6.

| Exit | ↗ | * | W | S | K | T | Am | FJ | Lo | Pe | Pi | Sp | TA | Wi |
|---|---|---|---|---|---|---|---|---|---|---|---|---|---|---|
| 3 | b | | | | s | | | | | | | | | |
| 1 | b | | | | | s | | | | | | | | |

Interstate 465 forms a 54-mile loop around Indianapolis. Exit numbering begins at US 31 and increases in a clockwise direction.

| Exit | ↗ | * | W | S | K | T | Am | FJ | Lo | Pe | Pi | Sp | TA | Wi |
|---|---|---|---|---|---|---|---|---|---|---|---|---|---|---|
| 52 | b | 1 | | | s | | | | | | | | | |
| 46 | b | | | | w | e | | | | | | | | |
| 42 | b | | | | w | | | | | | | | | |
| 27 | b | | s | | s | | | | | | | | | |
| 17 | b | | | | | w | | | | | | | | |
| 13ab | b | 1 | | n | | | | | | | | | | |
| 12ab | b | 1 | | | s | s | | | | | | | | |
| 4 | b | 1 | | | | | | • | | | • | | | |
| 2ab | b | 1 | | | | n | | | | | | | | |

Notes: 1) Shared with I-74

## Iowa

**Rest Area Usage:** There is a 24 hour stay limit, no camping or overnight parking is permitted. **Road Conditions:** 515-288-1047 (weather) **State Police:** *General*, 515-281-5824; *Emergency*, 911 or 800-525-5555 or *55 on cell phone **Tourism Contact:** Iowa Division of Tourism, 200 E Grand Ave, Des Moines IA 50309. *Phone*: 800-345-4692 or 515-242-4705. *Internet*: www.traveliowa.com

I-29 runs north to south for 152 miles from the South Dakota state line to the Missouri state line. A 4-mile section in Council Bluffs is also I-80.

N ↕ S

| Mile Marker | ↗ | * | | | | | | | | | | | | |
|---|---|---|---|---|---|---|---|---|---|---|---|---|---|---|
| 149 | b | 1 | • | | | • | • | • | • | | | • | | |
| 139 | b | 2 | • | • | | • | • | • | • | • | • | • | | |
| 110 | b | | | • | | • | • | • | | • | • | • | | |
| 91 | b | | | | • | | | | | | | | | |
| 80 | sb | | | • | | • | • | • | | • | | • | | |
| 78 | nb | | | • | | • | • | • | | • | | • | | |
| 38 | b | | | • | | • | • | • | • | • | • | • | | |

Notes: 1) West at exit to Welcome Center; 2) Welcome Center sb, Rest Area nb

| | Exit | ⤢ | * | W | S | K | T | Am | FJ | Lo | Pe | Pi | Sp | TA | Wi |
|---|---|---|---|---|---|---|---|---|---|---|---|---|---|---|---|
| N | 144a | b | | | | | e+ | | | | | | | | |
| ↕ | 143 | b | | | e | | | | | | | | | | |
| | 3 | b | 1 | w | w | | | | | | | | | • | |
| S | 1 | b | 1 | | | | | | | | | • | | | |

Notes: 1) Shared with I-80 / Follows I-80 numbering

**35**

Interstate 35 runs north to south for 219 miles from the Minnesota state line to the Missouri state line. Part of the Interstate is also I-80.

| | Mile Marker | ⤢ | * | (?) | (arrow) | (trees) | (restrooms) | (phone) | (picnic table) | (vending) | (map) | (pets) | (handicap) | (camera) | (other) |
|---|---|---|---|---|---|---|---|---|---|---|---|---|---|---|---|
| | 214 | b | 1 | • | | | • | • | • | • | • | • | • | | |
| | 120 | nb | | | • | | • | • | • | • | • | | • | | |
| N | 119 | sb | | | • | | • | • | • | • | • | | • | | |
| ↕ | 94 | b | | | • | | • | • | • | • | | • | • | | |
| | 125 | b | 2 | • | | | • | • | • | | | | • | | |
| S | 53 | nb | | | | • | | | | | | | | | |
| | 51 | sb | | | | • | | | | | | | | | |
| | 32 | b | | | • | | • | • | • | • | • | • | • | | |
| | 7 | b | | • | | | • | • | • | • | • | • | • | | |

Notes: 1) West at exit to Welcome Center; 2) East at exit to Welcome Center / Shared with I-80 / Follows I-80 numbering

| | Exit | ⤢ | * | W | S | K | T | Am | FJ | Lo | Pe | Pi | Sp | TA | Wi |
|---|---|---|---|---|---|---|---|---|---|---|---|---|---|---|---|
| N | 144 | b | | | | | | | • | | | | | | |
| ↕ | 90 | b | | w | | | | | | | | | | | |
| | 126 | b | 1 | | | | | | | | | • | | | |
| S | 125 | b | 1 | | | | | | • | | | | | | |

Notes: 1) Shared with I-80 / Follows I-80 numbering

**80**

Interstate 80 runs east to west for 307 miles from the Illinois state line to the Nebraska state line. A portion of the Interstate is also I-35.

| Mile Marker | ⤢ | * | (?) | (arrow) | (trees) | (restrooms) | (phone) | (picnic table) | (vending) | (map) | (pets) | (handicap) | (camera) | (other) |
|---|---|---|---|---|---|---|---|---|---|---|---|---|---|---|
| 306 | b | 1 | • | | | • | • | • | | | • | • | • | |
| 300 | b | | | • | | • | • | • | • | • | • | • | | |
| 270 | b | 2 | • | • | | • | • | • | • | • | • | • | | |

E ↕ W

| Mile Marker | ⇗ | * | | | | | | | | | | | | |
|---|---|---|---|---|---|---|---|---|---|---|---|---|---|---|
| 237 | b | | | • | | • | • | • | • | • | • | • | | |
| 225 | b | 3 | • | | | • | • | • | • | | | • | | |
| 208 | b | 4 | | • | | • | • | • | • | • | • | • | | |
| 180 | b | | | • | | • | • | • | • | • | • | • | | |
| 147 | b | | | • | | • | • | • | • | • | • | • | | |
| 125 | b | 5 | • | | | • | • | • | | | | • | | |
| 119 | b | | | • | | • | • | • | • | • | • | • | | |
| 81 | eb | | | • | | • | • | • | • | • | • | • | | |
| 80 | wb | | | • | | • | • | • | • | • | • | • | | |
| 32 | b | | | | • | | | | | | | | | |
| 19 | b | 6 | • | • | | • | • | • | • | • | • | • | | |

Notes: 1) North at exit to Welcome Center; 2) Welcome Center wb, Rest Area eb; 3) South at exit to Welcome Center; 4) No Vending Machines wb; 5) South at exit to Welcome Center / Shared with I-35; 6) Welcome Center eb, Rest Area wb

E ↕ W

| Exit | ⇗ | * | W | S | K | T | Am | FJ | Lo | Pe | Pi | Sp | TA | Wi |
|---|---|---|---|---|---|---|---|---|---|---|---|---|---|---|
| 292 | b | | | | | | | • | | | | | | |
| 284 | b | | | | | | • | | | | • | | • | |
| 240 | b | | n | | | s | | | | | | | | |
| 168 | b | | n | | | | | | | | | | | |
| 142 | b | | | | | | • | | | | | | | |
| 136 | b | | | | n | | | | | | | | | |
| 126 | b | 1 | | | | | | | | | • | | | |
| 125 | b | 1 | | | | | | • | | | | | | |
| 5 | b | | | | | n | | | | | | | | |
| 3 | b | 2 | s | s | | | | | | | | | • | |
| 1 | b | 2 | | | | | | | | | • | | | |

Notes: 1) Also I-35; 2) Also I-29

I-235 is a 14-mile route in Des Moines that runs through the downtown area. It begins at I-35 exit 72 and ends at I-35/80 exit 137.

| Exit | ⇗ | * | W | S | K | T | Am | FJ | Lo | Pe | Pi | Sp | TA | Wi |
|---|---|---|---|---|---|---|---|---|---|---|---|---|---|---|
| 3 | b | | n | n | | | | | | | | | | |
| 1 | b | | | | | n | | | | | | | | |

Interstate 380 is a 72-mile spur route off I-80 that connects Iowa City with Waterloo. It is a north/south route.

N ↕ S

| Mile Marker | | * | ? | | | | | | | | | | | |
|---|---|---|---|---|---|---|---|---|---|---|---|---|---|---|
| 13 | b | | | • | | • | • | • | • | • | | • | | |

| Exit | | * | W | S | K | T | Am | FJ | Lo | Pe | Pi | Sp | TA | Wi |
|---|---|---|---|---|---|---|---|---|---|---|---|---|---|---|
| 72 | b | | w | | | w | | | | | | | | |
| 68 | b | | | | | | | • | | | | | | |
| 24b | b | | w | w | | | | | | | | | | |

680

Interstate 680 is a 42-mile route connecting I-80 exit 27 in Iowa with I-80 exit 446 in Nebraska, west of Omaha. A portion of the Interstate is shared with I-29. It provides an alternate route around Omaha and Council Bluffs for I-80 travelers.

| Mile Marker | | * | ? | | | | | | | | | | | |
|---|---|---|---|---|---|---|---|---|---|---|---|---|---|---|
| 18 | wb | | | • | | • | • | • | | | | • | | |
| 16 | eb | | | • | | • | • | • | | | | • | | |
| 15 | wb | | | • | | • | | • | | | | • | | |

# Kansas

**Rest Area Usage:** Parking, including overnight parking, is limited to one night. Camping is not permitted. **Road Conditions:** 800-585-7623 (general) **State Police:** *General*, 785-296-6800; *Emergency*, 911 or *47 on cell phone **Tourism Contact:** Kansas Travel & Tourism Division, 700 SW Harrison St, Ste 1300, Topeka KS 66603. *Phone*: 800-252-6727 or 785-296-2009. *Internet*: www.travelks.com

35

I-35 runs north to south for 235 miles from the Missouri state line to the Oklahoma state line. A portion of the Interstate is also the Kansas Turnpike.

| Mile Marker | | * | ? | | | | | | | | | | | |
|---|---|---|---|---|---|---|---|---|---|---|---|---|---|---|
| 175 | b | | | • | | • | • | • | • | | • | • | | |
| 98 | b | 1 | | • | | • | • | • | | | • | • | | |

| Mile Marker | ↗ | * | ? | Arrow | Trees | Restrooms | Phone | Picnic | Vending | RV | Pet | Handicap | Camera | Truck |
|---|---|---|---|---|---|---|---|---|---|---|---|---|---|---|
| 65 | b | 1 | | • | | • | • | • | | | • | • | | |
| 26 | b | 1 | | • | | • | • | • | | | • | • | | |

Notes: 1) Service Area, Gas, Food

| Exit | ↗ | * | W | S | K | T | Am | FJ | Lo | Pe | Pi | Sp | TA | Wi |
|---|---|---|---|---|---|---|---|---|---|---|---|---|---|---|
| 228b | b | | | | e | | | | | | | | | |
| 227 | b | | e | | | | | | | | | | | |
| 224 | b | | | e | | | | | | | | | | |
| 220 | b | | | | | e | | | | | | | | |
| 218 | b | | | | w | | | | | | | | | |
| 215 | b | | | | | | • | | | | | | | |
| 183ab | b | | w | | | | | | | | | | | |
| 155 | b | | | | | | | | | | | | • | |
| 128 | b | | w | | | | | | | | | | | |
| 127 | b | | | | | | | • | | | | | | |
| 71 | b | | e | | | | | | | | | | | |
| 50 | b | | | | w | w+ | | | | | | | | |
| 42 | b | | | | w | | | | | | | | | |

N ↕ S

70

I-70 runs east to west for 423 miles from the Missouri state line to the Colorado state line. A segment is also the Kansas Turnpike.

| Mile Marker | ↗ | * | ? | Arrow | Trees | Restrooms | Phone | Picnic | Vending | RV | Pet | Handicap | Camera | Truck |
|---|---|---|---|---|---|---|---|---|---|---|---|---|---|---|
| 414 | b | | | | • | | • | | | | | | | |
| 209 | b | 1 | | • | | • | • | • | | | • | • | | |
| 188 | b | 1 | | • | | • | • | • | | | • | • | | |
| 336 | b | | | • | | • | • | • | | • | • | • | | |
| 310 | b | | | • | | • | • | • | | • | • | • | | |
| 294 | b | | | • | | • | • | • | | • | • | • | | |
| 265 | b | | | • | | • | • | • | | • | • | • | | |
| 224 | b | | | • | | • | • | • | | • | • | • | | |
| 187 | b | | | • | | • | • | • | | • | • | • | | |
| 132 | b | | | • | | • | • | • | • | • | • | • | | |
| 97 | b | | | • | | • | • | • | • | • | • | • | | |
| 48 | b | | | • | | • | • | • | • | • | • | • | | |
| 7 | b | 2 | • | • | | • | • | • | • | • | • | • | | |

E ↕ W

Notes: 1) Service Area, Gas, Food; 2) Welcome Center eb, Rest Area wb.

E ↕ W

| Exit | | * | W | S | K | T | Am | FJ | Lo | Pe | Pi | Sp | TA | Wi |
|---|---|---|---|---|---|---|---|---|---|---|---|---|---|---|
| 224 | b | 1 | s | | | | | | | | | | | |
| 356ab | b | | s | s | s | s | | | | | | | | |
| 298 | b | | n | | | | | | | | | | | |
| 253 | b | | | | | | | • | | | | | | |
| 252 | b | | | | | | • | | | • | | | | |
| 159 | b | | n | | | | | | | | | | | |
| 76 | b | | | | | | • | | | | | | | |
| 53 | b | | n | | | | | | | | | | | |
| 17 | b | | n | | | | | | | | | | | |

Notes: 1) Kansas Turnpike

Interstate 135 runs north to south for 95 miles between Salina and Wichita.

N ↕ S

| Mile Marker | | * | | | | | | | | | | | | |
|---|---|---|---|---|---|---|---|---|---|---|---|---|---|---|
| 68 | b | | | • | | • | • | • | | • | • | • | | |
| 23 | b | | | • | | • | • | • | • | • | • | • | | |

| Exit | | * | W | S | K | T | Am | FJ | Lo | Pe | Pi | Sp | TA | Wi |
|---|---|---|---|---|---|---|---|---|---|---|---|---|---|---|
| 89 | b | | e | e | | e | | | | | | | | |
| 60 | b | | w | | | | | | | | | | | |
| 31 | b | | | | | | • | | | | | | | |
| 30 | b | | w | | | | | | | | | | | |
| 1ab | b | | | | w | | | | | | | | | |

Interstate 235 in Wichita is 16 miles long. It connects I-135 exit 1 with I-135 exit 11 in northern Wichita.

| Exit | | * | W | S | K | T | Am | FJ | Lo | Pe | Pi | Sp | TA | Wi |
|---|---|---|---|---|---|---|---|---|---|---|---|---|---|---|
| 7 | b | | w | w | | | | | | | | | | |

Interstate 435 is an 83-mile loop around Kansas City. Exit numbering begins at Lackman Road in Kansas and increases in a clockwise direction. See Missouri for that state's part of the Interstate.

| Exit | ↗ | * | W | S | K | T | Am | FJ | Lo | Pe | Pi | Sp | TA | Wi |
|---|---|---|---|---|---|---|---|---|---|---|---|---|---|---|
| 79 | b | | S+ | | | | | | | | | | | |
| 6 | b | | e | | | e | | | | | | | | |
| 3 | b | | | | e | | | | | | | | | |

Interstate 470 in Topeka is an 11-mile route that connects I-70 exit 355 with I-70 exit 182. A portion of it is also the Kansas Turnpike.

| Exit | ↗ | * | W | S | K | T | Am | FJ | Lo | Pe | Pi | Sp | TA | Wi |
|---|---|---|---|---|---|---|---|---|---|---|---|---|---|---|
| 5 | b | | e | | | | | | | | | | | |
| 2 | b | | | | | w | | | | | | | | |
| 1b | b | | w | w | w | | | | | | | | | |

# Kentucky

**Rest Area Usage:** There is a 4 hour stay limit, no camping or overnight parking is permitted. **Road Conditions:** 800-459-7623 (general) **State Police:** *General*, 502-695-6300; *Emergency*, 800-222-5555 **Tourism Contact:** Kentucky Department of Travel Development, 500 Mero St, Ste 22, Frankfort KY 40601. *Phone*: 800-225-8747 or 502-564-4930. *Internet*: www.kentuckytourism.com

Interstate 24 runs east to west for 94 miles from the Tennessee state line to the Illinois state line.

| Mile Marker | ↗ | * | ? | | | | | | | | | | | |
|---|---|---|---|---|---|---|---|---|---|---|---|---|---|---|
| 93 | wb | | • | | | • | • | • | • | | • | • | | |
| 7 | b | 1 | • | | | • | • | • | • | | • | • | | |

Notes: 1) South at exit to Welcome Center

| E↕W Exit | ↗ | * | W | S | K | T | Am | FJ | Lo | Pe | Pi | Sp | TA | Wi |
|---|---|---|---|---|---|---|---|---|---|---|---|---|---|---|
| 89 | b | | | | | | | | | | • | | | |
| 86 | b | | | | | | • | • | | | • | | | • |

| Exit | | * | W | S | K | T | Am | FJ | Lo | Pe | Pi | Sp | TA | Wi |
|---|---|---|---|---|---|---|---|---|---|---|---|---|---|---|
| 7 | b | | | | s | | | | | | | | | |
| 4 | b | | s | s | | | | | | | | | | |
| 3 | b | | | | | | | | | | • | | | |

64

Interstate 64 runs east to west for 192 miles from the West Virginia state line to the Indiana state line.

| Mile Marker | | * | | | | | | | | | | | | |
|---|---|---|---|---|---|---|---|---|---|---|---|---|---|---|
| 174 | eb | | | • | | • | • | • | • | | • | • | | |
| 173 | wb | | • | | | • | • | • | • | | • | • | | |
| 141 | b | | | • | | • | • | • | • | | • | • | | |
| 108 | wb | | | • | | • | • | • | • | | • | • | | |
| 98 | eb | | | • | | • | • | • | • | | • | • | | |
| 60 | b | | | • | | • | • | • | • | | • | • | | |
| 29 | b | 1 | • | • | | • | • | • | • | | • | • | | |

Notes: 1) Welcome Center eb, Rest Area wb.

| Exit | | * | W | S | K | T | Am | FJ | Lo | Pe | Pi | Sp | TA | Wi |
|---|---|---|---|---|---|---|---|---|---|---|---|---|---|---|
| 185 | b | | | | | | | • | | | | | | |
| 172 | b | | | | n | | | | | | • | | | |
| 161 | b | | | | | | • | | | | | | | |
| 137 | b | | s | | | | | | | | | | | |
| 110 | b | | s | | | | | | | | | | | |
| 94 | b | | s | | s | | | | | | | • | | |
| 53ab | b | | n | | n | | | | | | | | | |
| 43 | b | | | | | | • | • | | | | | | |
| 32 | b | | n | | | | | | | | | | | |
| 28 | b | | | | | | | | | | • | | | |
| 17 | b | | | s | | | | | | | | | | |
| 15 | b | | s | | | s | | | | | | | | |

65

Interstate 65 runs north to south for 138 miles from the Indiana state line to the Tennessee state line.

| Mile Marker | | * | | | | | | | | | | | | |
|---|---|---|---|---|---|---|---|---|---|---|---|---|---|---|
| 114 | sb | | • | | | • | • | • | • | | • | • | | |
| 82 | sb | | | • | | • | • | • | • | | • | • | | |

| Mile Marker | | * | | | | | | | | | | | | |
|---|---|---|---|---|---|---|---|---|---|---|---|---|---|---|
| 81 | nb | | | • | | • | • | • | • | | • | • | | |
| 55 | sb | | | • | | • | • | • | • | | • | • | | |
| 39 | nb | | | • | | • | • | • | • | | • | • | | |
| 30 | sb | | | • | | • | • | • | • | | • | • | | |
| 1 | nb | | • | | | • | • | • | • | | • | • | | |

| Exit | | * | W | S | K | T | Am | FJ | Lo | Pe | Pi | Sp | TA | Wi |
|---|---|---|---|---|---|---|---|---|---|---|---|---|---|---|
| 128 | b | | | e | | | | | | | | | | |
| 121 | b | | | | | | | | | | • | | | |
| 116 | b | | | | | | | | • | | | | | |
| 105 | b | | | | | | • | | | | | | | |
| 86 | b | | | | | | | | | • | • | | | |
| 81 | b | | | | | | • | | | | | | | |
| 22 | b | | w+ | | w | | | | | | | | | |
| 6 | b | | | | | | | | | | • | | | • |
| 2 | b | | | | | | | • | | | | | | |

I-71 runs north to south for 96 miles from the Ohio state line to I-64 exit 6 in Louisville. A portion of the Interstate is also I-75.

| Mile Marker | | * | | | | | | | | | | | | |
|---|---|---|---|---|---|---|---|---|---|---|---|---|---|---|
| 177 | b | 1 | • | • | | • | • | • | • | • | | • | | |
| 13 | b | | | • | | • | • | • | • | | • | • | | |

Notes: 1) Welcome Center sb, Rest Area nb / Shared with I-75 / Follows I-75 numbering

| Exit | | * | W | S | K | T | Am | FJ | Lo | Pe | Pi | Sp | TA | Wi |
|---|---|---|---|---|---|---|---|---|---|---|---|---|---|---|
| 182 | b | 1 | w | w | | w | | | | | | | | |
| 181 | b | 1 | | | w | | | | | | | | • | |
| 175 | b | 1 | | | | | | | | | • | | • | |
| 44 | b | | w | | | | | | | | | | | |
| 28 | b | | | | | | | | | | • | | | • |
| 22 | b | | e | | | | | | | | | | | |

Notes: 1) Shared with I-75 / Follows I-75 numbering

Interstate 75 runs north to south for 192 miles from the Ohio state line to the Tennessee state line. A portion of it is shared with I-71.

| Mile Marker | ↗ | * | ? | | | | | | | | | | | |
|---|---|---|---|---|---|---|---|---|---|---|---|---|---|---|
| 177 | b | 1 | • | • | | • | • | • | • | • | | • | | |
| 127 | b | | | • | | • | • | • | • | | • | • | | |
| 82 | b | | | • | | • | • | • | • | | • | • | | |
| 1 | nb | | • | | | • | • | • | • | | • | • | | |

Notes: 1) Welcome Center sb, Rest Area nb / Shared with I-71

| Exit | ↗ | * | W | S | K | T | Am | FJ | Lo | Pe | Pi | Sp | TA | Wi |
|---|---|---|---|---|---|---|---|---|---|---|---|---|---|---|
| 182 | b | 1 | w | w | | w | | | | | | | | |
| 181 | b | 1 | | | w | | | | | | | | • | |
| 175 | b | 1 | | | | | | | | | • | | • | |
| 171 | b | | | | | | | • | | | | | | |
| 159 | b | | e | | | | | | | | | | | |
| 129 | b | | | | | | | | | | • | | | |
| 126 | b | | | | w | | | | | | | | | |
| 120 | b | | | | | | • | | | | | | | |
| 108 | b | | | | | w | | | | | | | | |
| 87 | b | | e+ | | | | | | | | | | | |
| 76 | b | | e | | | | | | | | | | | |
| 41 | b | | | | e | | | | | | | | | |
| 38 | b | | e | | | | | | | | | | | |
| 29 | b | | | | | | | | | | • | | | |
| 11 | b | | w | | | | | | | | | | | • |

Notes: 1) Shared with I-71

Interstate 264 in Louisville is a 23-mile route. It forms an open loop that connects I-64 exit 1 with I-71 exit 5.

| Exit | ↗ | * | W | S | K | T | Am | FJ | Lo | Pe | Pi | Sp | TA | Wi |
|---|---|---|---|---|---|---|---|---|---|---|---|---|---|---|
| 18ab | b | | | | s | | | | | | | | | |
| 14 | b | | | | n | | | | | | | | | |

I-265 is a 35-mile route through southern Louisville. It connects I-71 exit 9 with US 31.

| Exit | ↗ | * | W | S | K | T | Am | FJ | Lo | Pe | Pi | Sp | TA | Wi |
|---|---|---|---|---|---|---|---|---|---|---|---|---|---|---|
| 32 | b | | e | | | w | | | | | | | | |

# Louisiana

**Rest Area Usage:** There is no limit to length of stay, however, no camping or overnight parking is permitted. **Road Conditions:** No central phone number. *Internet*: www.dotd.state.la.us **State Police:** *General*, 225-925-6006; *Emergency*, 911 **Tourism Contact:** Louisiana Office of Tourism, PO Box 94291, Baton Rouge LA 70804. *Phone*: 800-994-8626 or 225-342-8119. *Internet*: www.louisianatravel.com **Notes:** Louisiana offers increased security at their rest areas with patrols between 6 p.m. and 6 a.m.

**10** Interstate 10 runs east to west for 274 miles from the Mississippi state line to the Texas state line.

| Mile Marker | ⇗ | * | ? | | | | | | | | | | | |
|---|---|---|---|---|---|---|---|---|---|---|---|---|---|---|
| 270 | wb | | • | | | • | • | • | | | • | • | | |
| 181 | b | | | • | | • | • | • | | • | • | • | | |
| 121 | b | | | • | | • | • | • | | • | • | • | | |
| 67 | b | | | • | | • | • | • | | • | • | • | | |
| 1 | eb | | • | | | • | • | • | | | • | • | | |

| Exit | ⇗ | * | W | S | K | T | Am | FJ | Lo | Pe | Pi | Sp | TA | Wi |
|---|---|---|---|---|---|---|---|---|---|---|---|---|---|---|
| 266 | b | | s | | | | | | | | | | • | |
| 263 | b | | | | | | | | | | • | | | |
| 244 | b | | n | n | | | | | | | | | | |
| 239ab | b | | | | n | | | | | | | | | |
| 228 | b | | | | n | | | | | | | | | |
| 225 | b | | s | | s | | | | | | | | | |
| 223ab | b | | s | | | | | | | | | | | |
| 221 | b | | | n | | | | | | | | | | |
| 209 | b | | | | | | | | | | • | | | |
| 163 | b | | s | s | | | | | | | | | | |
| 158 | b | | | | s | | | | | | | | | |
| 157a | b | | s | | | | | | | | | | | |
| 151 | b | | n | | | | | | • | | | | | |
| 109 | b | | | | | | | | | | • | | | |
| 103a | b | | s | | s | | | | | | | | | |
| 101 | b | | | | | | | | | | | • | • | |
| 100 | b | | | n | | | | | | | | | | |

| Exit | ↗ | * | W | S | K | T | Am | FJ | Lo | Pe | Pi | Sp | TA | Wi |
|---|---|---|---|---|---|---|---|---|---|---|---|---|---|---|
| 87 | b | | | | | | • | | | | | | | |
| 82 | b | | s | | | | | | | | | | | |
| 64 | b | | s | | | | | | | | | | | |
| 43 | b | | | | | | | | • | | | | | |
| 23 | b | | n | | | | | | | | | | | |
| 20 | b | | | | | | | | | | • | | | |

## 12

Interstate 12 runs east to west for about 85 miles between I-10 exit 159 in Baton Rouge and I-10 exit 267.

| Mile Marker | ↗ | * | ? | ↗ | 🌲 | 🚻 | ☎ | 🛈 | | | | ♿ | | |
|---|---|---|---|---|---|---|---|---|---|---|---|---|---|---|
| 60 | b | | | • | | • | • | • | | | • | • | | |

| Exit | ↗ | * | W | S | K | T | Am | FJ | Lo | Pe | Pi | Sp | TA | Wi |
|---|---|---|---|---|---|---|---|---|---|---|---|---|---|---|
| 83 | b | | | | | | | | | | | • | | |
| 80 | b | | s | s | | | | | | | | | | |
| 63ab | b | | n | | | | | | | | | | | |
| 40 | b | | | | | | | | | • | • | | | |
| 15 | b | | n | | | | | | | | | | | |
| 10 | b | | n | | | | | | | | • | | | |
| 7 | b | | s | | | | | | | | | | | |
| 6 | b | | | | n | | | | | | | | | |

## 20

Interstate 20 runs east to west for 189 miles from the Mississippi state line to the Texas state line.

| Mile Marker | ↗ | * | ? | ↗ | 🌲 | 🚻 | ☎ | 🛈 | | | | ♿ | | |
|---|---|---|---|---|---|---|---|---|---|---|---|---|---|---|
| 184 | b | 1 | • | • | | • | • | • | | • | • | • | | |
| 150 | b | | | • | | • | • | • | | • | • | • | | |
| 97 | wb | | | • | | • | • | • | | • | • | • | | |
| 95 | eb | | | • | | • | • | • | | • | • | • | | |
| 58 | b | | | • | | • | • | • | | • | • | • | | |
| 2 | eb | | • | | | • | • | • | | • | • | • | | |

Notes: 1) Welcome Center wb, Rest Area eb

| Exit | ↗ | * | W | S | K | T | Am | FJ | Lo | Pe | Pi | Sp | TA | Wi |
|---|---|---|---|---|---|---|---|---|---|---|---|---|---|---|
| 171 | b | | | | | | | | • | | | | • | |

E ↕ W

| Exit | ⤢ | * | W | S | K | T | Am | FJ | Lo | Pe | Pi | Sp | TA | Wi |
|---|---|---|---|---|---|---|---|---|---|---|---|---|---|---|
| 138 | b | | n | | | | | | | | • | | | |
| 120 | b | | | s | | | | | | | | | | |
| 114 | b | | n | | s | | | | | | | | | |
| 112 | b | | | | | | | | | | | | | • |
| 85 | b | | n | | | | | | | | | | | |
| 33 | b | | | | | | | | | | • | | | |
| 22 | b | | | | n | | | | | | | | | |
| 10 | b | | s | | | | | | | | | | | |
| 8 | b | | | | | | | | | • | • | | | |
| 5 | b | | | | | | • | | | | | | | |
| 3 | b | | | | | | | • | | | | | | |

**49** Interstate 49 runs north to south for 206 miles from I-20 exit 17 in Shreveport to I-10 exit 103 in Lafayette.

| Mile Marker | ⤢ | * | Information | Highway sign arrow | Picnic area | Restrooms | Telephone | Picnic tables | Vending | RV dump | Pet area | Handicapped access | | |
|---|---|---|---|---|---|---|---|---|---|---|---|---|---|---|
| 35 | b | | | • | | • | | • | | • | • | • | | |

N ↕ S

| Exit | ⤢ | * | W | S | K | T | Am | FJ | Lo | Pe | Pi | Sp | TA | Wi |
|---|---|---|---|---|---|---|---|---|---|---|---|---|---|---|
| 138 | b | | e+ | | | | | | | | | | | |
| 83 | b | | e+ | e+ | | e+ | | | | | | | | |
| 80 | b | | | w+ | | | | | | | | | | |
| 18 | b | | w | | | | | | | | | | | |
| 1a | b | 1 | s | | s | | | | | | | | | |

Notes: 1) On US 167

**55** Interstate 55 runs north to south for 66 miles from the Mississippi state line to I-10 exit 209.

| Mile Marker | ⤢ | * | Information | Highway sign arrow | Picnic area | Restrooms | Telephone | Picnic tables | Vending | RV dump | Pet area | Handicapped access | | |
|---|---|---|---|---|---|---|---|---|---|---|---|---|---|---|
| 65 | sb | | • | | | • | • | • | | • | • | • | | |

N ↕ S

| Exit | ⤢ | * | W | S | K | T | Am | FJ | Lo | Pe | Pi | Sp | TA | Wi |
|---|---|---|---|---|---|---|---|---|---|---|---|---|---|---|
| 31 | b | | e | | | | | | | | • | | | |
| 1 | b | | | | | | | | | | • | | | |

Interstate 59 runs north to south for 11 miles from the Mississippi state line to I-10/12 in Slidell.

| Mile Marker | | * | | | | | | | | | | | | |
|---|---|---|---|---|---|---|---|---|---|---|---|---|---|---|
| 1 | sb | 1 | • | | | • | • | • | | | • | • | | |

Notes: 1) Welcome Center is closing December 2002 and will reopen in October 2003

Interstate 210 in Lake Charles is 12 miles long. It begins on I-10 exit 25 and ends at I-10 exit 34.

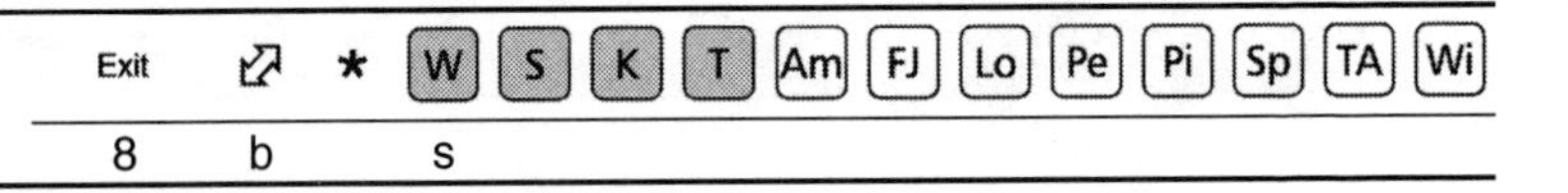

| Exit | | * | W | S | K | T | Am | FJ | Lo | Pe | Pi | Sp | TA | Wi |
|---|---|---|---|---|---|---|---|---|---|---|---|---|---|---|
| 8 | b | | s | | | | | | | | | | | |

Interstate 220 in Shreveport is 17 miles long. It begins on I-20 at exit 11 and ends at I-20 exit 26.

| Exit | | * | W | S | K | T | Am | FJ | Lo | Pe | Pi | Sp | TA | Wi |
|---|---|---|---|---|---|---|---|---|---|---|---|---|---|---|
| 12 | b | | s | | s+ | | | | | | | | | |

## Maine

**Rest Area Usage:** There is no limit to length of stay, however, no camping or overnight parking is permitted. **Road Conditions:** 207-624-3595 (weather) **State Police:** *General*, 207-624-7000; *Emergency*, 911 **Tourism Contact:** Maine Office of Tourism, 59 Statehouse Station, Augusta ME 04333. *Phone*: 888-624-6345 or 207-287-5711. *Internet*: www.visitmaine.com

I-95 runs north to south for 298 miles from the United States/Canada border to New Hampshire. A segment is also the Maine Turnpike. Exit numbers are based on the consecutive numbering system.

| Mile Marker | | * | | | | | | | | | | | | |
|---|---|---|---|---|---|---|---|---|---|---|---|---|---|---|
| 295 | b | 1 | | • | | • | • | • | | | • | • | | |
| 245 | nb | | | | • | | | | | | | | • | |
| 236 | b | | | • | | • | • | • | | | • | • | | |

| Mile Marker | (exit icon) | * | (info) | (arrow) | (trees) | (restrooms) | (phone) | (picnic) | (vending) | (RV) | (pets) | (handicap) | (camera) | (truck) |
|---|---|---|---|---|---|---|---|---|---|---|---|---|---|---|
| 192 | b | | | | • | | | | | | | | | |
| 172 | sb | | • | | | • | • | • | • | | • | • | | |
| 169 | nb | | • | | | • | • | • | • | | • | • | | |
| 141 | b | | | • | | • | • | • | | | • | • | | |
| 111 | sb | | | • | | • | • | • | • | | • | • | | |
| 107 | nb | | | • | | • | • | • | • | | • | • | | |
| 71 | sb | | | | • | | | | | | | | | |
| 62 | b | 2 | • | | | • | • | • | • | | | • | | |
| 24 | b | 3 | | • | | • | • | • | | | • | • | | |
| 3 | nb | | • | | | • | • | • | • | | • | • | | |

Notes: 1) West at exit 62 to Rest Area; 2) East at exit 17 to Welcome Center; 3) Turnpike Service Area, Gas, Food

| Exit | (exit icon) | * | W | S | K | T | Am | FJ | Lo | Pe | Pi | Sp | TA | Wi |
|---|---|---|---|---|---|---|---|---|---|---|---|---|---|---|
| 62 | b | | w | | | | | | | | | | | |
| 49 | b | | w | e | w | | | | | | | | | |
| 39 | b | | w | | | | | | | | | | | |
| 34 | b | | | | e | | | | | | | | | |
| 33 | b | | e | | | | | | | | | | | |
| 31 | b | | e | e | | | | | | | | | | |
| 30 | b | | | | e | | | | | | | | | |
| 15 | b | | e | | | | | | | | | | | |
| 7 | b | 1 | e | e | | | | | | | | | | |
| 4 | b | 1 | e | | | | | | | | | | | |
| 2 | b | | | | | | • | | | | | | | |

Notes: 1) Maine Turnpike numbering

Interstate 495 is about 50 miles long. It begins on I-95 at exit 9 and ends back on I-95 at exit 29. It is also part of the Maine Turnpike. Exit numbers are based on the consecutive numbering system.

| Mile Marker | (exit icon) | * | (info) | (arrow) | (trees) | (restrooms) | (phone) | (picnic) | (vending) | (RV) | (pets) | (handicap) | (camera) | (truck) |
|---|---|---|---|---|---|---|---|---|---|---|---|---|---|---|
| 95 | nb | 1 | | • | | • | • | • | | | • | • | | |
| 81 | sb | 1 | | • | | • | • | • | | | • | • | | |
| 57 | nb | 1 | | • | | • | • | • | | | • | • | | |
| 56 | sb | 1 | | • | | • | • | • | | | • | • | | |

Notes: 1) Service Area, Gas, Food

## Maryland

**Rest Area Usage:** There is a 3 hour stay limit, no camping or overnight parking is permitted. **Road Conditions:** 800-327-3125 (weather) **State Police:** *General*, 410-486-3101; *Emergency*, 911 **Tourism Contact:** Maryland Office of Tourism Development, 217 E Redwood St, 9th Fl, Baltimore MD 21202. *Phone*: 800-543-1036 or 410-767-3400. *Internet*: www.mdisfun.org

**68** Interstate 68 runs east to west for about 82 miles from I-70 exit 1 near Hancock to the West Virginia state line.

E ↕ W

| Mile Marker | | * | | | | | | | | | | | | |
|---|---|---|---|---|---|---|---|---|---|---|---|---|---|---|
| 75 | eb | | | | | | | | | | | | | • |
| 74 | b | | | • | | • | • | • | • | | | • | | |
| 72 | wb | | | | | | | | | | | | | • |
| 64 | b | | | | • | | • | | | | | | • | |
| 6 | eb | | • | | | • | • | • | • | | • | • | | |

| Exit | | * | W | S | K | T | Am | FJ | Lo | Pe | Pi | Sp | TA | Wi |
|---|---|---|---|---|---|---|---|---|---|---|---|---|---|---|
| 40 | b | | s | | | | | | | | | | | |

**70** Interstate 70 runs east to west for 94 miles from Baltimore at Cooks Lane to the Pennsylvania state line.

| Mile Marker | | * | | | | | | | | | | | | |
|---|---|---|---|---|---|---|---|---|---|---|---|---|---|---|
| 39 | b | | • | | | • | • | • | • | | • | • | | |

E ↕ W

| Exit | | * | W | S | K | T | Am | FJ | Lo | Pe | Pi | Sp | TA | Wi |
|---|---|---|---|---|---|---|---|---|---|---|---|---|---|---|
| 87ab | b | 1 | s+ | | | | | | | | | | | |
| 68 | b | | n | | | | | | | | | | | |
| 54 | b | | s | s | | | | | | | | | | |
| 24 | b | | | | | | | | | | • | | | |

Notes: 1) On US 40

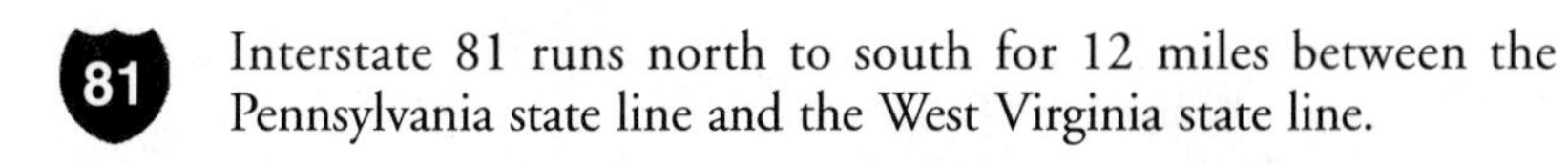

Interstate 81 runs north to south for 12 miles between the Pennsylvania state line and the West Virginia state line.

| Exit | | * | W | S | K | T | Am | FJ | Lo | Pe | Pi | Sp | TA | Wi |
|---|---|---|---|---|---|---|---|---|---|---|---|---|---|---|
| 6ab | b | | w | | | | | | | | | | | |
| 5 | b | | | e | e | e | | | | | | | | |

Interstate 83 runs north to south for 38 miles from the Pennsylvania state line to Fayette Street in downtown Baltimore.

| Exit | | * | W | S | K | T | Am | FJ | Lo | Pe | Pi | Sp | TA | Wi |
|---|---|---|---|---|---|---|---|---|---|---|---|---|---|---|
| 20 | b | | e | | | | | | | | | | | |
| 17 | b | | | e | | | | | | | | | | |

Interstate 95 runs north to south for 110 miles from the Delaware state line to the Virginia state line. A portion of it is shared with I-495.

| Mile Marker | | * | | | | | | | | | | | | |
|---|---|---|---|---|---|---|---|---|---|---|---|---|---|---|
| 96 | b | 1 | • | | | • | • | • | • | | • | • | | |
| 81 | b | 1 | | • | | • | • | • | • | | • | • | | |
| 37 | b | | • | | | • | • | • | • | | • | • | | |

Notes: 1) Service Area, Gas, Food

| Exit | | * | W | S | K | T | Am | FJ | Lo | Pe | Pi | Sp | TA | Wi |
|---|---|---|---|---|---|---|---|---|---|---|---|---|---|---|
| 109 | b | | | | | | | | | • | | | • | |
| 100 | b | | | | | | | • | | | | | | |
| 93 | b | | | | | | | | | | • | | | |
| 85 | b | | | | | e | | | | | | | | |
| 77ab | b | | w | | | | | | | | | | | |
| 67ab | b | | | | | e | | | | | | | | |
| 57 | b | | | | | | | | | | | | • | |
| 41 | b | | | | | | | | | | | | • | |
| 23 | b | | | | | w+ | | | | | | | | |
| 17 | b | 1 | | w | | | | | | | | | | |
| 4ab | b | 1 | | | e | | | | | | | | | |

Notes: 1) Shared with I-495

Interstate 97 runs north to south for 17 miles between I-695 in Ferndale and US 50 near Annapolis.

| Exit | ↗ | * | W | S | K | T | Am | FJ | Lo | Pe | Pi | Sp | TA | Wi |
|---|---|---|---|---|---|---|---|---|---|---|---|---|---|---|
| 12 | b | | e | | | e | | | | | | | | |

Interstate 270 is 32 miles long. It connects I-70 exit 53 in Frederick with I-495 near Bethesda.

| Mile Marker | ↗ | * | | | | | | | | | | | | |
|---|---|---|---|---|---|---|---|---|---|---|---|---|---|---|
| 28 | wb | | | | • | | | | | | | | • | |

| Exit | ↗ | * | W | S | K | T | Am | FJ | Lo | Pe | Pi | Sp | TA | Wi |
|---|---|---|---|---|---|---|---|---|---|---|---|---|---|---|
| 31ab | b | | n | n | | | | | | | | | | |
| 16 | b | | n | | | n | | | | | | | | |
| 11ab | b | | | n | | | | | | | | | | |

Interstate 495 forms a 64-mile loop around Washington, D.C. Portions of it are shared with I-95.

| Exit | ↗ | * | W | S | K | T | Am | FJ | Lo | Pe | Pi | Sp | TA | Wi |
|---|---|---|---|---|---|---|---|---|---|---|---|---|---|---|
| 17 | b | 1 | | w | | | | | | | | | | |
| 4ab | b | 1 | | | e | | | | | | | | | |

Notes: 1) Shared with I-95

Interstate 695 forms a 48-mile loop around Baltimore. Exit numbering begins at MD 173 and increases in a clockwise direction. Exit numbers are based on the consecutive numbering system.

| Exit | ↗ | * | W | S | K | T | Am | FJ | Lo | Pe | Pi | Sp | TA | Wi |
|---|---|---|---|---|---|---|---|---|---|---|---|---|---|---|
| 39 | b | | w | | | | | | | | | | | |
| 38 | b | | | e | | | | | | | | | | |
| 32ab | b | | | | n | | | | | | | | | |
| 30ab | b | | | | n | | | | | | | | | |
| 17 | b | | | e | | | | | | | | | | |
| 15ab | b | | w | | | | | | | | | | | |
| 3a | b | | w | | w | | | | | | | | | |

## Massachusetts

**Rest Area Usage:** There is no limit to length of stay, however, no camping or overnight parking is permitted. **Road Conditions:** 617-374-1234 (general) **State Police:** General, 617-740-7600; Emergency, 911 **Tourism Contact:** Massachusetts Office of Travel & Tourism, 10 Park Plaza, Ste 4510, Boston MA 02116. Phone: 800-227-6277. Internet: www.massvacation.com

**84** I-84 runs east to west for approximately 8 miles from I-90 exit 9 to the Connecticut state line. Exit numbers are based on the consecutive numbering system.

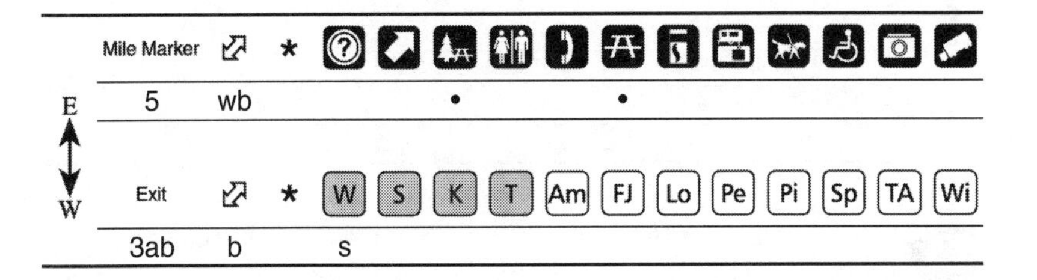

| Mile Marker | Direction | * | Info | Arrow | Trees | Restrooms | Phone | Picnic | Vending | RV | Pet | Handicap | Camera | Truck |
|---|---|---|---|---|---|---|---|---|---|---|---|---|---|---|
| 5 | wb | | | | • | | | • | | | | | | |

| Exit | Direction | * | W | S | K | T | Am | FJ | Lo | Pe | Pi | Sp | TA | Wi |
|---|---|---|---|---|---|---|---|---|---|---|---|---|---|---|
| 3ab | b | | s | | | | | | | | | | | |

**90** I-90 runs east to west for 136 miles from I-93 exit 20 in Boston to the New York state line. I-90 is also the Massachusetts Turnpike. Exit numbers are based on the consecutive numbering system.

| Mile Marker | Direction | * | Info | Arrow | Trees | Restrooms | Phone | Picnic | Vending | RV | Pet | Handicap | Camera | Truck |
|---|---|---|---|---|---|---|---|---|---|---|---|---|---|---|
| 117 | eb | 1 | • | | | • | • | • | • | | | • | | |
| 114 | wb | 1 | | • | | • | • | • | • | | | • | | |
| 105 | wb | 1 | | • | | • | • | • | • | | | • | | |
| 84 | wb | 1 | • | | | • | • | • | • | | | • | | |
| 80 | eb | 1 | • | | | • | • | • | • | | | • | | |
| 56 | wb | 1 | | • | | • | • | • | • | | | • | | |
| 55 | eb | 1 | | • | | • | • | • | • | | | • | | |
| 35 | eb | | | | | | | | | | | | | • |
| 29 | b | 1 | | • | | • | • | • | • | | | • | | |
| 12 | b | | | | • | | | | | | | | | |
| 8 | b | 2 | • | • | | • | • | • | | | | • | | |

Notes: 1) Service Area, Gas, Food; 2) Service Area, Gas, Food / Welcome Center eb, Rest Area wb

| Exit | ↗ | * | W | S | K | T | Am | FJ | Lo | Pe | Pi | Sp | TA | Wi |
|---|---|---|---|---|---|---|---|---|---|---|---|---|---|---|
| 13 | b | | | s | | s | | | | | | | | |
| 6 | b | | | | | | • | | | | | | | |

Interstate 91 runs north to south for 55 miles from the Vermont state line to the Connecticut state line. Exit numbers are based on the consecutive numbering system.

| Mile Marker | ↗ | * | | | | | | | | | | | | |
|---|---|---|---|---|---|---|---|---|---|---|---|---|---|---|
| 54 | b | | | | • | | | • | | | | | | |
| 34 | b | | | | • | | | | | | | | | |
| 18 | b | | | | • | | | • | | | | | • | |

| Exit | ↗ | * | W | S | K | T | Am | FJ | Lo | Pe | Pi | Sp | TA | Wi |
|---|---|---|---|---|---|---|---|---|---|---|---|---|---|---|
| 20 | b | | w | | | | | | | | | | | |
| 15 | b | | | | | e | | | | | | | | |

Interstate 93 runs north to south for 47 miles from the New Hampshire state line to I-95 exit 12 in Canton. Exit numbers are based on the consecutive numbering system.

| Exit | ↗ | * | W | S | K | T | Am | FJ | Lo | Pe | Pi | Sp | TA | Wi |
|---|---|---|---|---|---|---|---|---|---|---|---|---|---|---|
| 37c | b | | | | | w | | | | | | | | |
| 29 | b | | | | e | | | | | | | | | |
| 16 | b | | | | w | | | | | | | | | |

Interstate 95 runs north to south for 90 miles from the New Hampshire state line to the Rhode Island state line. Exit numbers are based on the consecutive numbering system.

| Mile Marker | ↗ | * | | | | | | | | | | | | |
|---|---|---|---|---|---|---|---|---|---|---|---|---|---|---|
| 89 | sb | | • | | | • | • | • | • | | | • | | |
| 46 | nb | 1 | | • | | • | • | | | | | • | | |
| 38 | sb | 1 | | • | | • | • | | | | | • | | |
| 33 | sb | | | | • | | • | • | | | | | | |
| 27 | sb | | | • | | • | • | • | • | | | • | | |
| 10 | b | 2 | • | • | | • | • | • | • | | • | • | | |

| Mile Marker | | * | | | | | | | | | | | | |
|---|---|---|---|---|---|---|---|---|---|---|---|---|---|---|
| 2 | nb | | | | • | | | | | | | | | |

Notes: 1) Service Area, Gas, Food; 2) Welcome Center nb, Rest Area sb

N ↕ S

| Exit | | * | W | S | K | T | Am | FJ | Lo | Pe | Pi | Sp | TA | Wi |
|---|---|---|---|---|---|---|---|---|---|---|---|---|---|---|
| 57 | b | | | | e | | | | | | | | | |
| 10 | b | | w+ | | | | | | | | | | | |
| 2ab | b | | | | e | | | | | | | | | |

**195** Interstate 195 runs east to west for 40 miles from I-495 exit 1 to the Rhode Island state line. Exit numbers are based on the consecutive numbering system.

E ↕ W

| Mile Marker | | * | | | | | | | | | | | | |
|---|---|---|---|---|---|---|---|---|---|---|---|---|---|---|
| 37 | eb | | | • | | • | • | • | | | • | • | | |
| 7 | wb | | | | • | | • | • | • | | | | | |
| 6 | eb | | | | | • | • | • | | | • | • | | |

| Exit | | * | W | S | K | T | Am | FJ | Lo | Pe | Pi | Sp | TA | Wi |
|---|---|---|---|---|---|---|---|---|---|---|---|---|---|---|
| 18 | b | | s+ | | s+ | | | | | | | | | |
| 12 | b | | s | | | | | | | | | | | |
| 1 | b | | s | s | | s | | | | | | | | |

**295** Interstate 295 is a 27-mile open loop route around Providence, Rhode Island. This portion in Massachusetts is 4 miles long. It runs from I-95 exit 4 to the Rhode Island state line. See Rhode Island for that portion of the Interstate.

| Exit | | * | W | S | K | T | Am | FJ | Lo | Pe | Pi | Sp | TA | Wi |
|---|---|---|---|---|---|---|---|---|---|---|---|---|---|---|
| 1ab | b | | e | | | e | | | | | | | | |

**495** Interstate 495 runs north to south for 120 miles from I-95 exit 59 near Amesbury to I-195 and MA 25 near Wareham. Exit numbers are based on the consecutive numbering system.

| Mile Marker | | * | | | | | | | | | | | | |
|---|---|---|---|---|---|---|---|---|---|---|---|---|---|---|
| 114 | sb | | | • | | • | • | • | • | | | • | | |

| Mile Marker | | * | | | | | | | | | | | | |
|---|---|---|---|---|---|---|---|---|---|---|---|---|---|---|
| 110 | nb | | | | • | | • | • | | | | | | |
| 87 | b | | | • | | • | • | • | • | | | • | | |
| 11 | b | | | | • | | | • | • | | | | | |

N ↕ S

| Exit | | * | W | S | K | T | Am | FJ | Lo | Pe | Pi | Sp | TA | Wi |
|---|---|---|---|---|---|---|---|---|---|---|---|---|---|---|
| 49 | b | | | | e | | | | | | | | | |
| 47 | b | | w+ | | | | | | | | | | | |
| 38 | b | | e | | w | | | | | | | | | |
| 19 | b | | | | w | | | | | | | | | |
| 18 | b | | e | | | | | | | | | | | |

## Michigan

**Rest Area Usage:** There is a 4 hour stay limit, no camping or overnight parking is permitted. **Road Conditions:** 800-381-8477 (weather), 888-305-7283 (construction) **State Police:** *General*, 517-332-2521; *Emergency*, 911 **Tourism Contact:** Travel Michigan, PO Box 30226, Lansing MI 48909. *Phone*: 800-784-7328. *Internet*: www.michigan.org

Interstate 69 runs north to south for 203 miles from Port Huron to the Indiana state line. Portions are shared with I-94 and I-96.

| Mile Marker | | * | | | | | | | | | | | | |
|---|---|---|---|---|---|---|---|---|---|---|---|---|---|---|
| 274 | b | 1 | • | | | • | • | • | | | • | • | | |
| 174 | sb | | | • | | • | • | • | | | • | • | | |
| 160 | nb | | | • | | • | • | • | | | • | • | | |
| 126 | nb | | | • | | • | • | • | | | • | • | | |
| 101 | sb | | | • | | • | • | • | | | • | • | | |
| 41 | sb | | | • | | • | • | • | | | • | • | | |
| 28 | nb | | | • | | • | • | • | | | • | • | | |
| 6 | nb | | • | | | • | • | • | • | | • | • | | |

N ↕ S

Notes: 1) Shared with I-94 / Follows I-94 numbering

| Exit | | * | W | S | K | T | Am | FJ | Lo | Pe | Pi | Sp | TA | Wi |
|---|---|---|---|---|---|---|---|---|---|---|---|---|---|---|
| 199 | b | | | e | e | | | | | | | | | |

| Exit | | * | W | S | K | T | Am | FJ | Lo | Pe | Pi | Sp | TA | Wi |
|---|---|---|---|---|---|---|---|---|---|---|---|---|---|---|
| 168 | b | | | | | | | | | | | • | | |
| 155 | b | | | | w+ | | | | | | | | | |
| 141 | b | | w | | w | | | | | | | | | |
| 139 | b | | | | | e | | | | | | | | |
| 87 | b | | | | | | | | | | | • | | |
| 61 | b | | e | | | | | | | | | | | |
| 36 | b | | | | e | | | | | | | | | |
| 25 | b | | | | | | • | | | | | | | |
| 13 | b | | e | | | | | | | | | | | |

N ↕ S

75

I-75 runs north to south for 395 miles from the United States/ Canada border to the Ohio state line.

| Mile Marker | | * | | | | | | | | | | | | |
|---|---|---|---|---|---|---|---|---|---|---|---|---|---|---|
| 394 | b | | • | | | • | • | • | | | | • | | |
| 389 | nb | | | • | | • | • | • | | | • | • | | |
| 346 | sb | | | • | | • | • | • | | | • | • | • | |
| 343 | b | | • | | | • | • | • | | | | • | | |
| 338 | b | | • | | | • | • | • | • | | | • | | |
| 328 | sb | | | • | | • | • | • | | | • | • | | |
| 317 | nb | | | • | | • | • | • | | | • | • | • | |
| 287 | sb | | | • | | • | • | • | • | | | • | | |
| 277 | nb | | | • | | • | • | • | • | | • | • | | |
| 262 | sb | | | • | | • | • | • | • | | • | • | | |
| 251 | nb | | | • | | • | • | • | • | | • | • | | |
| 235 | sb | | | • | | • | • | • | • | | • | • | | |
| 210 | nb | | | • | | • | • | • | • | | • | • | | |
| 201 | sb | | | • | | • | • | • | • | | • | • | | |
| 175 | nb | | | • | | • | • | • | • | | • | • | | |
| 158 | sb | | | • | | • | • | • | • | | • | • | | |
| 129 | b | | | • | | • | • | • | • | | • | • | | |
| 95 | b | | | • | | • | • | • | • | | • | • | | |
| 10 | nb | | • | | | • | • | • | • | | • | • | | |

N ↕ S

| Exit | | * | W | S | K | T | Am | FJ | Lo | Pe | Pi | Sp | TA | Wi |
|---|---|---|---|---|---|---|---|---|---|---|---|---|---|---|
| 392 | b | | e | | e | | | | | | | | | |
| 282 | b | | w | | w | | | | | | | | | |
| 254 | b | | | | w+ | | | | | | | | | |

| Exit | ↗ | * | W | S | K | T | Am | FJ | Lo | Pe | Pi | Sp | TA | Wi |
|---|---|---|---|---|---|---|---|---|---|---|---|---|---|---|
| 149ab | b | | | | w | | | | | | | | | |
| 144 | b | | | | | | | | | | • | | • | |
| 131 | b | | | | e | | | | | | | | | |
| 118 | b | | w | w | | | | | | | | | | |
| 117b | b | | | | e | w | | | | | | | | |
| 83ab | b | | | | w | | | | | | | | | |
| 77ab | b | | w+ | | | | | | | | | | | |
| 65ab | b | | | e | | | | | | | | | | |
| 63 | b | | | | e | | | | | | | | | |
| 42 | b | | | | w | | | | | | | | | |
| 37 | b | | | e | | | | | | | | | | |
| 32 | b | | | | | | • | | | | | | | |
| 18 | b | | | | | | | | | | • | | | |
| 15 | b | | | | | | | | | | • | | • | |

Interstate 94 runs east to west for 275 miles from Port Huron to the Indiana state line. A portion of it is shared with I-69.

| Mile Marker | ↗ | * | Information | Arrow | Picnic area | Restrooms | Phone | Picnic table | Vending | Map/Info board | Pet area | Handicap access | Camera | Other |
|---|---|---|---|---|---|---|---|---|---|---|---|---|---|---|
| 274 | b | 1 | • | | | • | • | • | | | • | • | | |
| 255 | eb | | | • | | • | • | • | | | • | • | | |
| 251 | wb | | | • | | • | • | • | | | • | • | | |
| 168 | eb | | | • | | • | • | • | • | | • | • | | |
| 150 | wb | | | • | | • | • | • | • | | • | • | | |
| 135 | eb | | | • | | • | • | • | • | | • | • | | |
| 113 | wb | | | • | | • | • | • | • | | • | • | | |
| 96 | eb | | | • | | • | • | • | • | | • | • | | |
| 85 | wb | | | • | | • | • | • | • | | • | • | | |
| 72 | eb | | | • | | • | • | • | | | • | • | | |
| 42 | wb | | | • | | • | • | • | • | | • | • | | |
| 36 | eb | | | • | | • | • | • | • | | • | • | | |
| 0.5 | eb | | • | | | • | • | • | • | | • | • | | |

Notes: 1) Shared with I-69

| Exit | ↗ | * | W | S | K | T | Am | FJ | Lo | Pe | Pi | Sp | TA | Wi |
|---|---|---|---|---|---|---|---|---|---|---|---|---|---|---|
| 243 | b | | | | n | n | | | | | • | | | |
| 232 | b | | | | s | | | | | | | | | |
| 231 | b | | | n | | n | | | | | | | | |

| Exit | ⇗ | * | W | S | K | T | Am | FJ | Lo | Pe | Pi | Sp | TA | Wi |
|---|---|---|---|---|---|---|---|---|---|---|---|---|---|---|
| 205 | b | | | | | | | | | | • | | | |
| 202ab | b | | s | | | | | | | | | | | |
| 190 | b | | n | | | | | | | | | | | |
| 187 | b | | | | s | | | | | | | | | |
| 181 | b | | n | | | | | | | | | | | |
| 175 | b | | | | | s | | | | | | | | |
| 172 | b | | | | n | | | | | | | | | |
| 167 | b | | | | | | | | | | • | | • | |
| 142 | b | | | | s+ | | | | | | | | | |
| 138 | b | | | | | s | | | | | | | | |
| 137 | b | | | s | s | | | | | | | | | |
| 104 | b | | | | | | • | | | | • | | | |
| 97 | b | | s | s | | s | | | | | | | | |
| 76ab | b | | | s | s | s | | | | | | | | |
| 66 | b | | | | | | | | | | | • | | |
| 30 | b | | | | | | | • | | | | | | |
| 29 | b | | n | | | | | | | | | | | |
| 28 | b | | | | | n | | | | | | • | | |
| 16 | b | | | | | | | | | | • | | | |
| 12 | b | | | | | | | | | | | | • | |

96

I-96 is 191 miles long. It runs east to west from I-75 in Detroit to US 31 near Muskegon. A portion is shared with I-69 and I-275.

| Mile Marker | ⇗ | * | ? | | | | | | | | | | | |
|---|---|---|---|---|---|---|---|---|---|---|---|---|---|---|
| 161 | eb | | | • | | • | • | • | • | | • | • | | |
| 141 | wb | | | • | | • | • | • | • | | • | • | | |
| 135 | eb | | | • | | • | • | • | • | | • | • | | |
| 111 | wb | | | • | | • | • | • | • | | • | • | | |
| 87 | eb | | | • | | • | • | • | • | | • | • | | |
| 79 | wb | | | • | | • | • | • | • | | • | • | | |
| 63 | eb | | | • | | • | • | • | • | | • | • | | |
| 45 | wb | | | • | | • | • | • | • | | | • | | |
| 25 | eb | | | • | | • | • | • | | | • | • | | |
| 8 | wb | | | • | | • | • | • | • | | • | • | | |

| Exit | ⇗ | * | W | S | K | T | Am | FJ | Lo | Pe | Pi | Sp | TA | Wi |
|---|---|---|---|---|---|---|---|---|---|---|---|---|---|---|
| 176 | b | | s | | | | | | | | | | | |

| E↕W | Exit | ↗ | * | W | S | K | T | Am | FJ | Lo | Pe | Pi | Sp | TA | Wi |
|---|---|---|---|---|---|---|---|---|---|---|---|---|---|---|---|
| | 167 | b | 1 | | | | s | | | | | | | | |
| | 145 | b | | | | s | s | | | | | | | | |
| | 104 | b | | | n | | n | | | | | | | | |
| | 98 | b | | | | | | • | | | | | | | |
| | 86 | b | | | | | | | | | | • | | | |
| | 77 | b | | | | | | | | | | | • | | |
| | 67 | b | | | | | | | | | | • | | | |
| | 43ab | b | | n | s | | s | | | | | | | | |
| | 30ab | b | | n | n | n | n | | | | | | | | |
| | 16 | b | | | | | | | | | | • | | | |
| | 1ab | b | | n+ | n+ | | n+ | | | | | | | | |

Notes: 1) Shared with I-275

**196** Interstate 196 is 81 miles long. It runs east to west from I-96 in Grand Rapids to I-94 at Benton Harbor.

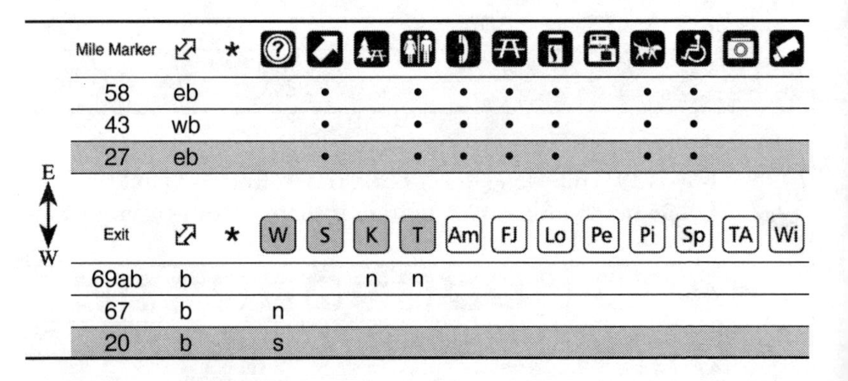

| E↕W | Mile Marker | ↗ | * | Info | Ramp | Trees | Restrooms | Phone | Picnic | Vending | RV | Pets | Handicap | | |
|---|---|---|---|---|---|---|---|---|---|---|---|---|---|---|---|
| | 58 | eb | | | • | | • | • | • | • | | • | • | | |
| | 43 | wb | | | • | | • | • | • | • | | • | • | | |
| | 27 | eb | | | • | | • | • | • | • | | • | • | | |

| E↕W | Exit | ↗ | * | W | S | K | T | Am | FJ | Lo | Pe | Pi | Sp | TA | Wi |
|---|---|---|---|---|---|---|---|---|---|---|---|---|---|---|---|
| | 69ab | b | | | | n | n | | | | | | | | |
| | 67 | b | | n | | | | | | | | | | | |
| | 20 | b | | s | | | | | | | | | | | |

**275** Interstate 275 is a 36-mile spur route. It runs north to south connecting I-96 with I-75.

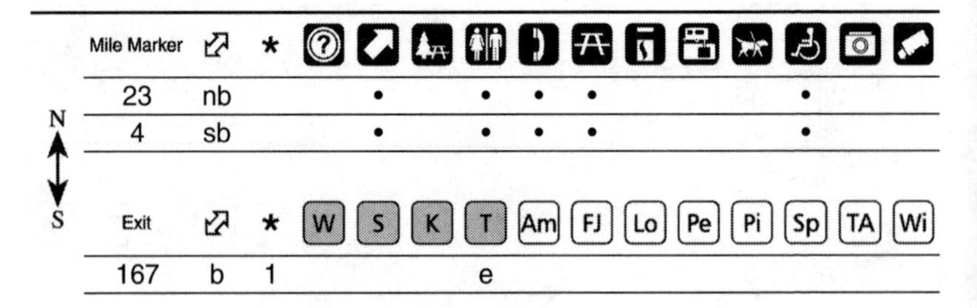

| N↕S | Mile Marker | ↗ | * | Info | Ramp | Trees | Restrooms | Phone | Picnic | Vending | RV | Pets | Handicap | | |
|---|---|---|---|---|---|---|---|---|---|---|---|---|---|---|---|
| | 23 | nb | | | • | | • | • | • | | | | • | | |
| | 4 | sb | | | • | | • | • | • | | | | • | | |

| N↕S | Exit | ↗ | * | W | S | K | T | Am | FJ | Lo | Pe | Pi | Sp | TA | Wi |
|---|---|---|---|---|---|---|---|---|---|---|---|---|---|---|---|
| | 167 | b | 1 | | | | e | | | | | | | | |

| Exit | ⇗ | * | W | S | K | T | Am | FJ | Lo | Pe | Pi | Sp | TA | Wi |
|---|---|---|---|---|---|---|---|---|---|---|---|---|---|---|
| 28 | b | | | | w | | | | | | | | | |
| 25 | b | | | | w | w | | | | | | | | |

Notes: 1) Shared with I-96 / Follows I-96 numbering

Interstate 475 in Flint is 16 miles long. It connects I-75 exit 111 with I-75 exit 125, providing a route through Flint.

| Exit | ⇗ | * | W | S | K | T | Am | FJ | Lo | Pe | Pi | Sp | TA | Wi |
|---|---|---|---|---|---|---|---|---|---|---|---|---|---|---|
| 13 | b | | | | s | | | | | | | | | |

Interstate 696 is a 27-mile route in Detroit. It runs east to west between I-94 and I-96.

| Exit | ⇗ | * | W | S | K | T | Am | FJ | Lo | Pe | Pi | Sp | TA | Wi |
|---|---|---|---|---|---|---|---|---|---|---|---|---|---|---|
| 10 | b | | | | n | | | | | | | | | |

## Minnesota

**Rest Area Usage:** There is a 6 hour stay limit, no camping or overnight parking is permitted. **Road Conditions:** 800-542-0220 or 651-284-0511 (weather) **State Police:** *General*, 651-282-6871; Emergency, 911 **Tourism Contact:** Minnesota Office of Tourism, 500 Metro Square, 121 7th Place E, St Paul MN 55101. *Phone*: 800-657-3700 or 651-296-5029. *Internet*: www.exploreminnesota.com

Interstate 35 runs north to south for 260 miles from Duluth to the Iowa state line. I-35 splits south of Minneapolis into I-35E and I-35W. It comes together again north of Minneapolis.

| N ↕ S | Mile Marker | ⇗ | * | ? | | | | | | | | | | | |
|---|---|---|---|---|---|---|---|---|---|---|---|---|---|---|---|
| | 250 | b | | • | | | • | • | • | • | | • | • | • | |
| | 226 | nb | | | • | | • | • | • | • | | • | • | | |
| | 208 | sb | | | • | | • | • | • | • | | • | • | | |
| | 198 | nb | | | • | | • | • | • | • | | • | • | | |
| | 154 | nb | | | • | | • | • | • | • | | • | • | | |

| Mile Marker | ⤢ | * | ? | Arrow | Trees | Restrooms | Phone | Picnic | Vending | RV | Pets | Handicap | Camera | Truck |
|---|---|---|---|---|---|---|---|---|---|---|---|---|---|---|
| 131 | sb | | | • | | • | • | • | • | | • | • | | |
| 75 | sb | | | • | | • | • | • | • | | • | • | | |
| 68 | nb | | | • | | • | • | • | • | | • | • | | |
| 35 | b | | | • | | • | • | • | • | | • | • | | |
| 1 | nb | | • | | | • | • | • | • | | • | • | | |

| Exit | ⤢ | * | W | S | K | T | Am | FJ | Lo | Pe | Pi | Sp | TA | Wi |
|---|---|---|---|---|---|---|---|---|---|---|---|---|---|---|
| 252 | b | | | | w | | | | | | | | | |
| 237 | b | | w+ | | | | | | | | | | | |
| 171 | b | | | | | | | | | | | • | | |
| 169 | b | | e | | | | | | | | | | | |
| 131 | b | | e | | | e | | | | | | | | |
| 115 | b | 1 | w | | | w | | | | | | | | |
| 109 | b | 1 | | | w | | | | | | | | | |
| 97 | b | 1 | e | | | | | | | | | | | |
| 93 | b | 1 | | | | w | | | | | | | | |
| 88b | b | 1 | | | | w | | | | | | | | |
| 56 | b | | e | | | | | | | | | | | |
| 55 | b | | | | e+ | | | | | | | | | |
| 42ab | b | | e | | | | • | | | | | | | |
| 41 | b | | | | | w | | | | | | | | |
| 11 | b | | | | | | | | | | | | • | |

Notes: 1) I-35E

Interstate 35W is a 41-mile route that separates from I-35 at exit 88 and rejoins I-35 at exit 127.

| Exit | ⤢ | * | W | S | K | T | Am | FJ | Lo | Pe | Pi | Sp | TA | Wi |
|---|---|---|---|---|---|---|---|---|---|---|---|---|---|---|
| 21ab | b | | | | | w | | | | | | | | |
| 1 | b | | | | w | w | | | | | | | | |

Interstate 90 runs east to west for 277 miles from the Wisconsin state line to the South Dakota state line.

| Mile Marker | ⤢ | * | ? | Arrow | Trees | Restrooms | Phone | Picnic | Vending | RV | Pets | Handicap | Camera | Truck |
|---|---|---|---|---|---|---|---|---|---|---|---|---|---|---|
| 275 | wb | | • | | | • | • | • | • | | • | • | • | |
| 244 | eb | | | • | | • | • | • | • | | • | • | • | |

| Mile Marker | | * | | | | | | | | | | | | |
|---|---|---|---|---|---|---|---|---|---|---|---|---|---|---|
| 222 | wb | | | • | | • | • | • | • | | • | • | | |
| 202 | eb | | | • | | • | • | • | • | | • | • | | |
| 171 | wb | | | • | | • | • | • | • | | • | • | | |
| 162 | eb | | | • | | • | • | • | • | | • | • | | |
| 118 | b | | | • | | • | • | • | • | | • | • | • | |
| 72 | wb | | | • | | • | • | • | • | | • | • | • | |
| 69 | eb | | | • | | • | • | • | • | | • | • | • | |
| 25 | wb | | | • | | • | • | • | • | | • | • | | |
| 24 | eb | | | • | | • | • | • | • | | • | • | | |
| 0 | eb | | • | | | • | • | • | • | | • | • | | |

| Exit | | * | W | S | K | T | Am | FJ | Lo | Pe | Pi | Sp | TA | Wi |
|---|---|---|---|---|---|---|---|---|---|---|---|---|---|---|
| 177 | b | | | | n | n | | | | | | | | |
| 154 | b | | s+ | | | | | | | | | | | |
| 146 | b | | | | | | • | | | | | | | |
| 119 | b | | s | | | | | | | | | | | |
| 102 | b | | | | s | | | | | | | | | |
| 43 | b | | s | | s | | | | | | | | | |

94

Interstate 94 runs east to west for 259 miles from the Wisconsin state line to the North Dakota state line. A portion of it is shared with I-694.

| Mile Marker | | * | | | | | | | | | | | | |
|---|---|---|---|---|---|---|---|---|---|---|---|---|---|---|
| 256 | wb | | • | | | • | • | • | • | | • | • | | |
| 215 | eb | | | • | | • | • | • | • | | | • | | |
| 187 | eb | | | • | | • | • | • | • | | • | • | | |
| 177 | wb | | | • | | • | • | • | • | | • | • | | |
| 152 | b | | | • | | • | • | • | • | | • | • | | |
| 105 | wb | | | • | | • | • | • | • | | • | • | | |
| 100 | eb | | | • | | • | • | • | • | | • | • | | |
| 69 | wb | | | • | | • | • | • | • | | • | • | | |
| 60 | eb | | | • | | • | • | • | • | | • | • | | |
| 2 | eb | | • | | | • | • | • | • | | • | • | | |

| Exit | | * | W | S | K | T | Am | FJ | Lo | Pe | Pi | Sp | TA | Wi |
|---|---|---|---|---|---|---|---|---|---|---|---|---|---|---|
| 245 | b | | | | | s | | | | | | | | |
| 239ab | b | | | | n | n | | | | | | | | |

| Exit | | * | W | S | K | T | Am | FJ | Lo | Pe | Pi | Sp | TA | Wi |
|---|---|---|---|---|---|---|---|---|---|---|---|---|---|---|
| 238 | b | | | | n | n | | | | | | | | |
| 229 | b | | | | | s | | | | | | | | |
| 34 | b | 1 | | | | s | | | | | | | | |
| 215 | b | | | | n | | | | | | | | | |
| 213 | b | | | | | s | | | | | | | | |
| 207 | b | | | | | | | | | | | | • | |
| 193 | b | | | | n | | | | | | | | | |
| 183 | b | | | | | | • | | | | | | | |
| 167ab | b | | | n+ | | | | | | | | | | |
| 103 | b | | n | | | n | | | | | | | | |
| 54 | b | | s | | n | n | | | | | | | | |
| 2 | b | | | | | n+ | | | | | | | | |

Notes: 1) Shared with I-694 / Follows I-694 numbering

Interstate 494 forms a partial loop around Minneapolis/Saint Paul. It is 42 miles long and connects I-94 exit 249 with I-94 exit 216.

| Exit | | * | W | S | K | T | Am | FJ | Lo | Pe | Pi | Sp | TA | Wi |
|---|---|---|---|---|---|---|---|---|---|---|---|---|---|---|
| 59 | b | | | | | s | | | | | | | | |
| 67 | b | | | n+ | n+ | n+ | | | | | | | | |
| 3 | b | | s | | | | | | | | | | | |
| 6a | b | | | | | s | | | | | | | | |
| 11ab | b | | s | | | s | | | | | | | | |
| 23 | b | | | | | e | | | | | | | | |

Interstate 694 is 34 miles long. It connects I-94 exit 249 with I-94 near exit 215. A portion is also I-94.

| Exit | | * | W | S | K | T | Am | FJ | Lo | Pe | Pi | Sp | TA | Wi |
|---|---|---|---|---|---|---|---|---|---|---|---|---|---|---|
| 57 | b | | | | w | | | | | | | | | |
| 50 | b | | e | | e | | | | | | | | | |
| 43a | b | | | | | s | | | | | | | | |
| 38ab | b | | | | | s | | | | | | | | |
| 34 | b | 1 | | | | s | | | | | | | | |

Notes: 1) Shared with I-94

# Mississippi

**Rest Area Usage:** There is no limit to length of stay and overnight parking is permitted. Camping is not allowed. **Road Conditions:** 601-987-1211 (weather), 601-359-7301 (construction) **State Police:** *General*, 601-987-1530; *Emergency*, 911 **Tourism Contact:** Mississippi Division of Tourism Development, PO Box 849, Jackson MS 39205. *Phone*: 800-927-6378 or 601-359-3297. *Internet*: www.visitmississippi.org **Notes:** 24-hour security is provided at nearly all of Mississippi's rest areas.

10

Interstate 10 runs east to west for 77 miles from the Alabama state line to the Louisiana state line.

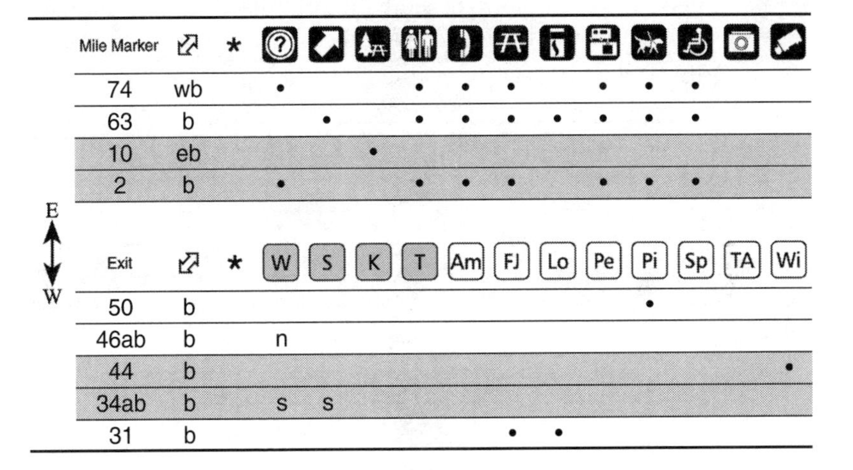

| Mile Marker | | * | ? | | | | | | | | | | | |
|---|---|---|---|---|---|---|---|---|---|---|---|---|---|---|
| 74 | wb | | • | | | • | • | • | | • | • | • | | |
| 63 | b | | | • | | • | • | • | • | • | • | • | | |
| 10 | eb | | | | • | | | | | | | | | |
| 2 | b | | • | | | • | • | • | | • | • | • | | |

| Exit | | * | W | S | K | T | Am | FJ | Lo | Pe | Pi | Sp | TA | Wi |
|---|---|---|---|---|---|---|---|---|---|---|---|---|---|---|
| 50 | b | | | | | | | | | | • | | | |
| 46ab | b | | n | | | | | | | | | | | |
| 44 | b | | | | | | | | | | | | | • |
| 34ab | b | | s | s | | | | | | | | | | |
| 31 | b | | | | | | | • | • | | | | | |

20

Interstate 20 runs east to west for 154 miles from the Alabama state line to the Louisiana state line. Portions are shared with I-59 and I-55.

| Mile Marker | | * | ? | | | | | | | | | | | |
|---|---|---|---|---|---|---|---|---|---|---|---|---|---|---|
| 164 | wb | 1 | • | | | • | • | • | | • | • | • | | |
| 90 | eb | | | • | | • | • | • | • | • | • | • | | |
| 75 | wb | | | • | | • | • | • | • | • | • | • | | |
| 6 | eb | | | | • | | | | | | | | | |
| 1 | b | | • | | | • | • | | | | | • | | |

Notes: 1) Shared with I-59 / Follows I-59 numbering

E ↕ W

| Exit | ⇗ | * | W | S | K | T | Am | FJ | Lo | Pe | Pi | Sp | TA | Wi |
|---|---|---|---|---|---|---|---|---|---|---|---|---|---|---|
| 160 | b | 1 | | | | | | | | | | | • | |
| 154ab | b | 1 | s | | s | | | | | | | | | |
| 109 | b | | s | | | | | | | | | | | |
| 88 | b | | n | | | | | | | | | | | |
| 54 | b | | n | | | | | | | | | | | |
| 47 | b | | | | | | | • | | | | | | • |
| 45 | b | 2 | | | | | | | | • | • | | | |
| 42ab | b | | s | | | | | | | | | | | |
| 40ab | b | | s | | | | | | | | | | | |
| 36 | b | | n | | | | | | | | | | | |
| 1c | b | | s | | | | | | | | | | | |

Notes: 1) Shared with I-59 / Follows I-59 numbering; 2) Shared with I-55

**55**

Interstate 55 runs north to south for 291 miles from the Tennessee state line to the Louisiana state line. A small portion is shared with I-20.

N ↕ S

| Mile Marker | ⇗ | * | ? | ↗ | 🌲 | 🚻 | ☎ | Picnic | Vending | Map | Pets | ♿ | Camera | Truck |
|---|---|---|---|---|---|---|---|---|---|---|---|---|---|---|
| 279 | sb | | • | | | • | • | • | | • | • | • | | |
| 276 | nb | | | • | | • | • | • | • | • | • | • | | |
| 240 | b | | | • | | • | • | • | | • | • | • | | |
| 204 | sb | | | | • | | • | | | | | | | |
| 202 | nb | | | | • | | • | | | | | | | |
| 173 | sb | | | • | | • | • | • | | • | • | • | | |
| 163 | nb | | | • | | • | • | • | | • | • | • | | |
| 121 | sb | | | | • | | | • | | | | | | |
| 117 | nb | | | | • | | | • | | | | | | |
| 54 | b | | | • | | • | • | • | • | • | • | • | | |
| 26 | nb | | | | • | | | | | | | | | |
| 23 | sb | | | | • | | | | | | | | | |
| 3 | nb | | • | | | • | • | • | | • | • | • | | |

N ↕ S

| Exit | ⇗ | * | W | S | K | T | Am | FJ | Lo | Pe | Pi | Sp | TA | Wi |
|---|---|---|---|---|---|---|---|---|---|---|---|---|---|---|
| 291 | b | | | | e | | | | | | | | | |
| 289 | b | | e | | | w | | | | | | | | |
| 243ab | b | | w | | | e | | | | | | | | |
| 206 | b | | e | | | | | | | | | | | |
| 119 | b | | | | | | | | • | | | | | |

| | Exit | ↗ | * | W | S | K | T | Am | FJ | Lo | Pe | Pi | Sp | TA | Wi |
|---|---|---|---|---|---|---|---|---|---|---|---|---|---|---|---|
| N | 103 | b | | e | e | | w | | | | | | | | |
| | 102b | b | | | | w | | | | | | | | | |
| | 45 | b | 1 | | | | | | | | | • | | | |
| | 61 | b | | e | | | | | | | | | | | |
| S | 51 | b | | | | | | • | | | | | | | |
| | 40 | b | | e | | | | | | | | | | | |
| | 18 | b | | e | | | | | | | | | | | |

Notes: 1) Shared with I-20 / Follows I-20 numbering

59

Interstate 59 runs north to south for 172 miles from the Alabama state line to the Louisiana state line. A portion of it is shared with I-20.

| | Mile Marker | ↗ | * | | | | | | | | | | | | |
|---|---|---|---|---|---|---|---|---|---|---|---|---|---|---|---|
| N | 164 | sb | 1 | • | | | • | • | • | | • | • | • | | |
| | 109 | sb | | | | • | | | | | | | | | |
| | 106 | nb | | | | • | | | | | | | | | |
| | 56 | b | | | | • | | | | | | | | | |
| S | 13 | sb | | | | • | | | | | | | | | |
| | 8 | nb | | | | • | | | | | | | | | |
| | 3 | nb | | • | | | • | • | • | | • | • | • | | |

Notes: 1) Shared with I-20

| | Exit | ↗ | * | W | S | K | T | Am | FJ | Lo | Pe | Pi | Sp | TA | Wi |
|---|---|---|---|---|---|---|---|---|---|---|---|---|---|---|---|
| N | 160 | b | 1 | | | | | | | | | | | • | |
| | 154ab | b | 1 | e | | e | | | | | | | | | |
| | 65ab | b | | w | w | | | | | | | | | | |
| S | 4 | b | | e | | | | | | | | | | | |

Notes: 1) Shared with I-20

220

I-220 in Jackson is 12 miles long. It travels between I-20 and I-55.

| Exit | ↗ | * | W | S | K | T | Am | FJ | Lo | Pe | Pi | Sp | TA | Wi |
|---|---|---|---|---|---|---|---|---|---|---|---|---|---|---|
| 1ab | b | | | | w | | | | | | | | | |

## Missouri

**Rest Area Usage:** There is no limit to length of stay and overnight parking is permitted. Camping or sleeping outside of vehicle is not allowed. **Road Conditions:** 800-222-6400 (weather) **State Police:** *General*, 573-751-3313; *Emergency*, 800-525-5555 or *55 on cell phone **Tourism Contact:** Missouri Division of Tourism, PO Box 1055, Jefferson City MO 65102. *Phone*: 800-877-1234 or 573-751-4133. *Internet*: www.visitmo.com

**29** Interstate 29 runs north to south for 124 miles from the Iowa state line to I-70 in Kansas City. A small segment is also I-35.

N ↕ S

| Mile Marker | | * | | | | | | | | | | | | |
|---|---|---|---|---|---|---|---|---|---|---|---|---|---|---|
| 109 | sb | | • | | | • | • | • | • | | • | • | | |
| 82 | b | | | • | | • | • | • | • | | • | • | | |
| 27 | b | | | • | | • | • | • | • | | • | • | | |

| Exit | | * | W | S | K | T | Am | FJ | Lo | Pe | Pi | Sp | TA | Wi |
|---|---|---|---|---|---|---|---|---|---|---|---|---|---|---|
| 50 | b | | w | | | | | | | | | | | |
| 44 | b | | w | | | | | | | | | | | |
| 8 | b | | e | | | | | | | | | | | |
| 6 | b | | | | w | | | | | | | | | |
| 1c | b | | | e | e | | | | | | | | | |

**35** Interstate 35 runs north to south for 115 miles from the Iowa state line to the Kansas state line. Portions are also shared with I-29 and I-70.

N ↕ S

| Mile Marker | | * | | | | | | | | | | | | |
|---|---|---|---|---|---|---|---|---|---|---|---|---|---|---|
| 81 | b | | | • | | • | • | • | • | | • | • | | |
| 35 | sb | | | • | | • | • | • | • | | • | • | | |
| 34 | nb | | | • | | • | • | • | • | | • | • | | |

| Exit | | * | W | S | K | T | Am | FJ | Lo | Pe | Pi | Sp | TA | Wi |
|---|---|---|---|---|---|---|---|---|---|---|---|---|---|---|
| 92 | b | | w | | | | | | | | | | | |
| 54 | b | | w | | | | | | | | | | | |

| Exit | | * | W | S | K | T | Am | FJ | Lo | Pe | Pi | Sp | TA | Wi |
|---|---|---|---|---|---|---|---|---|---|---|---|---|---|---|
| 26 | b | | | | | | • | | | | | | | |
| 16 | b | | w | | e | | | | | | | | | |

Interstate 44 runs east to west for 291 miles from I-55 in Saint Louis to the Oklahoma state line.

E ↕ W

| Mile Marker | | * | ? | | | | | | | | | | | |
|---|---|---|---|---|---|---|---|---|---|---|---|---|---|---|
| 235 | b | | | • | | • | • | • | | | • | • | | |
| 178 | b | | | • | | • | • | • | • | | • | • | | |
| 111 | b | | | • | | • | • | • | • | | • | • | | |
| 52 | b | | | • | | • | • | • | • | | • | • | | |
| 2 | b | 1 | • | • | | • | • | • | • | | | • | | |

Notes: 1) Welcome Center eb, Rest Area wb

E ↕ W

| Exit | | * | W | S | K | T | Am | FJ | Lo | Pe | Pi | Sp | TA | Wi |
|---|---|---|---|---|---|---|---|---|---|---|---|---|---|---|
| 286 | b | | | n+ | | | | | | | | | | |
| 277 | b | | n | | n | | | | | | | | | |
| 261 | b | | n | | | | | | | | | | | |
| 226 | b | | s | | | | | • | | | | | | |
| 208 | b | | s | | | | | | | | | | | |
| 184 | b | | s | | s | | | | | | | | | |
| 161ab | b | | s | | | | | | | | | | | |
| 129 | b | | s | | n | | | | | | | | | |
| 127 | b | | | | | | • | | | | | | | |
| 100 | b | | s | | | | | | | | | | | |
| 88 | b | | | | | | | | | | | | • | |
| 80ab | b | | s | | s | | | | | | | | | |
| 77 | b | | s | | | | | | | | | | | |
| 46 | b | | | | | | | | | | | | • | |
| 11a | b | | | | | | | • | | | | | | |
| 8ab | b | | n | n | n | | | | | | | | | |
| 4 | b | | | | | | | | • | • | • | | | |

55

Interstate 55 runs north to south for 210 miles from the Illinois state line to the Arkansas state line.

| Mile Marker | | * | ? | | | | | | | | | | | |
|---|---|---|---|---|---|---|---|---|---|---|---|---|---|---|
| 160 | b | | | • | | • | • | • | • | | • | • | | |

| Mile Marker | | * | | | | | | | | | | | | |
|---|---|---|---|---|---|---|---|---|---|---|---|---|---|---|
| 110 | b | | | • | | • | • | • | • | | • | • | | |
| 42 | b | 1 | • | • | | • | • | • | • | | • | • | | |
| 3 | b | | | • | | • | • | • | • | | • | • | | |

Notes: 1) Welcome Center nb, Rest Area sb

N ↕ S

| Exit | | * | W | S | K | T | Am | FJ | Lo | Pe | Pi | Sp | TA | Wi |
|---|---|---|---|---|---|---|---|---|---|---|---|---|---|---|
| 197 | b | | | | e | | | | | | | | | |
| 191 | b | | e | | e | | | | | | | | | |
| 190 | b | | | | | w | | | | | | | | |
| 175 | b | | e | | e | | | | | | | | | |
| 174ab | b | | e+ | | | | | | | | | | | |
| 143 | b | | | | | | • | | | | | | | |
| 129 | b | | w | | | | | | | | | | | |
| 99 | b | | w | | | | | | | | | | | |
| 96 | b | | w | w | e+ | w | | | | | | | | |
| 66b | b | | w+ | | | | | | | | | | | |
| 58 | b | | | | | | | • | | | | | • | |
| 40 | b | | | | | | | | | | • | | | |
| 19 | b | | | | | | | | | | | | | • |

57

Interstate 57 runs north to south for 22 miles from the Illinois state line to I-55 near Sikeston.

| Exit | | * | W | S | K | T | Am | FJ | Lo | Pe | Pi | Sp | TA | Wi |
|---|---|---|---|---|---|---|---|---|---|---|---|---|---|---|
| 10 | b | | w | | | | | | | | • | | | |

64

Officially, I-64 is a 15-mile route running east to west from the Illinois state line to I-270. However, the limited-access highway continues west another 13 miles to the Missouri River as US 40.

| Exit | | * | W | S | K | T | Am | FJ | Lo | Pe | Pi | Sp | TA | Wi |
|---|---|---|---|---|---|---|---|---|---|---|---|---|---|---|
| 32b | b | | | | | s | | | | | | | | |
| 16 | b | 1 | s | | | | | | | | | | | |
| 14 | b | 1 | | | | n | | | | | | | | |

Notes: 1) US 40 exit

Interstate 70 runs east to west from the Illinois state line to the Kansas state line. It is 252 miles long.

| Mile Marker | | * | | | | | | | | | | | | |
|---|---|---|---|---|---|---|---|---|---|---|---|---|---|---|
| 198 | b | | | • | | • | • | • | • | | • | • | | |
| 169 | wb | | | • | | • | • | • | • | | • | • | | |
| 167 | eb | | | • | | • | • | • | • | | • | • | | |
| 104 | b | | | • | | • | • | • | • | | • | • | | |
| 57 | b | | | • | | • | • | • | • | | • | • | | |

| Exit | | * | W | S | K | T | Am | FJ | Lo | Pe | Pi | Sp | TA | Wi |
|---|---|---|---|---|---|---|---|---|---|---|---|---|---|---|
| 234 | b | | | n | n | n | | | | | | | | |
| 228 | b | | | | s | | | | | | | | | |
| 227 | b | | s | s | | | | | | | | | | |
| 225 | b | | | | | s | | | | | | | | |
| 217 | b | | | | s | | | | | | | | | |
| 208 | b | | s | | | | | | | | | | | |
| 203 | b | | | | | | | | | | | | • | |
| 193 | b | | n | | | | | | | | | | | |
| 188 | b | | | | | | | • | | | | | | |
| 148 | b | | | | | | | | | • | | | | |
| 128 | b | | s | s | | | | | | | | | | |
| 124 | b | | s | | s | | | | | | | | | |
| 103 | b | | n | | | | | | | | | | | |
| 101 | b | | | | | | | | | | • | | | |
| 58 | b | | | | | | | | | | | | • | |
| 49 | b | | | | | | | | | | | | | • |
| 28 | b | | s | | | | | | | • | | | • | |
| 24 | b | | | | | | | | | | • | | | |
| 20 | b | | s | | s | | | | | | | | | |
| 15b | b | | n | n | | n | | | | | | | | |
| 12 | b | | | s | n | | | | | | | | | |

Interstate 255 in Saint Louis is 4 miles long. It runs between the Illinois state line and I-55.

| Exit | | * | W | S | K | T | Am | FJ | Lo | Pe | Pi | Sp | TA | Wi |
|---|---|---|---|---|---|---|---|---|---|---|---|---|---|---|
| 2 | b | | n | | | | | | | | | | | |
| 1a | b | | | s | n | | | | | | | | | |

Interstate 270 is 36 miles long. It forms a partial loop around Saint Louis. Exit numbering begins at I-55 and increases in a clockwise direction.

| Mile Marker | | * | | | | | | | | | | | | |
|---|---|---|---|---|---|---|---|---|---|---|---|---|---|---|
| 34 | b | | • | | | • | • | • | | | | • | | |

| Exit | | * | W | S | K | T | Am | FJ | Lo | Pe | Pi | Sp | TA | Wi |
|---|---|---|---|---|---|---|---|---|---|---|---|---|---|---|
| 31ab | b | | | | s+ | | | | | | | | | |
| 30 | b | | | | | n | | | | | | | | |
| 29 | b | | s | s | | | | | | | | | | |
| 20b | b | | | | e | e | | | | | | | | |
| 1ab | b | | | s | | | | | | | | | | |

Interstate 435 is an 83-mile loop around Kansas City. Exit numbering begins at Lackman Road in Kansas and increases in a clockwise direction. See Kansas for that state's part of the Interstate.

| Exit | | * | W | S | K | T | Am | FJ | Lo | Pe | Pi | Sp | TA | Wi |
|---|---|---|---|---|---|---|---|---|---|---|---|---|---|---|
| 69 | b | | e | | | | | | | | | | | |
| 57 | b | | | | | | | • | | | | | | |

Interstate 470 in Kansas City is 17 miles long. It connects I-70 in Blue Springs with US 71 and I-435 in Grandview.

| Exit | | * | W | S | K | T | Am | FJ | Lo | Pe | Pi | Sp | TA | Wi |
|---|---|---|---|---|---|---|---|---|---|---|---|---|---|---|
| 15 | b | | n | | | | | | | | | | | |
| 10a | b | | s | | | | | | | | | | | |

## Montana

**Rest Area Usage:** There is no limit to length of stay and overnight parking is permitted. Camping or sleeping outside of vehicle is not allowed. **Road Conditions:** 800-226-7623 (weather) **State Police:** *General*, 406-444-3780; *Emergency*, 911 **Tourism Contact:** Travel Montana, PO Box 200533, Helena MT 59620. *Phone*: 800-847-4868 or 406-444-2654. *Internet*: www.visitmt.com

I-15 runs north to south for 398 miles from the US/Canada border to the Idaho state line. A portion of it is also shared with I-90.

| N↕S Mile Marker | | * | | | | | | | | | | | | |
|---|---|---|---|---|---|---|---|---|---|---|---|---|---|---|
| 397 | b | 1 | | • | | • | • | • | | | • | • | | |
| 361 | nb | | | | • | | | | | | | | | |
| 319 | b | | | • | | • | • | • | | | • | • | | |
| 288 | b | | | | • | | | | | | | | | |
| 245 | sb | | | | • | | | | | | | | • | |
| 239 | b | | | • | | • | • | • | | | • | • | | |
| 222 | b | | | | • | | | | | | | | | |
| 205 | sb | | | | • | | | | | | | | | |
| 178 | b | | | • | | • | • | • | | | • | • | | |
| 161 | nb | | | | • | | | | | | | | | |
| 138 | b | | | | • | | | • | | | | | • | |
| 130 | sb | | | | • | | | | | | | | • | |
| 109 | b | | | • | | • | • | • | | | • | • | | |
| 55 | sb | | | | • | | | | | | | | | |
| 34 | b | | | | • | | | | | | | | | |

Notes: 1) West at exit to Rest Area

| N↕S Exit | | * | W | S | K | T | Am | FJ | Lo | Pe | Pi | Sp | TA | Wi |
|---|---|---|---|---|---|---|---|---|---|---|---|---|---|---|
| 282 | b | | e+ | e+ | | | | | | | | | | |
| 280 | b | | | | | | | • | | | | | | |
| 278 | b | | | | e+ | e+ | | | | | | | | |
| 193 | b | | | | w | w | | | | | | | | |
| 192ab | b | | e | | | | | | | | | | | |
| 127 | b | 1 | e | | e | | | | | | | | | |
| 122 | b | 1 | | | | | | • | | | | | | |

Notes: 1) Shared with I-90

Interstate 90 is about 552 miles long. It runs east to west from the Wyoming state line to the Idaho state line. A portion is shared with I-15.

| Mile Marker | | * | | | | | | | | | | | | |
|---|---|---|---|---|---|---|---|---|---|---|---|---|---|---|
| 476 | eb | | | • | | • | • | • | | | • | • | | |
| 475 | wb | | | • | | • | • | • | | | • | • | | |
| 419 | b | | | • | | • | • | • | | | • | • | | |

E ↕ W

| Mile Marker | ↗ | * | | | | | | | | | | | | |
|---|---|---|---|---|---|---|---|---|---|---|---|---|---|---|
| 381 | b | | | • | | • | • | • | | | • | • | | |
| 321 | b | | | | • | | | | | | | | | |
| 305 | b | | | • | | • | • | • | | | • | • | | |
| 238 | eb | | | | | | | | | | | | | • |
| 237 | eb | | | | • | | | | | | | | | |
| 235 | b | | | | • | | | | | | | | | |
| 210 | wb | | | | • | | | | | | | | | |
| 169 | eb | | | • | | • | • | • | | | • | • | | |
| 167 | wb | | | • | | • | • | • | | | • | • | | |
| 143 | b | | | • | | • | • | • | | | • | • | | |
| 128 | b | | | | • | | | | | | | | | |
| 73 | wb | | | | • | | | | | | | | | |
| 72 | eb | | | | • | | | | | | | | | |
| 58 | b | 1 | | • | | • | • | • | | | • | • | | |
| 4 | b | | | • | | • | | • | | | • | • | | |

Notes: 1) Seasonal camping at a National Forest campground accessed from this area

E ↕ W

| Exit | ↗ | * | W | S | K | T | Am | FJ | Lo | Pe | Pi | Sp | TA | Wi |
|---|---|---|---|---|---|---|---|---|---|---|---|---|---|---|
| 495 | b | | | | | | | • | | | | | | |
| 455 | b | | | | | | | • | | | | | | |
| 452 | b | | n+ | | n+ | | | | | | | | | |
| 306 | b | | s | | s | | | | | | | | | |
| 305 | b | | | | | s | | | | | | | | |
| 298 | b | | | | | | | • | | | | | | |
| 127 | b | 1 | s | | s | | | | | | | | | |
| 122 | b | 1 | | | | | | • | | | | | | |
| 101 | b | | s+ | | | s+ | | | | | | | | |
| 96 | b | | | | | | • | | | | | | | |

Notes: 1) Shared with I-15 / Follows I-15 numbering

**94** Interstate 94 runs east to west from the North Dakota state line to I-90 near Billings. It is about 250 miles long.

E ↕ W

| Mile Marker | ↗ | * | | | | | | | | | | | | |
|---|---|---|---|---|---|---|---|---|---|---|---|---|---|---|
| 242 | eb | | | • | | • | • | • | | | • | | | |
| 193 | eb | | | • | | • | • | • | | | • | • | | |
| 114 | eb | | | • | | • | • | • | | | • | • | | |
| 113 | wb | | | • | | • | • | • | | | • | • | • | |

E ↕ W

| Mile Marker | | * | | | | | | | | | | | | |
|---|---|---|---|---|---|---|---|---|---|---|---|---|---|---|
| 65 | b | | | • | | • | • | • | | | • | • | | |
| 41 | eb | | | • | | • | • | • | | | • | • | | |
| 38 | wb | | | • | | • | • | • | | | • | • | | |

| Exit | | * | W | S | K | T | Am | FJ | Lo | Pe | Pi | Sp | TA | Wi |
|---|---|---|---|---|---|---|---|---|---|---|---|---|---|---|
| 213 | b | | | | s | | | | | | | | | |
| 138 | b | | n | | n | | | | | | | | | |

## Nebraska

**Rest Area Usage:** There is a 8 hour stay limit, no camping or parking overnight is permitted. **Road Conditions:** 511 (weather, in state), 800-906-9069 or 402-471-4533 (weather, out of state) **State Police:** *General*, 402-471-4680; *Emergency*, 911 **Tourism Contact:** Nebraska Tourism Information Center, PO Box 98907, Lincoln NE 68509. *Phone*: 800-228-4307. *Internet*: www.visitnebraska.org

Interstate 80 runs east to west for 455 miles from the Iowa state line to the Wyoming state line.

E ↕ W

| Mile Marker | | * | | | | | | | | | | | | |
|---|---|---|---|---|---|---|---|---|---|---|---|---|---|---|
| 431 | wb | | | • | | • | • | • | • | | • | • | | |
| 425 | eb | | | • | | • | • | • | • | | • | • | | |
| 405 | wb | | | • | | • | • | • | • | | • | • | | |
| 381 | eb | | | • | | • | • | • | • | | • | • | | |
| 375 | wb | | | • | | • | • | • | • | | • | • | | |
| 355 | wb | | | • | | • | • | • | • | | • | • | | |
| 350 | eb | | | • | | • | • | • | • | | • | • | | |
| 316 | wb | | | • | | • | • | • | • | | • | • | | |
| 314 | eb | | | • | | • | • | • | • | | • | • | | |
| 270 | wb | | | • | | • | • | • | • | | • | • | | |
| 269 | eb | | | • | | • | • | • | • | | • | • | | |
| 227 | wb | | | • | | • | • | • | • | | • | • | | |
| 226 | eb | | | • | | • | • | • | • | | • | • | | |
| 194 | b | | | • | | • | • | • | • | | • | • | | |

| Mile Marker | ↗ | * | | | | | | | | | | | | |
|---|---|---|---|---|---|---|---|---|---|---|---|---|---|---|
| 159 | b | | | • | | • | • | • | • | | • | • | | |
| 132 | wb | | | • | | • | • | • | • | | • | • | | |
| 124 | eb | | | • | | • | • | • | • | | • | • | | |
| 99 | eb | | | | • | | | | | | | | • | |
| 87 | wb | | | • | | • | • | • | • | | • | • | | |
| 82 | eb | | | • | | • | • | • | • | | • | • | | |
| 61 | wb | | | • | | • | • | • | • | | • | • | | |
| 51 | eb | | | • | | • | • | • | • | | • | • | | |
| 25 | wb | | | • | | • | • | • | • | | • | • | | |
| 9 | eb | | | • | | • | • | • | • | | • | • | | |

| Exit | ↗ | * | W | S | K | T | Am | FJ | Lo | Pe | Pi | Sp | TA | Wi |
|---|---|---|---|---|---|---|---|---|---|---|---|---|---|---|
| 445 | b | | | n | | | | | | | | | | |
| 432 | b | | | | | | | • | | | | | | |
| 403 | b | | s+ | s+ | | | | | | | | | | |
| 353 | b | | | | | | | | | • | | | | |
| 312 | b | | | | | | • | | | | | | | |
| 305 | b | | | | | | | | | | | | • | |
| 300 | b | | | | | | • | | | | | | | |
| 272 | b | | n | | | | | | | | | | | |
| 257 | b | | | | | | • | | | | | | | |
| 237 | b | | n | | | | | | | | | | | |
| 179 | b | | | | | | | • | | | | | | |
| 177 | b | | n | | | | | | | | | | | |
| 126 | b | | | | | | | | | | | | • | |
| 107 | b | | | | | | • | | | | | | | |

Interstate 680 in Omaha is 13 miles long. It runs between I-80 and the Iowa state line.

| Exit | ↗ | * | W | S | K | T | Am | FJ | Lo | Pe | Pi | Sp | TA | Wi |
|---|---|---|---|---|---|---|---|---|---|---|---|---|---|---|
| 5 | b | | w | | | | | | | | | | | |

## Nevada

**Rest Area Usage:** There is a 24 hour stay limit unless otherwise posted. Camping and overnight parking are permitted. **Road Conditions:** 877-687-6237 (weather) **State Police:** *General*, 775-687-5300; *Emergency*, 911 or *647 on cell phone **Tourism Contact:** Nevada Commission on Tourism, 401 N Carson St, Carson City NV 89701. *Phone*: 800-237-0774 or 775-687-4322. *Internet*: www.travelnevada.com

### 15

Interstate 15 runs north to south for 124 miles from the Arizona state line to the California state line.

| Mile Marker | | * | | | | | | | | | | | | |
|---|---|---|---|---|---|---|---|---|---|---|---|---|---|---|
| 122 | b | | • | | | • | • | | | | | • | | |
| 110 | b | 1 | | | • | | | | | | | | | |
| 96 | b | 1 | | | • | | | | | | | | | |
| 87 | b | | | | • | | | | | | | | | |
| 12 | b | | • | | | • | • | | | | | • | | |

N ↕ S

Notes: 1) Truck parking

| Exit | | * | W | S | K | T | Am | FJ | Lo | Pe | Pi | Sp | TA | Wi |
|---|---|---|---|---|---|---|---|---|---|---|---|---|---|---|
| 54 | b | | | | | | | | | • | | | | |
| 48 | b | | e+ | | | | | | | | • | | | |
| 46 | b | | | | | | | • | | | | | | |
| 33 | b | | | | | | | | | | | | • | |

N ↕ S

### 80

Interstate 80 is 411 miles long. It runs east to west from the Utah state line to the California state line.

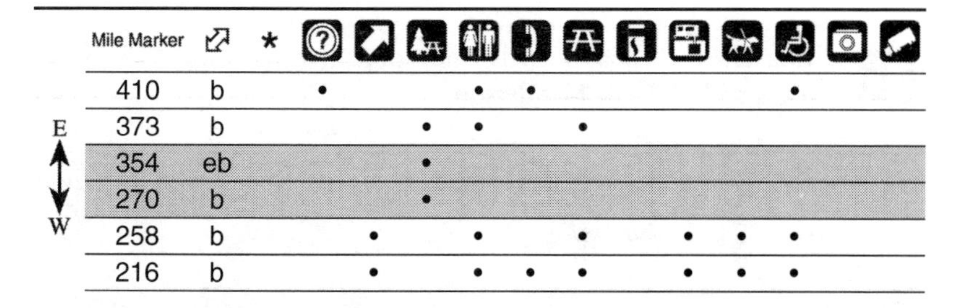

| Mile Marker | | * | | | | | | | | | | | | |
|---|---|---|---|---|---|---|---|---|---|---|---|---|---|---|
| 410 | b | | • | | | • | • | | | | | • | | |
| 373 | b | | | | • | • | | • | | | | | | |
| 354 | eb | | | | • | | | | | | | | | |
| 270 | b | | | | • | | | | | | | | | |
| 258 | b | | | • | | • | | • | | • | • | • | | |
| 216 | b | | | • | | • | • | • | | • | • | • | | |

E ↕ W

| Mile Marker | ↗ | * | | | | | | | | | | | | |
|---|---|---|---|---|---|---|---|---|---|---|---|---|---|---|
| 187 | b | | | • | | • | • | • | | • | • | • | | |
| 158 | b | | | • | | • | • | • | | • | • | • | | |
| 83 | b | | | • | | • | • | • | | | | • | | |
| 42 | wb | | | • | | • | • | • | | • | • | • | | |
| 27 | eb | | | | • | | | | | | | | • | |
| 6 | b | | | | • | | | | | | | | • | |
| 4 | eb | | | | • | | | | | | | | • | |

| Exit | ↗ | * | W | S | K | T | Am | FJ | Lo | Pe | Pi | Sp | TA | Wi |
|---|---|---|---|---|---|---|---|---|---|---|---|---|---|---|
| 410 | b | | | | | | | | | | • | | | |
| 352 | b | | | | | | | • | | | | | | |
| 301 | b | | n | | n | | | | | | | | | |
| 280 | b | | | | | | | | | | • | | | |
| 231 | b | | | | | | | • | | | | | | |
| 176 | b | | s | | | | | • | | | | | | |
| 151 | b | | | | | | | | | | | | • | |
| 129 | b | | | | | | | | | | | | • | |
| 46 | b | | | | | | | | | | • | | | |
| 21 | b | | | | | | • | | | | | | | |
| 19 | b | | | | | n | | | | | | | • | |
| 15 | b | | n+ | | | | | | | | | | | |
| 10 | b | | | | s | | | | | | | | | |

215

Interstate 215 near Las Vegas is about 11 miles long. It runs between I-15 and I-515.

| Exit | ↗ | * | W | S | K | T | Am | FJ | Lo | Pe | Pi | Sp | TA | Wi |
|---|---|---|---|---|---|---|---|---|---|---|---|---|---|---|
| 5 | b | | s | s | | | | | | | | | | |

515

Interstate 515 is about 21 miles long. It runs from I-15 in Las Vegas to US 93 in Henderson.

| Exit | ↗ | * | W | S | K | T | Am | FJ | Lo | Pe | Pi | Sp | TA | Wi |
|---|---|---|---|---|---|---|---|---|---|---|---|---|---|---|
| 68 | b | | w | w | | | | | | | | | | |
| 64 | b | | w | | | | | | | | | | | |

# New Hampshire

**Rest Area Usage:** There is a 4 hour stay limit unless emergency conditions exist. No camping or overnight parking is permitted. **Road Conditions:** 800-918-9993 or 603-271-6900 (weather) **State Police:** *General*, 603-271-2575; *Emergency*, 800-852-3411 **Tourism Contact:** New Hampshire Division of Travel & Tourism Development, PO Box 1856, Concord NH 03302. *Phone*: 800-386-4664 or 603-271-2665. *Internet*: www.visitnh.gov

**89** Interstate 89 runs north to south for 61 miles from the Vermont state line to I-93 in Concord. Exit numbers are based on the consecutive numbering system.

N ↕ S

| Mile Marker | Direction | * | ? | Arrow | Trees | Restrooms | Phone | Picnic Table | Fountain | Vending | Pets | Handicapped | Icon | Icon |
|---|---|---|---|---|---|---|---|---|---|---|---|---|---|---|
| 57 | sb | | • | | | • | • | • | • | | • | • | | |
| 40 | nb | | | • | | • | • | • | • | | • | • | | |
| 26 | sb | | | • | | • | • | • | • | | • | • | | |

| Exit | Direction | * | W | S | K | T | Am | FJ | Lo | Pe | Pi | Sp | TA | Wi |
|---|---|---|---|---|---|---|---|---|---|---|---|---|---|---|
| 20 | b | | w | | e | | | | | | | | | |

**93** Interstate 93 runs north to south for 132 miles from the Vermont state line to the Massachusetts state line. Exit numbers are based on the consecutive numbering system.

N ↕ S

| Mile Marker | Direction | * | ? | Arrow | Trees | Restrooms | Phone | Picnic Table | Fountain | Vending | Pets | Handicapped | Icon | Icon |
|---|---|---|---|---|---|---|---|---|---|---|---|---|---|---|
| 130 | b | 1 | • | | | • | • | • | | | • | • | • | |
| 61 | sb | | | • | | • | • | • | • | | • | • | | |
| 51 | nb | | | • | | • | • | • | • | | • | • | | |
| 31 | b | | | • | | • | • | • | • | | | • | | |
| 1 | nb | | • | | | • | • | • | • | | • | • | | |

Notes: 1) West at exit 44 to Welcome Center

| Exit | Direction | * | W | S | K | T | Am | FJ | Lo | Pe | Pi | Sp | TA | Wi |
|---|---|---|---|---|---|---|---|---|---|---|---|---|---|---|
| 42 | b | | w | | | | | | | | | | | |
| 20 | b | | w | | | | | | | | | | | |

| | Exit | ↗ | * | W | S | K | T | Am | FJ | Lo | Pe | Pi | Sp | TA | Wi |
|---|---|---|---|---|---|---|---|---|---|---|---|---|---|---|---|
| N | 14 | b | | e+ | | | | | | | | | | | |
| ↕ | 5 | b | | e+ | | | | | | | | | | | |
| | 4 | b | | | | w | | | | | | | | | |
| S | 1 | b | | | | e | e | | | | | | | | |

Interstate 95 runs north to south for 16 miles from the Maine state line to the Massachusetts state line. Exit numbers are based on the consecutive numbering system.

| Mile Marker | ↗ | * | (info) | (direction) | (picnic area) | (restrooms) | (phone) | (picnic tables) | (vending) | (map) | (pets) | (handicapped) | (camera) | (truck) |
|---|---|---|---|---|---|---|---|---|---|---|---|---|---|---|
| 0.5 | nb | | • | | | • | • | • | • | | • | • | | |

| | Exit | ↗ | * | W | S | K | T | Am | FJ | Lo | Pe | Pi | Sp | TA | Wi |
|---|---|---|---|---|---|---|---|---|---|---|---|---|---|---|---|
| N ↕ S | 5 | b | | | | w | | | | | | | | | |
| | 3 | b | | | | | | | | | | | | • | |
| | 1 | b | | e | w | | | | | | | | | | |

293

Interstate 293 is 11 miles long. It forms an open loop around Manchester. Exit numbers are based on the consecutive numbering system.

| Exit | ↗ | * | W | S | K | T | Am | FJ | Lo | Pe | Pi | Sp | TA | Wi |
|---|---|---|---|---|---|---|---|---|---|---|---|---|---|---|
| 1 | b | | s | n | | | | | | | | | | |

## New Jersey

**Rest Area Usage:** There is no limit to length of stay. Camping is not permitted but limited overnight parking is allowed. **Road Conditions:** 732-247-0900 (weather turnpike), 732-727-5929 (weather Garden State Pkwy) **State Police:** *General*, 609-882-2000; *Emergency*, 911 **Tourism Contact:** New Jersey Division of Travel & Tourism, PO Box 820, Trenton NJ 08625. *Phone*: 800-847-4865 or 609-292-2470. *Internet*: www.visitnj.org

Interstate 78 runs east to west for approximately 68 miles from the Holland Tunnel to the Pennsylvania state line.

| | Mile Marker | ⇗ | * | ? | ↗ | Tree | Restrooms | Phone | Picnic | Vending | RV | Pet | Handicap | Camera | Truck |
|---|---|---|---|---|---|---|---|---|---|---|---|---|---|---|---|
| E ↕ W | 32 | wb | | | | • | | | | | | | | • | |
| | 8 | b | | | | • | | | • | | | | | | |

| | Exit | ⇗ | * | W | S | K | T | Am | FJ | Lo | Pe | Pi | Sp | TA | Wi |
|---|---|---|---|---|---|---|---|---|---|---|---|---|---|---|---|
| E ↕ W | 15 | b | | s | | | | | | | | | | | |
| | 7 | b | | | | | | | | | | • | | • | |
| | 3 | b | | n+ | | | | | | | | | | | |

80

Interstate 80 runs east to west for 68 miles from the George Washington Bridge in Fort Lee to the Pennsylvania state line.

| | Mile Marker | ⇗ | * | ? | ↗ | Tree | Restrooms | Phone | Picnic | Vending | RV | Pet | Handicap | Camera | Truck |
|---|---|---|---|---|---|---|---|---|---|---|---|---|---|---|---|
| E ↕ W | 32 | b | 1 | | • | | | | | | | | | | |
| | 21 | b | 2 | | • | | | • | • | | | • | | • | |
| | 7 | eb | | • | | | • | • | • | • | | • | • | | |
| | 6 | wb | | | | • | | | | | | | | • | |
| | 1 | b | | | • | | • | • | • | | | • | | | |

Notes: 1) Truck rest area, no facilities; 2) No trucks / Scenic Vista only eb

| | Exit | ⇗ | * | W | S | K | T | Am | FJ | Lo | Pe | Pi | Sp | TA | Wi |
|---|---|---|---|---|---|---|---|---|---|---|---|---|---|---|---|
| E ↕ W | 53 | b | | | | | s | | | | | | | | |
| | 45 | b | | | | n | | | | | | | | | |
| | 28 | b | | s | | | | | | | | | | | |
| | 4 | b | | | | | | | | | | | | • | |

The New Jersey Turnpike is 118 miles long. It runs north to south from US 46 in Ridgefield Park to I-295 in Deepwater. Exit numbers are based on the consecutive numbering system.

| | Mile Marker | ⇗ | * | ? | ↗ | Tree | Restrooms | Phone | Picnic | Vending | RV | Pet | Handicap | Camera | Truck |
|---|---|---|---|---|---|---|---|---|---|---|---|---|---|---|---|
| N ↕ S | 115 | nb | 1 | | • | | • | • | • | • | | | • | | |
| | 112 | sb | 1 | | • | | • | • | • | • | | | • | | |
| | 102 | nb | 1 | | • | | • | • | • | • | | | • | | |
| | 94 | b | 1 | | • | | • | • | • | • | | | • | | |
| | 79 | nb | 1 | | • | | • | • | • | • | | | • | | |
| | 72 | sb | 1 | | • | | • | • | • | • | | | • | | |

| | Mile Marker | ↗ | * | ? | Arrow | Tree/Picnic | Restrooms | Phone | Picnic Table | Vending | Truck/RV | Pets | Handicap | Camera | Last |
|---|---|---|---|---|---|---|---|---|---|---|---|---|---|---|---|
| N | 59 | b | 1 | | • | | • | • | • | • | | | • | | |
| ↕ | 39 | nb | 1 | | • | | • | • | • | • | | | • | | |
| | 30 | sb | 1 | | • | | • | • | • | • | | | • | | |
| S | 5 | b | 1 | | • | | • | • | • | • | | | • | | |

Notes: 1) Service Area, Gas, Food

| Exit | ↗ | * | W | S | K | T | Am | FJ | Lo | Pe | Pi | Sp | TA | Wi |
|---|---|---|---|---|---|---|---|---|---|---|---|---|---|---|
| 9 | b | | | e | | | | | | | | | | |
| 7 | b | | | | | | | | | • | • | | | |

Interstate 195 is 34 miles long. It runs east to west from the Garden State Parkway to I-295 in White Horse.

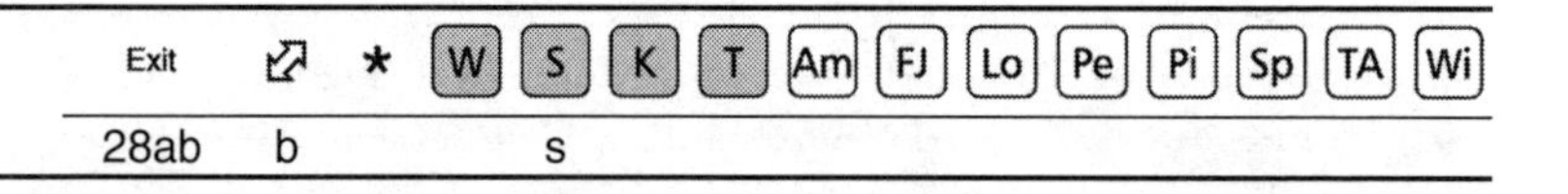

| Exit | ↗ | * | W | S | K | T | Am | FJ | Lo | Pe | Pi | Sp | TA | Wi |
|---|---|---|---|---|---|---|---|---|---|---|---|---|---|---|
| 28ab | b | | | s | | | | | | | | | | |

Interstate 287 is about 68 miles long. It primarily runs north to south from the New York state line to US 1 in the Metuchen borough.

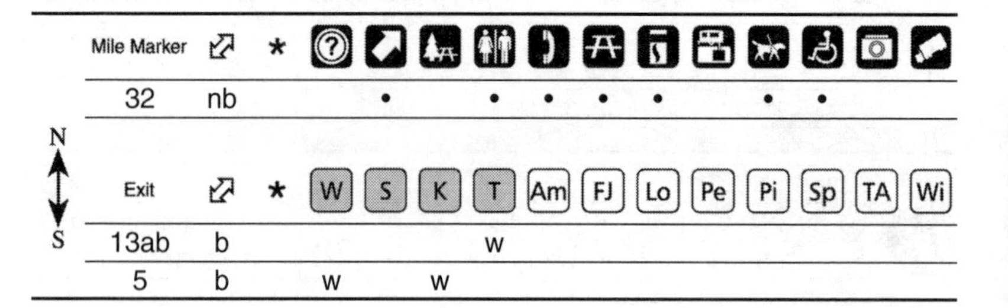

| Mile Marker | ↗ | * | ? | Arrow | Tree/Picnic | Restrooms | Phone | Picnic Table | Vending | Truck/RV | Pets | Handicap | Camera | Last |
|---|---|---|---|---|---|---|---|---|---|---|---|---|---|---|
| 32 | nb | | | • | | • | • | • | • | | • | • | | |

N ↕ S

| Exit | ↗ | * | W | S | K | T | Am | FJ | Lo | Pe | Pi | Sp | TA | Wi |
|---|---|---|---|---|---|---|---|---|---|---|---|---|---|---|
| 13ab | b | | | | | w | | | | | | | | |
| 5 | b | | w | | w | | | | | | | | | |

Interstate 295 primarily runs north to south for 68 miles from US 1 in Trenton to the Delaware state line.

| Mile Marker | ↗ | * | ? | Arrow | Tree/Picnic | Restrooms | Phone | Picnic Table | Vending | Truck/RV | Pets | Handicap | Camera | Last |
|---|---|---|---|---|---|---|---|---|---|---|---|---|---|---|
| 58 | b | | | | • | | | | | | | | • | |
| 50 | b | | | • | | • | • | • | • | | • | • | | |
| 2 | nb | | • | | | • | • | • | • | • | • | • | | |

| | Exit | ⇗ | * | W | S | K | T | Am | FJ | Lo | Pe | Pi | Sp | TA | Wi |
|---|---|---|---|---|---|---|---|---|---|---|---|---|---|---|---|
| N ↕ S | 67ab | b | | e+ | | | e+ | | | | | | | | |
| | 57 | b | | | | | | | | | • | • | | | |
| | 47ab | b | | w | | w | e | | | | | | | | |
| | 36ab | b | | | | w | | | | | | | | | |
| | 29ab | b | | | | e | | | | | | | | | |
| | 18 | b | | | | | | | | | | | | • | |
| | 2 | b | | | | | | • | • | | | • | | | |

## New Mexico

**Rest Area Usage:** There is a 24 hour stay limit and overnight parking is permitted. Camping or sleeping outside of vehicle is not allowed. **Road Conditions:** 800-432-4269 (weather) **State Police:** *General*, 505-827-9300; *Emergency*, 911 **Tourism Contact:** New Mexico Department of Tourism, 491 Old Santa Fe Trail, Santa Fe NM 87503. *Phone*: 800-545-2070 or 505-827-7400. *Internet*: www.newmexico.org

**10** Interstate 10 runs east to west for 164 miles from the Texas state line to the Arizona state line.

| | Mile Marker | ⇗ | * | ? | | | | | | | | | | | |
|---|---|---|---|---|---|---|---|---|---|---|---|---|---|---|---|
| E ↕ W | 164 | wb | | • | | | • | • | • | • | | • | • | | |
| | 135 | eb | | | • | | • | | • | • | | • | • | • | |
| | 120 | eb | | | | • | | | | | | | | | |
| | 61 | wb | | | • | | • | | • | • | | • | • | | |
| | 53 | eb | | | • | | • | | • | • | | • | • | | |
| | 20 | b | | • | | | • | • | | | | | • | | |

| | Exit | ⇗ | * | W | S | K | T | Am | FJ | Lo | Pe | Pi | Sp | TA | Wi |
|---|---|---|---|---|---|---|---|---|---|---|---|---|---|---|---|
| E ↕ W | 139 | b | | | | | | | | | | • | | • | |
| | 132 | b | | | | | | | | • | | | | | |
| | 83 | b | | | | s | | | | | | | | | |
| | 82ab | b | | | | s | | | | | | | | | |
| | 24 | b | | | | | | | | | | • | | | |
| | 20 | b | | | | | | | | • | | | | | |

Interstate 25 runs north to south for 462 miles from the Colorado state line to I-10 in Las Cruces.

N ↕ S

| Mile Marker | ↗ | * | ? | | | | | | | | | | | |
|---|---|---|---|---|---|---|---|---|---|---|---|---|---|---|
| 451 | b | 1 | • | | | • | • | • | | | | • | | |
| 434 | b | | | • | | • | | • | | | • | • | | |
| 376 | sb | | | • | | • | • | • | | | • | • | | |
| 374 | nb | | | • | | • | | • | | | • | • | | |
| 360 | b | | | | • | | | • | | | | | | |
| 325 | b | | | | • | | | • | | | | | | |
| 269 | nb | | | • | | • | • | • | | | • | • | | |
| 267 | sb | | | • | | • | • | • | | | • | • | | |
| 167 | b | | | • | | • | | • | • | | • | • | | |
| 165 | b | | | | • | | | | | | | | | |
| 114 | b | | | • | | • | | • | • | | • | • | | |
| 67 | b | | | | • | | | • | | | | | | |
| 27 | nb | | | | • | | | • | | | | | • | |
| 23 | b | | | • | | • | | • | • | | • | • | | |

Notes: 1) West at exit 451 to Welcome Center

N ↕ S

| Exit | ↗ | * | W | S | K | T | Am | FJ | Lo | Pe | Pi | Sp | TA | Wi |
|---|---|---|---|---|---|---|---|---|---|---|---|---|---|---|
| 450 | b | 1 | | | w | | | | | | | | | |
| 278 | b | | w+ | w+ | | | | | | | | | | |
| 227 | b | | | | | | | | | | | | • | |
| 195 | b | | e+ | | | | | | | | | | | |
| 6ab | b | | | | e | | | | | | | | | |
| 3 | b | | w | | | e | | | | | | | | |

Notes: 1) Can also be accessed from exit 451

40

Interstate 40 is about 374 miles long. It runs east to west from the Texas state line to the California state line.

E ↕ W

| Mile Marker | ↗ | * | ? | | | | | | | | | | | |
|---|---|---|---|---|---|---|---|---|---|---|---|---|---|---|
| 373 | wb | | • | | | • | • | • | | | • | • | | |
| 302 | b | | | • | | • | • | • | | | • | • | | |
| 252 | b | | | • | | • | • | • | | | • | • | | |
| 220 | b | | | | • | | | | | | | | | |
| 207 | b | | | • | | • | | • | | | • | • | | |
| 113 | b | | | | • | | | | | | | | • | |

| Mile Marker | ↗ | * | Info | Arrow | Trees | Restrooms | Phone | Picnic | Vending | Food | Pets | Handicap | Camera | Dump |
|---|---|---|---|---|---|---|---|---|---|---|---|---|---|---|
| 102 | b | 1 | | • | | • | • | • | | | • | • | | |
| 22 | b | 2 | • | | | • | • | • | • | • | • | • | | |
| 3 | eb | | | • | | • | • | • | | | • | • | | |

Notes: 1) South at exit 102 to Rest Area; 2) North at exit 22 to Welcome Center

| | Exit | ↗ | * | W | S | K | T | Am | FJ | Lo | Pe | Pi | Sp | TA | Wi |
|---|---|---|---|---|---|---|---|---|---|---|---|---|---|---|---|
| | 333 | b | | | | n+ | | | | • | | | | | |
| | 277 | b | | | | | | | | • | | | | • | |
| | 194 | b | | | | | | • | | | | | | | |
| E | 165 | b | | s | s | | n | | | | | | | | |
| ↕ | 160 | b | | n | | s | | | | | | | | | |
| | 158 | b | | | | | | | | • | | | | | |
| W | 153 | b | | | | | | | • | | | | | | |
| | 85 | b | | n | | | | | | | | | | | |
| | 79 | b | | | | | | | | • | • | | | | |
| | 20 | b | | n | | n | | | | | | | | | |
| | 16 | b | | | | | | | | • | | | | • | |

## New York

**Rest Area Usage:** There is a 8 hour stay limit, camping and overnight parking are not permitted. **Road Conditions:** 800-847-8929 (weather Thruway) **State Police:** *General*, 518-436-2825; *Emergency*, 911 **Tourism Contact:** New York State Department of Economic Development, Division of Tourism, PO Box 2603, Albany NY 12220. *Phone*: 800-456-8369 or 518-474-4116. *Internet*: www.iloveny.com

I-81 runs north to south for 184 miles from the United States/ Canada border to the Pennsylvania state line. Exit numbers are based on the consecutive numbering system.

| | Mile Marker | ↗ | * | Info | Arrow | Trees | Restrooms | Phone | Picnic | Vending | Food | Pets | Handicap | Camera | Dump |
|---|---|---|---|---|---|---|---|---|---|---|---|---|---|---|---|
| | 178 | sb | | | • | | • | • | • | | | • | • | | |
| N | 174 | nb | | | • | | • | • | • | • | | • | • | | |
| ↕ | 168 | sb | | | | • | | | • | | | | | | |
| S | 161 | nb | | | | • | | | | | | | | | |
| | 156 | b | | | | • | | | | | | | | | |

N ↕ S

| Mile Marker | ⤢ | * | (?) | ↗ | Trees | Restrooms | Phone | Picnic | Vending | Food | Pets | Handicap | Camera | RV |
|---|---|---|---|---|---|---|---|---|---|---|---|---|---|---|
| 149 | nb | | | | • | | • | | | | | | | |
| 147 | sb | | | • | | • | • | • | • | | • | • | | |
| 134 | b | | | | • | | | | | | | | | |
| 101 | sb | | | • | | • | • | • | • | | • | • | | |
| 60 | nb | | | • | | • | • | • | • | | • | • | | |
| 45 | nb | | | | • | | | • | | | | | | |
| 33 | sb | | | • | | • | • | • | • | | • | • | | |
| 14 | nb | | | • | | • | • | • | | | | • | | |
| 2 | nb | | • | | | • | • | • | • | | • | • | | |

N ↕ S

| Exit | ⤢ | * | W | S | K | T | Am | FJ | Lo | Pe | Pi | Sp | TA | Wi |
|---|---|---|---|---|---|---|---|---|---|---|---|---|---|---|
| 48 | b | | | | | | • | | | | | | | |
| 45 | b | | w | w | w | | | | | | | | | |
| 44 | b | | | | e+ | | | | | | | | | |
| 26 | b | | | | e | | | | | | | | | |
| 25 | b | | | | | | | | | | • | | | |
| 3 | b | | | | | | | | | | • | | • | |

**84** Interstate 84 runs east to west for 72 miles from the Connecticut state line to the Pennsylvania state line. Exit numbers are based on the consecutive numbering system.

E ↕ W

| Mile Marker | ⤢ | * | (?) | ↗ | Trees | Restrooms | Phone | Picnic | Vending | Food | Pets | Handicap | Camera | RV |
|---|---|---|---|---|---|---|---|---|---|---|---|---|---|---|
| 55 | b | | | • | | • | • | • | • | | • | • | | |
| 24 | wb | | | • | | • | • | • | • | | • | • | | |
| 17 | eb | | | • | | • | • | • | • | | • | • | | |
| 3 | b | | | | • | | | | | | | | | |

| Exit | ⤢ | * | W | S | K | T | Am | FJ | Lo | Pe | Pi | Sp | TA | Wi |
|---|---|---|---|---|---|---|---|---|---|---|---|---|---|---|
| 13 | b | | n | n | | | | | | | | | | |
| 7 | b | | s | | | | | | | | | | | |
| 5 | b | | | | | | | | | | | | • | |
| 4 | b | | n | n | n | | | | | | | | | |

**86** Interstate 86 is 386 miles long. It runs east to west between I-87 and the Pennsylvania state line. The Interstate is not entirely completed. Parts are identified as NY Hwy 17. Exit numbers are based on the consecutive numbering system.

| Mile Marker | Direction | * | Info | Arrow | Tree | Restrooms | Phone | Picnic | Vending | RV | Pet | Handicapped | Camera | Sign |
|---|---|---|---|---|---|---|---|---|---|---|---|---|---|---|
| 313 | eb | | | • | | • | • | • | • | | • | • | | |
| 295 | wb | | | • | | • | • | • | • | | • | • | | |
| 276 | wb | | | | • | | | | | | | | | |
| 265 | eb | | | | • | | | • | | | | | | |
| 212 | eb | | | • | | • | • | • | • | | • | • | | |
| 199 | wb | | | • | | • | • | • | • | | • | • | | |
| 160 | eb | | | • | | • | • | • | • | | • | • | | |
| 147 | wb | | | • | | • | • | • | • | | • | • | | |
| 125 | eb | | | | • | | | | | | | | • | |
| 101 | eb | | | • | | • | • | • | • | | • | • | | |
| 41 | eb | | | | • | | • | • | | | | | | |
| 40 | wb | | | | • | | • | • | | | | | | |

| Exit | Direction | * | W | S | K | T | Am | FJ | Lo | Pe | Pi | Sp | TA | Wi |
|---|---|---|---|---|---|---|---|---|---|---|---|---|---|---|
| 130a | b | | s | | | | | | | | | | | |
| 120 | b | | n | n | s | | | | | | | | | |
| 105 | b | | n | | | | | | | | | | | |
| 72 | b | | | | s | | | | | | | | | |
| 67 | b | 1 | s | s | | s | | | | | | | | |
| 63 | b | | | | | | • | | | | | | | |
| 53 | b | 2 | | | n | | | | | | | | | |
| 51 | b | | s | s | | | | | | | | | | |
| 38 | b | | | | n | | | | | | | | | |
| 37 | b | | | | | | • | | | | | | | |
| 34 | b | | s | | | | | | | | | | | |
| 25 | b | 3 | s+ | | s+ | | | | | | | | | |
| 16 | b | | | | | | • | | | | | | | |

Notes: 1) On NY 434; 2) On Center Street / Interstate is not limited-access at this point; 3) On Constitution

Interstate 87 runs north to south for about 334 miles from the United States/Canada border to I-278 in New York City. Portions are also I-287 and the New York Thruway. Exit numbers are based on the consecutive numbering system.

| Mile Marker | Direction | * | Info | Arrow | Tree | Restrooms | Phone | Picnic | Vending | RV | Pet | Handicapped | Camera | Sign |
|---|---|---|---|---|---|---|---|---|---|---|---|---|---|---|
| 162 | b | | • | | | • | • | • | | | • | • | | |
| 123 | b | | | • | | • | • | • | | | • | • | | |
| 99 | b | | | • | | • | • | • | | | • | • | | |

| Mile Marker | ⤢ | * | Info | Welcome | Picnic Area | Restrooms | Phone | Picnic Table | Vending | RV | Pet Area | Handicapped | Camera | Truck |
|---|---|---|---|---|---|---|---|---|---|---|---|---|---|---|
| 83 | b | 1 | | • | | • | • | • | • | | • | • | • | |
| 65 | sb | | | | • | | | • | | | | | | |
| 63 | nb | | | | • | | | • | | | | | | |
| 43 | b | | | • | | • | • | • | • | | • | • | | |
| 14 | nb | | | • | | • | • | • | • | | • | • | | |
| 139 | sb | 2 | | | • | | • | • | | | | | | |
| 127 | b | 3 | | • | | • | • | • | • | | | • | | |
| 103 | nb | 3 | | • | • | • | • | • | • | | | • | | |
| 99 | nb | 2 | | | • | | • | • | | | | | | |
| 96 | sb | 3 | | • | | • | • | • | • | | | • | | |
| 66 | sb | 3 | | • | | • | • | • | • | | | • | | |
| 65 | nb | 3 | | • | | • | • | • | • | | | • | | |
| 34 | sb | 3 | | • | | • | • | • | • | | | • | | |
| 33 | nb | 3 | | • | | • | • | • | • | | | • | | |
| 6 | nb | 3 | | • | | • | • | • | • | | | • | | |

N ↕ S

Notes: 1) Scenic Vista nb; 2) Follows NY Thruway numbering; 3) Service Area, Gas, Food / Follows NY Thruway numbering

| Exit | ⤢ | * | W | S | K | T | Am | FJ | Lo | Pe | Pi | Sp | TA | Wi |
|---|---|---|---|---|---|---|---|---|---|---|---|---|---|---|
| 37 | b | | e | e | w | | | | | | | | | |
| 19 | b | | e | | | | | | | | | | | |
| 15 | b | | e | | | e | | | | | | | | |
| 9 | b | | e | | w | | | | | | | | | |
| 6 | b | | e | e | | | | | | | | | | |
| 2 | b | | | | | e | | | | | | | | |
| 17 | b | 1 | e+ | | | | | | | | | | | |
| 14b | b | 2 | w | | | | | | | | | | | |
| 12 | b | 3 | | | | w | | | | | | | | |

N ↕ S

Notes: 1) Follows NY Thruway numbering / On NY 300; 2) Follows NY Thruway numbering / Shared with I-287; 3) Follows NY Thruway numbering

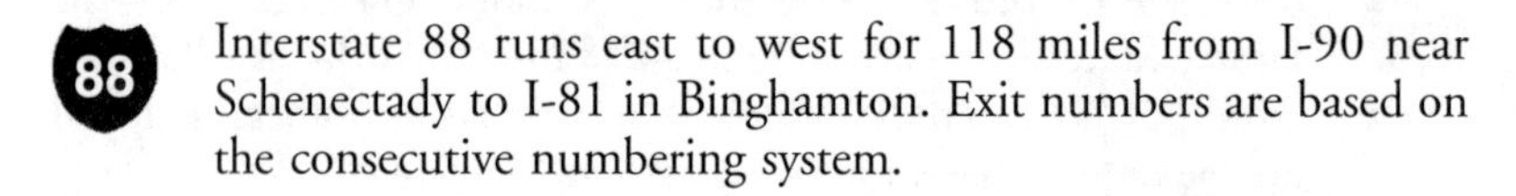


Interstate 88 runs east to west for 118 miles from I-90 near Schenectady to I-81 in Binghamton. Exit numbers are based on the consecutive numbering system.

| Mile Marker | ⤢ | * | Info | Welcome | Picnic Area | Restrooms | Phone | Picnic Table | Vending | RV | Pet Area | Handicapped | Camera | Truck |
|---|---|---|---|---|---|---|---|---|---|---|---|---|---|---|
| 79 | wb | | | • | | • | • | • | • | | • | • | | |
| 73 | eb | | | • | | • | • | • | • | | • | • | | |
| 43 | wb | | | • | | • | • | • | • | | • | • | | |

| Mile Marker | | * | | | | | | | | | | | | |
|---|---|---|---|---|---|---|---|---|---|---|---|---|---|---|
| 39 | eb | | | • | | • | • | • | • | | • | • | | |

| Exit | | * | W | S | K | T | Am | FJ | Lo | Pe | Pi | Sp | TA | Wi |
|---|---|---|---|---|---|---|---|---|---|---|---|---|---|---|
| 21 | b | | n+ | | | | | | | | | | | |
| 15 | b | | s | | s | | | | | | | | | |
| 9 | b | | | | n | | | | | | | | | |

90

I-90 runs east to west for 385 miles from the Massachusetts state line to the Pennsylvania state line. Most of it is also the New York Thruway. Exit numbers are based on the consecutive numbering system.

| Mile Marker | | * | | | | | | | | | | | | |
|---|---|---|---|---|---|---|---|---|---|---|---|---|---|---|
| 18 | wb | | | • | | • | • | • | • | | • | • | | |
| 153 | eb | 1 | | • | | • | • | • | • | | | • | | |
| 168 | wb | 1 | | • | | • | • | • | • | | | • | | |
| 172 | eb | 1 | | • | | • | • | • | • | | | • | | |
| 184 | b | 2 | | | • | | • | | | | | | | |
| 210 | b | 1 | | • | | • | • | • | • | | | • | | |
| 227 | wb | 1 | | • | | • | • | • | • | | | • | | |
| 244 | eb | 1 | | • | | • | • | • | • | | | • | | |
| 250 | eb | 2 | | | • | | • | • | | | | | | |
| 256 | wb | 2 | | | • | | • | • | | | | | | |
| 266 | wb | 1 | | • | | • | • | • | • | | | • | | |
| 280 | eb | 1 | | • | | • | • | • | • | | | • | | |
| 292 | wb | 1 | | • | | • | • | • | • | | | • | | |
| 310 | eb | 1 | | • | | • | • | • | • | | | • | | |
| 318 | wb | 2 | | | • | | • | • | | | | | | |
| 324 | wb | 1 | | • | | • | • | • | • | | | • | | |
| 337 | eb | 1 | | • | | • | • | • | • | | | • | | |
| 350 | wb | 1 | | • | | • | • | • | • | | | • | | |
| 353 | eb | 2 | | | • | | • | • | | | | | | |
| 366 | eb | 1 | | • | | • | • | • | • | | | • | | |
| 376 | wb | 1 | | • | | • | • | • | • | | | • | | |
| 397 | eb | 1 | | • | | • | • | • | • | | | • | | |
| 412 | wb | 1 | | • | | • | • | • | • | | | • | | |
| 442 | b | 2 | | | • | | • | • | | | | | | |
| 447 | b | 1 | | • | | • | • | • | • | | | • | | |

Notes: 1) Service Area, Gas, Food / Follows NY Thruway numbering; 2) Follows NY Thruway numbering

E ↕ W

| Exit | | * | W | S | K | T | Am | FJ | Lo | Pe | Pi | Sp | TA | Wi |
|---|---|---|---|---|---|---|---|---|---|---|---|---|---|---|
| B3 | b | | | | | | • | | | | | | | |
| 9 | b | | n | | | | | | | | | | | |
| 1S | b | | s | s | | | | | | | | | | |
| 28 | b | 1 | | | | | • | | | | | | • | |
| 30 | b | 1 | n | | n | | | | | | | | | |
| 31 | b | 1 | n | | | | | | | | | | | |
| 33 | b | 1 | n | | | | | | | | | | | |
| 36 | b | 1 | | | | | • | | | | • | | | |
| 42 | b | 1 | | | | | • | | | | | | | |
| 45 | b | 1 | | | n | | | | | | | | | |
| 48 | b | 1 | s | | s+ | | | • | | | | | • | |
| 49 | b | 1 | n+ | | | n+ | | | | | | | | |
| 52 | b | 1 | n | s | s | n | • | | | | | | | |
| 55 | b | 1 | | s | | | | | | | | | | |
| 59 | b | 1 | s | | | | | | | | | | | |

Notes: 1) Follows NY Thruway numbering

I-95 runs north to south for 24 miles from the Connecticut state line to the New Jersey state line. Exit numbers are based on the consecutive numbering system.

| Exit | | * | W | S | K | T | Am | FJ | Lo | Pe | Pi | Sp | TA | Wi |
|---|---|---|---|---|---|---|---|---|---|---|---|---|---|---|
| 11 | b | | | | e | | | | | | | | | |

Interstate 190 is 28 miles long. It generally runs north to south from the United States/Canada border in Lewiston to I-90 in Buffalo. Exit numbers are based on the consecutive numbering system.

| Exit | | * | W | S | K | T | Am | FJ | Lo | Pe | Pi | Sp | TA | Wi |
|---|---|---|---|---|---|---|---|---|---|---|---|---|---|---|
| 23 | b | | w | w | e | | | | | | | | | |

Interstate 287 is 31 miles long. It runs from I-95 to the New Jersey state line. Portions are shared with I-87 and the New York Thruway. Exit numbers are based on the consecutive numbering system.

| Exit | | * | W | S | K | T | Am | FJ | Lo | Pe | Pi | Sp | TA | Wi |
|---|---|---|---|---|---|---|---|---|---|---|---|---|---|---|
| 14b | b | 1 | s | | | | | | | | | | | |

| Exit | ↗ | * | W | S | K | T | Am | FJ | Lo | Pe | Pi | Sp | TA | Wi |
|---|---|---|---|---|---|---|---|---|---|---|---|---|---|---|
| 2 | b | | | s | | | | | | | | | | |

Notes: 1) Follows NY Thruway numbering / Shared with I-87

I-290 in Buffalo is about 10 miles long. It connects I-90 with I-190. Exit numbers are based on the consecutive numbering system.

| Exit | ↗ | * | W | S | K | T | Am | FJ | Lo | Pe | Pi | Sp | TA | Wi |
|---|---|---|---|---|---|---|---|---|---|---|---|---|---|---|
| 3ab | b | | | | s | | | | | | | | | |

390

Interstate 390 is about 80 miles long. It generally runs north to south from Rochester to I-86 near Bath. Exit numbers are based on the consecutive numbering system.

| Exit | ↗ | * | W | S | K | T | Am | FJ | Lo | Pe | Pi | Sp | TA | Wi |
|---|---|---|---|---|---|---|---|---|---|---|---|---|---|---|
| 13 | b | | w | w | | w | | | | | | | | |
| 12 | b | | | | | | • | | | | | | | |
| 5 | b | | | | | | | | | | | | • | |

490

Interstate 490 is about 38 miles long. It departs I-90 at exit 47, runs through Rochester, and rejoins I-90 at exit 45. Exit numbers are based on the consecutive numbering system.

| Exit | ↗ | * | W | S | K | T | Am | FJ | Lo | Pe | Pi | Sp | TA | Wi |
|---|---|---|---|---|---|---|---|---|---|---|---|---|---|---|
| 29 | b | | | | n | | | | | | | | | |
| 2 | b | | | | | | • | | | | | | | |

495

Interstate 495 on Long Island is 66 miles long. It begins in New York City and runs east to Calverton. Exit numbers are based on the consecutive numbering system.

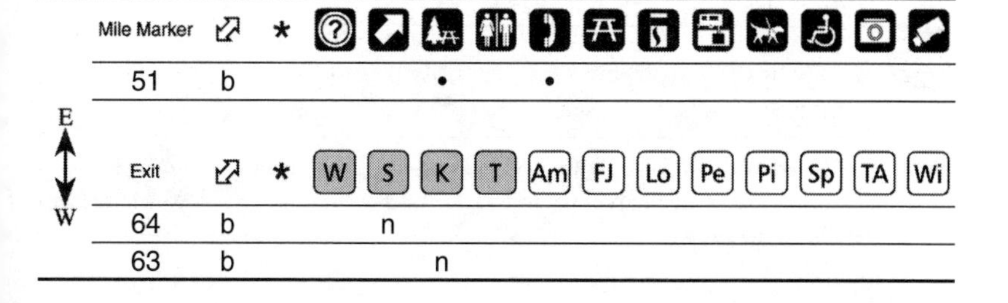

| Mile Marker | ↗ | * | ? | | | | | | | | | | | |
|---|---|---|---|---|---|---|---|---|---|---|---|---|---|---|
| 51 | b | | | | • | | • | | | | | | | |

E ↕ W

| Exit | ↗ | * | W | S | K | T | Am | FJ | Lo | Pe | Pi | Sp | TA | Wi |
|---|---|---|---|---|---|---|---|---|---|---|---|---|---|---|
| 64 | b | | | n | | | | | | | | | | |
| 63 | b | | | | n | | | | | | | | | |

## North Carolina

**Rest Area Usage:** There is a 4 hour stay limit, camping and overnight parking are not permitted. **Road Conditions:** No central phone number. *Internet*: www.ncsmartlink.org **State Police:** *General*, 919-733-7952; *Emergency*, 911 **Tourism Contact:** North Carolina Travel & Tourism, 301 N Wilmington St, Raleigh NC 27699. *Phone*: 800-847-4862 or 919-733-4171. *Internet*: www.visitnc.com

Interstate 26 runs east to west for 40 miles from the South Carolina state line to I-40 near Asheville.

E ↕ W

| Mile Marker | ⤢ | * | | | | | | | | | | | | |
|---|---|---|---|---|---|---|---|---|---|---|---|---|---|---|
| 36 | wb | | • | | | • | • | • | • | | | • | | |
| 10 | b | | | • | | • | • | • | • | | | • | | |

| Exit | ⤢ | * | W | S | K | T | Am | FJ | Lo | Pe | Pi | Sp | TA | Wi |
|---|---|---|---|---|---|---|---|---|---|---|---|---|---|---|
| 18ab | b | | s | | s | | | | | | | | | |
| 2 | b | | | | s | | | | | | | | | |

Interstate 40 runs east to west for 420 miles from Wilmington to the Tennessee state line. Part of it is also I-85.

E ↕ W

| Mile Marker | ⤢ | * | | | | | | | | | | | | |
|---|---|---|---|---|---|---|---|---|---|---|---|---|---|---|
| 364 | b | | | • | | • | • | • | • | | • | • | | |
| 324 | b | | | • | | • | • | • | • | | • | • | | |
| 139 | b | 1 | | • | | • | • | • | • | | | • | | |
| 177 | b | | | • | | • | • | • | • | | • | • | | |
| 136 | b | | | • | | • | • | • | • | • | • | • | | |
| 82 | b | | | • | | • | • | • | • | • | • | • | | |
| 67 | eb | 2 | | | | | | | | | | | | • |
| 10 | b | 3 | • | • | | • | • | • | • | | • | • | | |

Notes: 1) Shared with I-85 / Follows I-85 numbering; 2) There are 3 Runaway Truck Ramps between milemarker 67 and 71 for eastbound travelers; 3) Welcome Center eb, Rest Area wb

| Exit | | * | W | S | K | T | Am | FJ | Lo | Pe | Pi | Sp | TA | Wi |
|---|---|---|---|---|---|---|---|---|---|---|---|---|---|---|
| 298ab | b | | | s | | | | | | | | | | |
| 287 | b | | | s | | | | | | | | | | |
| 270 | b | | n | | | | | | | | | | | |
| 157 | b | 1 | | | | | | | | • | | | | |
| 152 | b | 1 | | | | | | | | | • | | | |
| 150 | b | 1 | | | | | | • | | | | | | |
| 145 | b | 1 | | | n | | | | | | | | | |
| 141 | b | 1 | n | | n | | | | | | | | | |
| 138 | b | 1 | | | | | | | | | | | • | |
| 124 | b | 1 | | | s | | | | | | | | | |
| 214ab | b | | s | s | s | s | | | | | | | | |
| 192 | b | | | | s | | | | | | | | | |
| 189 | b | | | s | | | | | | | | | | |
| 188 | b | 2 | n | | | | | | | | | | | |
| 184 | b | | | | s | | | | | | | | | |
| 170 | b | | s | | | | • | | | | | | | |
| 151 | b | | n | | | | | | | | | | | |
| 130 | b | | | | n | | | | | | | | | |
| 126 | b | | s | s | s | | | | | | | | | |
| 125 | b | | | | s | | | | | | | | | |
| 123 | b | | n+ | | | | | | | | | | | |
| 103 | b | | s | | | | | | | | | | | |
| 53ab | b | 3 | | | n+ | | | | | | | | | |
| 37 | b | | | | | | | | | | | | • | |
| 27 | b | | s+ | | | | | | | | | | | |
| 24 | b | | | | | | | | | | • | | | |

Notes: 1) Also I-85 / Follows I-85 numbering; 2) Off US 421; 3) On US 74

Interstate 77 runs north to south for 105 miles from the Virginia state line to the South Carolina state line.

| Mile Marker | | * | | | | | | | | | | | | |
|---|---|---|---|---|---|---|---|---|---|---|---|---|---|---|
| 105 | sb | | • | | | • | • | • | • | | • | • | | |
| 72 | nb | | | • | | • | • | • | • | | • | • | | |
| 63 | sb | | | • | | • | • | • | • | | • | • | | |
| 39 | b | | | • | | • | • | • | | | | • | | |
| 1 | nb | | • | | | • | • | • | • | | • | • | | |

| Exit | ↗ | * | W | S | K | T | Am | FJ | Lo | Pe | Pi | Sp | TA | Wi |
|---|---|---|---|---|---|---|---|---|---|---|---|---|---|---|
| 50 | b | | | | e | | | | | | | | | |
| 36 | b | | e | | e | | | | | | | | | |
| 25 | b | | | | | e | | | | | | | | |
| 16b | b | | | | | | • | | | | | | | |
| 13 | b | | | | | | | | | | • | | | |
| 5 | b | | | | | e | | | | | | | | |
| 4 | b | | | e | | | | | | | | | | |

85

Interstate 85 runs north to south for 234 miles from the Virginia state line to the South Carolina state line. Part of it is shared with I-40.

| Mile Marker | ↗ | * | [Information] | [Arrow] | [Picnic area] | [Restrooms] | [Phone] | [Picnic table] | [Drinking fountain] | [Vending] | [Pet area] | [Handicap] | [Camera] | [RV/Truck] |
|---|---|---|---|---|---|---|---|---|---|---|---|---|---|---|
| 231 | sb | | • | | | • | • | • | • | | • | • | | |
| 199 | b | | | • | | • | • | • | • | | • | • | | |
| 139 | b | 1 | | • | | • | • | • | • | | | • | | |
| 100 | b | | | • | | • | • | • | • | | • | • | | |
| 59 | b | | | • | | • | • | • | • | | • | • | | |
| 6 | sb | | | • | | • | • | • | • | | • | • | | |
| 2 | nb | | • | | | • | • | • | • | | • | • | | |

Notes: 1) Shared with I-40

| Exit | ↗ | * | W | S | K | T | Am | FJ | Lo | Pe | Pi | Sp | TA | Wi |
|---|---|---|---|---|---|---|---|---|---|---|---|---|---|---|
| 213 | b | | | | w | | | | | | | | | |
| 212 | b | | w | | | | | | | | | | | |
| 204 | b | | w | | | | | | | | | | | |
| 177a | b | | | | w | | | | | | | | | |
| 164 | b | | w | | | | | | | | | | | |
| 157 | b | 1 | | | | | | | | • | | | | |
| 152 | b | 1 | | | | | | | | | • | | | |
| 150 | b | 1 | | | | | | • | | | | | | |
| 145 | b | 1 | | | w | | | | | | | | | |
| 141 | b | 1 | w | | w | | | | | | | | | |
| 138 | b | 1 | | | | | | | | | | | • | |
| 124 | b | 1 | | | e | | | | | | | | | |
| 121 | b | | | | e | | | | | | | | | |
| 103 | b | | | | e | | | | | | | | | |
| 91 | b | | w | | | | | | | | | | | |
| 76ab | b | | | | w | | | | | | | | | |

| Exit | ↗ | * | W | S | K | T | Am | FJ | Lo | Pe | Pi | Sp | TA | Wi |
|---|---|---|---|---|---|---|---|---|---|---|---|---|---|---|
| 75 | b | | w | | | | | | | | | | | |
| 63 | b | | | | | | | | | | • | | | |
| 58 | b | | | | | w | | | | | | | | |
| 45 | b | | e | e | | | | | | | | | | |
| 39 | b | | | | | | | | | | • | | | |
| 22 | b | | | e | | | | | | | | | | |
| 21 | b | | e | | e | | | | | | | | | |
| 20 | b | | | | e | e | | | | | | | | |
| 5 | b | | | | | | • | | | | | | | |

N ↕ S

Notes: 1) Shared with I-40

95

Interstate 95 is 182 miles long. It runs north to south from the Virginia state line to the South Carolina state line.

| Mile Marker | ↗ | * | | | | | | | | | | | | |
|---|---|---|---|---|---|---|---|---|---|---|---|---|---|---|
| 181 | sb | | • | | | • | • | • | • | | • | • | | |
| 142 | b | | | • | | • | • | • | • | | • | • | | |
| 99 | b | | | • | | • | • | • | • | | • | • | | |
| 60 | b | | | | • | | | | | | | | | |
| 48 | b | | | • | | • | • | • | • | | • | • | | |
| 5 | nb | | • | | | • | • | • | • | | • | • | | |

| Exit | ↗ | * | W | S | K | T | Am | FJ | Lo | Pe | Pi | Sp | TA | Wi |
|---|---|---|---|---|---|---|---|---|---|---|---|---|---|---|
| 180 | b | | | | | | | | | | • | | | |
| 173 | b | | w | | | | | | | | | | | |
| 121 | b | | e+ | | e+ | | | | | | | | | |
| 106 | b | | | | | | | | | | | | • | |
| 97 | b | | w+ | | | | | | | | | | | |
| 77 | b | | | | | | | | | | • | | | |
| 22 | b | | e | | | | | | | | | | | |
| 20 | b | | | | e | | | | | | | | | |

240

Interstate 240 in Asheville is 9 miles long. It departs I-40 at exit 46 and rejoins it at exit 53.

| Exit | ↗ | * | W | S | K | T | Am | FJ | Lo | Pe | Pi | Sp | TA | Wi |
|---|---|---|---|---|---|---|---|---|---|---|---|---|---|---|
| 7 | b | | | | s | | | | | | | | | |
| 3a | b | | | n | n | | | | | | | | | |

Interstate 440 forms a 16-mile partial loop around Raleigh. Exit numbering begins at I-40 exit 293 and increases in a clockwise direction.

| Exit | ↗ | * | W | S | K | T | Am | FJ | Lo | Pe | Pi | Sp | TA | Wi |
|---|---|---|---|---|---|---|---|---|---|---|---|---|---|---|
| 13ab | b | | | | e+ | | | | | | | | | |
| 2ab | b | | | | w | | | | | | | | | |

## North Dakota

**Rest Area Usage:** There is no limit to length of stay, however, no camping or overnight parking is permitted. **Road Conditions:** 701-328-7623 (weather) **State Police:** *General*, 701-328-2455; *Emergency*, 800-472-2121 or *2121 on cell phone **Tourism Contact:** North Dakota Department of Tourism, 604 E Boulevard Ave, Bismarck ND 58505. *Phone*: 800-435-5663. *Internet*: www.ndtourism.com

I-29 runs north to south for 218 miles from the United States/ Canada border to the South Dakota state line.

| Mile Marker | ↗ | * | | | | | | | | | | | | |
|---|---|---|---|---|---|---|---|---|---|---|---|---|---|---|
| 216 | b | 1 | • | | • | • | • | • | • | | • | • | | |
| 179 | b | | | • | | • | • | • | • | | • | • | | |
| 99 | b | | | • | | • | • | • | • | | • | • | | |
| 74 | b | | | • | | • | • | • | • | | • | • | | |
| 40 | b | | | • | | • | • | • | • | | • | • | | |
| 3 | nb | | • | | | • | • | • | | | • | • | | |

N ↕ S

Notes: 1) Welcome Center sb, Roadside Turnout nb

| Exit | ↗ | * | W | S | K | T | Am | FJ | Lo | Pe | Pi | Sp | TA | Wi |
|---|---|---|---|---|---|---|---|---|---|---|---|---|---|---|
| 138 | b | | e | e | e | e | • | | | | | | | |
| 64 | b | | w | w | w | w | | | | | | | | |
| 62 | b | | | | | | | • | | | | | | |

Interstate 94 runs east to west for 352 miles from the Minnesota state line to the Montana state line.

| Mile Marker | | * | ? | | | | | | | | | | | |
|---|---|---|---|---|---|---|---|---|---|---|---|---|---|---|
| 348 | b | 1 | • | | | • | • | • | • | | • | • | | |
| 304 | b | | | • | | • | • | • | • | | • | • | | |
| 254 | b | | | • | | • | • | • | • | | • | • | | |
| 224 | wb | | | • | | • | • | • | • | | • | • | | |
| 221 | eb | | | • | | • | • | • | • | | • | • | | |
| 168 | b | | | • | | • | • | • | • | | • | • | | |
| 152 | eb | | | | • | | | | | | | | • | |
| 135 | wb | | | | • | | | | | | | | • | |
| 119 | b | | | • | | • | • | • | | | • | • | | |
| 94 | b | | | • | | • | • | • | | • | • | • | | |
| 71 | b | | | • | | • | • | • | | • | • | • | | |
| 32 | b | 2 | | • | | • | • | • | • | | • | • | | |
| 21 | eb | | | | • | | | | | | | | • | |
| 15 | wb | | | • | | • | • | • | | | • | • | | |
| 12 | eb | | • | | | • | • | • | | | • | • | | |
| 1 | eb | | | | • | | | | | | | | | |

Notes: 1) North at exit 348 to Welcome Center; 2) T. Roosevelt Nat'l Park Visitor Center

| Exit | | * | W | S | K | T | Am | FJ | Lo | Pe | Pi | Sp | TA | Wi |
|---|---|---|---|---|---|---|---|---|---|---|---|---|---|---|
| 351 | b | | | | s | | | | | | | | | |
| 348 | b | | n+ | n+ | n+ | n+ | | | | • | | | | |
| 258 | b | | s | | s | | | | | | | | | |
| 159 | b | | | | n | | | | | | | | | |
| 61 | b | | n | | n | | | | | | | | | |
| 1 | b | | | | | | | • | | | | | | |

## Ohio

**Rest Area Usage:** There is a 3 hour stay limit, no camping or overnight parking is permitted. **Road Conditions:** 888-264-7623 (general), 614-644-7031 or 440-234-2030 (weather turnpike), 888-876-7453 (construction turnpike) **State Police:** *General*, 614-466-2660; *Emergency*, 877-772-8765 **Tourism Contact:** Ohio Division of Travel & Tourism, PO Box 1001, Columbus OH 43216. *Phone*: 800-282-5393 or 614-466-8844. *Internet*: www.ohiotourism.com

Interstate 70 runs east to west for 226 miles from the West Virginia state line to the Indiana state line.

| Mile Marker | | * | | | | | | | | | | | | |
|---|---|---|---|---|---|---|---|---|---|---|---|---|---|---|
| 211 | b | 1 | • | • | | • | • | • | • | | | • | • | |
| 189 | eb | | | • | | • | • | • | | | | • | • | |
| 163 | wb | | | • | | • | • | • | | | | | • | |
| 131 | b | | | • | | • | • | • | | | | | • | |
| 71 | b | | | • | | • | • | • | • | | | | • | |
| 3 | b | 2 | • | • | | • | • | • | • | | | • | • | |

Notes: 1) Welcome Center wb, Rest Area eb; 2) Welcome Center eb, Rest Area wb

| Exit | | * | W | S | K | T | Am | FJ | Lo | Pe | Pi | Sp | TA | Wi |
|---|---|---|---|---|---|---|---|---|---|---|---|---|---|---|
| 218 | b | | n | n | s | | | | | | | | | |
| 178 | b | | | | s | | | | | | • | | | |
| 160 | b | | | | | | | | • | | | | | |
| 126 | b | | | | | | • | | | | • | | • | |
| 122 | b | | | | | | | • | | | | | | |
| 112 | b | | n | | | | | | | | | | | |
| 110 | b | | | s | | s | | | | | | | | |
| 94 | b | | | s | | | | | | | • | | | |
| 91ab | b | | n | n | | | | | | | | | | |
| 79 | b | | | | | | | | | | • | | • | • |
| 36 | b | | n | | s | n | | | | | | • | | |
| 21 | b | | | | | | | | | | | • | | |
| 10 | b | | | | | | | | | | • | | • | |

Interstate 71 runs north to south for 248 miles from I-90 in Cleveland to the Kentucky state line.

| Mile Marker | | * | | | | | | | | | | | | |
|---|---|---|---|---|---|---|---|---|---|---|---|---|---|---|
| 225 | nb | | | • | | • | • | • | | | | • | • | |
| 224 | sb | | | • | | • | • | • | | | | • | • | |
| 196 | b | | | • | | • | • | • | • | | | • | • | |
| 180 | b | | | • | | • | • | • | • | | | • | • | |
| 128 | b | | | • | | • | • | • | • | | | • | • | |
| 68 | b | | | • | | • | • | • | • | | | • | • | |
| 34 | b | | • | | | • | • | • | • | | | • | • | • | |

| Exit | ⇗ | * | W | S | K | T | Am | FJ | Lo | Pe | Pi | Sp | TA | Wi |
|---|---|---|---|---|---|---|---|---|---|---|---|---|---|---|
| 235 | b | | | | w | | | | | | | | | |
| 234 | b | | w | | | | | | | | | | | |
| 231 | b | | | | | w | | | | | | | | |
| 226 | b | | | | w | | | | | | | | | |
| 209 | b | | | | | | | | | | • | | • | |
| 204 | b | | | | | | | | | | • | | | |
| 186 | b | | | | | | | | | | | | • | |
| 140 | b | | | | | | | | | | | | | • |
| 131 | b | | | | | | | • | | | • | | | |
| 121 | b | | w | | w | | | | | | | | | |
| 100 | b | | | | w | | | | | | | | | |
| 65 | b | | | | | | | | | | | | • | |
| 50 | b | | | | | | | | | | • | | | |
| 19 | b | | e | | | e | | | | | | | | |
| 8 | b | | w | w | w | | | | | | | | | |

N ↕ S

74

Interstate 74 is 19 miles long. It runs east to west from I-75 in Cincinnati to the Indiana state line.

| Exit | ⇗ | * | W | S | K | T | Am | FJ | Lo | Pe | Pi | Sp | TA | Wi |
|---|---|---|---|---|---|---|---|---|---|---|---|---|---|---|
| 14 | b | | | n | | | | | | | | | | |
| 1 | b | | | | s | | | | | | | | | |

75

Interstate 75 runs north to south for 211 miles from the Michigan state line to the Kentucky state line.

| Mile Marker | ⇗ | * | | | | | | | | | | | | |
|---|---|---|---|---|---|---|---|---|---|---|---|---|---|---|
| 179 | b | | • | | | • | • | • | • | | • | • | | |
| 153 | b | | | • | | • | • | • | • | | • | • | | |
| 114 | b | | | • | | • | • | • | • | | • | • | | |
| 81 | b | | | • | | • | • | • | • | | • | • | | |
| 27 | b | | • | | | • | • | • | • | | • | • | | |

N ↕ S

| Exit | ⇗ | * | W | S | K | T | Am | FJ | Lo | Pe | Pi | Sp | TA | Wi |
|---|---|---|---|---|---|---|---|---|---|---|---|---|---|---|
| 210 | b | | | | | | | | | | • | | | |
| 193 | b | | | | e | | | | | | | | | |
| 167 | b | | | | | | | | | • | | | | |

N ↕ S

| Exit | ⤢ | * | W | S | K | T | Am | FJ | Lo | Pe | Pi | Sp | TA | Wi |
|---|---|---|---|---|---|---|---|---|---|---|---|---|---|---|
| 164 | b | | | | | | | | | | • | | | |
| 135 | b | | | | | | | • | | | • | | | • |
| 125 | b | | e | e | e | | | | | | | | | |
| 92 | b | | w | | | | | | | | | | | |
| 74 | b | | w | | | | | | | | | | | |
| 60 | b | | | w | | | | | | | | | | |
| 44 | b | | e | | e | | | | | | | | | |
| 36 | b | | | | | | | | | | • | | | • |
| 32 | b | | w | | | w | | | | | | | | |
| 29 | b | | | | | | • | | | | | | | |
| 22 | b | | w | | | | | | | | | | | |

## 76

Interstate 76 runs east to west for 82 miles from the Pennsylvania state line to I-71 south of Medina. Part of it is also the Ohio Turnpike.

| Mile Marker | ⤢ | * | Info | Arrow | Trees | Restrooms | Phone | Picnic Table | Vending | Food | Pet Area | Handicap | Camera | Truck |
|---|---|---|---|---|---|---|---|---|---|---|---|---|---|---|
| 237 | b | 1 | | • | | • | • | • | | | | • | | |
| 45 | b | | | • | | • | • | • | | | • | • | | |

Notes: 1) Service Area, Gas, Food / Follows OH Tpk numbering

E ↕ W

| Exit | ⤢ | * | W | S | K | T | Am | FJ | Lo | Pe | Pi | Sp | TA | Wi |
|---|---|---|---|---|---|---|---|---|---|---|---|---|---|---|
| 232 | b | 1 | | | | | | | | | • | | | |
| 9 | b | | | | n | | | | | | | | | |
| 1 | b | | | | | | | | | | • | | • | |

Notes: 1) Also Ohio Turnpike / Follows turnpike numbering

## 77

Interstate 77 is 160 miles long. It runs north to south from I-90 in Cleveland to the West Virginia state line.

N ↕ S

| Mile Marker | ⤢ | * | Info | Arrow | Trees | Restrooms | Phone | Picnic Table | Vending | Food | Pet Area | Handicap | Camera | Truck |
|---|---|---|---|---|---|---|---|---|---|---|---|---|---|---|
| 141 | b | | | • | | • | • | • | • | | • | • | | |
| 85 | b | | | • | | • | • | • | | | • | • | | |
| 39 | nb | | | • | | • | • | • | | | • | • | | |
| 36 | sb | | | • | | • | • | • | | | • | • | | |
| 3 | nb | | • | | | • | • | • | • | | • | • | | |

| Exit | ⇗ | * | W | S | K | T | Am | FJ | Lo | Pe | Pi | Sp | TA | Wi |
|---|---|---|---|---|---|---|---|---|---|---|---|---|---|---|
| 159 | b | | | | | | | | | | | • | | |
| 145 | b | | | | | | | | | | • | | | |
| 137ab | b | | e | e | e | | | | | | | | | |
| 120 | b | | e | | e | | | | | | | | | |
| 111 | b | | w | e | | | | | | | | | • | |
| 109ab | b | | | | | w | | | | | | | | |
| 81 | b | | e | | | | | | | | | | | |
| 25 | b | | | | | | | | | | • | | | |
| 1 | b | | e | | w | | | | | | | | | |

80

I-80 runs east to west for 237 miles from the Pennsylvania state line to the Indiana state line. Portions are also I-90 and the Ohio Turnpike.

| Mile Marker | ⇗ | * | | | | | | | | | | | | |
|---|---|---|---|---|---|---|---|---|---|---|---|---|---|---|
| 237 | wb | | • | | | • | • | • | • | | • | • | | |
| 197 | b | 1 | | • | | • | • | • | | • | • | • | | |
| 170 | b | 2 | | • | | • | • | • | | | • | • | | |
| 139 | b | 3 | | • | | • | • | • | | • | • | • | | |
| 100 | b | 2 | | • | | • | • | • | | | • | • | | |
| 77 | b | 1 | | • | | • | • | • | | • | • | • | | |
| 49 | b | 2 | | • | | • | • | • | | | • | • | | |
| 21 | eb | 2 | | • | | • | • | • | | | • | • | | |
| 21 | wb | 4 | | • | | • | • | • | | • | • | • | | |

Notes: 1) Service Area, Gas, Food / Overnight RV parking with hookups / Follows OH Tpk numbering; 2) Service Area, Gas, Food / Follows OH Tpk numbering; 3) Service Area, Gas / Overnight RV parking / Follows OH Tpk numbering; 4) Service Area, Gas, Food / Overnight RV parking / Follows OH Tpk numbering

| Exit | ⇗ | * | W | S | K | T | Am | FJ | Lo | Pe | Pi | Sp | TA | Wi |
|---|---|---|---|---|---|---|---|---|---|---|---|---|---|---|
| 226 | b | | | | | | | | | • | • | | | |
| 223 | b | | | | | | | | | | • | | • | |
| 187 | b | 1 | s+ | | s+ | | | | | | | | | |
| 173 | b | 1 | | | | | | | | | • | | | |
| 161 | b | 1 | n | | | | | | | | | | | |
| 145 | b | 1 | n | n | n | | | | | | | | | |
| 71 | b | 2 | | | | | | | | • | • | | • | |
| 59 | b | 2 | | | n | | | | | | | | | |
| 34 | b | 2 | s+ | | | | | | | | | | | |

Notes: 1) Also Ohio Turnpike; 2) Also Ohio Turnpike and I-90

Interstate 90 runs east to west for 245 miles from the Pennsylvania state line to the Indiana state line. Part of it is also I-80 and the Ohio Turnpike.

| Mile Marker | | * | | | | | | | | | | | | |
|---|---|---|---|---|---|---|---|---|---|---|---|---|---|---|
| 242 | wb | | • | | | • | • | • | • | | | • | • | |
| 198 | b | | | • | | • | • | • | • | | | • | • | |
| 139 | b | 1 | | • | | • | • | • | | • | | • | • | |
| 100 | b | 2 | | • | | • | • | • | | | | • | • | |
| 77 | b | 3 | | • | | • | • | • | | • | | • | • | |
| 49 | b | 2 | | • | | • | • | • | | | | • | • | |
| 21 | eb | 2 | | • | | • | • | • | | | | • | • | |
| 21 | wb | 4 | | • | | • | • | • | | • | | • | • | |

Notes: 1) Service Area, Gas / Overnight RV parking / Follows OH Tpk numbering; 2) Service Area, Gas, Food / Follows OH Tpk numbering; 3) Service Area, Gas, Food / Overnight RV parking with hookups / Follows OH Tpk numbering; 4) Service Area, Gas, Food / Overnight RV parking / Follows OH Tpk numbering

| Exit | | * | W | S | K | T | Am | FJ | Lo | Pe | Pi | Sp | TA | Wi |
|---|---|---|---|---|---|---|---|---|---|---|---|---|---|---|
| 241 | b | | | | n | | | | | | | | | |
| 235 | b | | | | | | | | | | | • | • | |
| 223 | b | | | | | | | • | | | • | | | |
| 187 | b | | | s | | | | | | | | | | |
| 186 | b | | | | s | | | | | | | | | |
| 184a | b | | | | s | | | | | | | | | |
| 156 | b | | | | s | | | | | | | | | |
| 153 | b | | | | | s | | | | | | | | |
| 151 | b | | | | | | | | | | • | | | |
| 148 | b | | | | s | | | | | | | | | |
| 145 | b | | s | s | s | | | | | | | | | |
| 71 | b | 1 | | | | | | | | • | • | | • | |
| 59 | b | 1 | | | n | | | | | | | | | |
| 34 | b | 1 | s+ | | | | | | | | | | | |

Notes: 1) Also Ohio Turnpike and I-80

Interstate 270 is a 55-mile loop around Columbus. Exit numbering begins at US 62 and increases in a clockwise direction.

| Exit | | * | W | S | K | T | Am | FJ | Lo | Pe | Pi | Sp | TA | Wi |
|---|---|---|---|---|---|---|---|---|---|---|---|---|---|---|
| 13ab | b | | | | e | | | | | | | | | |

| Exit | ↗ | * | W | S | K | T | Am | FJ | Lo | Pe | Pi | Sp | TA | Wi |
|---|---|---|---|---|---|---|---|---|---|---|---|---|---|---|
| 15 | b | | w | | | | | | | | | | | |
| 20 | b | | | s+ | | | | | | | | | | |
| 32 | b | | w | w | | | | | | | | | | |
| 37 | b | | | | n | | | | | | | | | |
| 52 | b | | n | | | | | | | | | | | |

Interstate 271 is about 40 miles long. It runs north to south from I-90 near Willoughby Hills to I-71 near Medina. Part of it is also I-480.

| Mile Marker | ↗ | * | | | | | | | | | | | | |
|---|---|---|---|---|---|---|---|---|---|---|---|---|---|---|
| 8 | b | | | • | | • | • | • | | | • | • | | |

N ↕ S

| Exit | ↗ | * | W | S | K | T | Am | FJ | Lo | Pe | Pi | Sp | TA | Wi |
|---|---|---|---|---|---|---|---|---|---|---|---|---|---|---|
| 23 | b | | | e | | | | | | | | | | |
| 19 | b | | w | | | | | | | | | | | |
| 18 | b | | w | | | | | | | | | | | |

Interstate 275 around Cincinnati is 56 miles long. It is part of an 84-mile loop that also runs through Kentucky and Indiana. Exit numbers increase in a clockwise direction.

| Exit | ↗ | * | W | S | K | T | Am | FJ | Lo | Pe | Pi | Sp | TA | Wi |
|---|---|---|---|---|---|---|---|---|---|---|---|---|---|---|
| 63 | b | | e+ | | | | | | | | | | | |
| 57 | b | | | | e | | | | | | | | | |
| 47 | b | | | | | | | | | | | • | | |
| 46 | b | | | | n | | | | | | | | | |
| 42 | b | | s | s | | | | | | | | | | |
| 39 | b | | | | n | | | | | | | | | |
| 33 | b | | n | | | | | | | | | | | |

280

Interstate 280 is 12 miles long. It connects I-80/90 with I-75 in Toledo.

| Exit | ↗ | * | W | S | K | T | Am | FJ | Lo | Pe | Pi | Sp | TA | Wi |
|---|---|---|---|---|---|---|---|---|---|---|---|---|---|---|
| 1 | b | | | | | | • | • | | • | | | | |

I-475 is 20 miles long. It forms a partial loop around Toledo. Exit numbers increase in a clockwise direction.

| Exit | | * | W | S | K | T | Am | FJ | Lo | Pe | Pi | Sp | TA | Wi |
|---|---|---|---|---|---|---|---|---|---|---|---|---|---|---|
| 13 | b | | | | e | | | | | | | | | |
| 8ab | b | | | w | | w | | | | | | | | |

Interstate 480 is 42 miles long. It runs east to west from I-80 near Streetsboro to I-80 near North Ridgeville.

| Exit | | * | W | S | K | T | Am | FJ | Lo | Pe | Pi | Sp | TA | Wi |
|---|---|---|---|---|---|---|---|---|---|---|---|---|---|---|
| 15 | b | | | | s | | | | | | | | | |
| 13 | b | | s | s | | | | | | | | | | |
| 6ab | b | | n | | | | | | | | | | | |

Interstate 675 in Dayton is about 27 miles long. It runs north to south from I-75 near Miamisburg to I-70 near Fairborn.

| Exit | | * | W | S | K | T | Am | FJ | Lo | Pe | Pi | Sp | TA | Wi |
|---|---|---|---|---|---|---|---|---|---|---|---|---|---|---|
| 17 | b | | e | e | | | | | | | | | | |
| 10 | b | | | | w | | | | | | | | | |
| 7 | b | | e | | | | | | | | | | | |
| 2 | b | | | | w | | | | | | | | | |

N ↕ S

## Oklahoma

**Rest Area Usage:** There is no limit to length of stay and overnight parking is permitted. Camping is not allowed. **Road Conditions:** 405-425-2385 (weather) **State Police:** General, 405-425-2424; Emergency, 911 **Tourism Contact:** Oklahoma Department of Tourism, PO Box 52002, Oklahoma City OK 73152. Phone: 800-652-6552 or 405-521-2409. Internet: www.travelok.com

Interstate 35 runs north to south for 236 miles from the Kansas state line to the Texas state line. Portions are also shared with I-40 and I-44.

| Mile Marker | | * | | | | | | | | | | | | |
|---|---|---|---|---|---|---|---|---|---|---|---|---|---|---|
| 225 | b | 1 | • | • | | • | • | • | • | | • | • | | |

N ↕ S

| Mile Marker | ↗ | * | Info | Arrow | Trees | Restrooms | Phone | Picnic Table | Vending | RV | Pet | Accessible | Camera | Pencil |
|---|---|---|---|---|---|---|---|---|---|---|---|---|---|---|
| 209 | b | | | | • | | | | | | | | | |
| 195 | b | | | | • | | | | | | | | | |
| 173 | sb | | | | • | | | | | | | | | |
| 171 | nb | | | | • | | | | | | | | | |
| 59 | b | | | • | | • | • | • | | • | • | • | | |
| 49 | b | | | | • | | | | | | | | • | |
| 46 | b | | | | • | | | | | | | | • | |
| 3 | b | 2 | • | • | | • | • | • | • | | | • | | |

Notes: 1) Welcome Center sb, Rest Area nb; 2) Welcome Center nb, Rest Area sb

N ↕ S

| Exit | ↗ | * | W | S | K | T | Am | FJ | Lo | Pe | Pi | Sp | TA | Wi |
|---|---|---|---|---|---|---|---|---|---|---|---|---|---|---|
| 211 | b | | | | | | | | • | | | | | |
| 137 | b | 1 | | | | | • | • | • | | | | | |
| 127 | b | 2 | | | | | | | | • | • | | | |
| 120 | b | | | | | | | | • | | | | | |
| 116 | b | | w | | | | | | | | | | | |
| 109 | b | | e | | | e | | | | | | | | |
| 106 | b | | | | | | | | • | | | | | |
| 72 | b | | e | | | | | | • | | | | | |
| 32 | b | | | | | | | | • | | | | | |

Notes: 1) Shared with I-44; 2) Shared with I-40

**40** Interstate 40 runs east to west for 331 miles from the Arkansas state line to the Texas state line. Part of it is shared with I-35.

E ↕ W

| Mile Marker | ↗ | * | Info | Arrow | Trees | Restrooms | Phone | Picnic Table | Vending | RV | Pet | Accessible | Camera | Pencil |
|---|---|---|---|---|---|---|---|---|---|---|---|---|---|---|
| 316 | eb | | | • | | • | • | • | • | • | • | • | | |
| 314 | wb | | • | | | • | • | • | • | • | • | • | | |
| 283 | b | | | | • | | | | | | | | • | |
| 251 | b | | | | • | | | | | | | | | |
| 197 | b | | | • | | • | • | • | | • | • | • | | |
| 111 | eb | | | | • | | | • | | | | | | |
| 94 | wb | | | | • | | | • | | | | | | |
| 10 | b | 1 | • | • | | • | • | • | | • | • | • | | |

Notes: 1) Welcome Center eb, Rest Area wb

| Exit | ↗ | * | W | S | K | T | Am | FJ | Lo | Pe | Pi | Sp | TA | Wi |
|---|---|---|---|---|---|---|---|---|---|---|---|---|---|---|
| 325 | b | | | | | | | | | | • | | | |

| Exit | ↗ | * | W | S | K | T | Am | FJ | Lo | Pe | Pi | Sp | TA | Wi |
|---|---|---|---|---|---|---|---|---|---|---|---|---|---|---|
| 308 | b | | n | | | | | | | | | | | |
| 287 | b | | | | | | | | • | | | | | |
| 264ab | b | | n+ | | | | | | | | | | | |
| 240ab | b | | n | | | | | | | | | | | |
| 221 | b | | | | | | | | • | | | | | |
| 200 | b | | | | | | | | • | | | | | |
| 186 | b | | | s+ | | | | | | | | | | |
| 185 | b | | n | | | | | | | | | | | |
| 166 | b | | | | | | | | • | | | | | |
| 157a | b | | | s | | | | | | | | | | |
| 127 | b | 1 | | | | | | | | • | • | | | |
| 144 | b | | n | s | | | | | | | | | | |
| 142 | b | | | | | | | | | | | | • | |
| 140 | b | | | | | | | • | • | | | | • | • |
| 136 | b | | n | | | | | | | | | | | |
| 123 | b | | n | | | | | | | | | | | |
| 108 | b | | | | | | | | • | | | | | |
| 82 | b | | n | | | | | | | | | | | |
| 71 | b | | | | | | | | • | | | | | |
| 65 | b | | | | n | | | | | | | | | |
| 41 | b | | | | | | | | • | | | | | |
| 26 | b | | | | | | | | | | | | • | |
| 20 | b | | | | | | | • | | | | | | |
| 7 | b | | | | | | | | • | | | | | |

Notes: 1) Also I-35 / Follows I-35 numbering

44

Interstate 44 runs east to west for about 329 miles from the Missouri state line to the Texas state line. Part of it is shared with I-35. Much of I-44 is part of Oklahoma's toll-highway system.

| Mile Marker | ↗ | * | ? | ↗ | Tree/Picnic | Restrooms | Phone | Picnic Table | Vending | RV | Pet | Handicap | Camera | Other |
|---|---|---|---|---|---|---|---|---|---|---|---|---|---|---|
| 314 | wb | 1 | • | | | • | • | • | | | | • | | |
| 312 | eb | | | | • | | • | • | | | | | | |
| 310 | wb | | | | • | | • | • | | | | | | |
| 299 | eb | | | | • | | | • | | | | | | |
| 288 | b | 2 | | • | | • | • | • | | | | • | | |
| 271 | wb | | | | • | | | • | | | | | | |
| 269 | eb | | | | • | | | • | | | | | | |
| 256 | wb | | | | • | | • | • | | | | | | |

| Mile Marker | | * | ? | | | | | | | | | | | |
|---|---|---|---|---|---|---|---|---|---|---|---|---|---|---|
| 207 | wb | 1 | | • | | • | • | • | | | | • | | |
| 205 | wb | | | | • | | | • | | | | | | |
| 204 | eb | | | | • | | | • | | | | | | |
| 197 | eb | 2 | | • | | • | • | • | | | | • | | |
| 191 | wb | | | | • | | | • | | | | | | |
| 189 | eb | | | | • | | | • | | | | | | |
| 178 | b | 2 | | • | | • | • | • | | | | • | | |
| 171 | eb | | | | • | | • | • | | | | | | |
| 166 | wb | | | | • | | • | • | | | | | | |
| 153 | b | | | | • | | • | • | | | | | | |
| 100 | eb | | | | • | | | • | | | | | | |
| 96 | wb | | | | • | | | • | | | | | | |
| 85 | b | 2 | | • | | • | • | • | | | | • | | |
| 63 | wb | | | | • | | | • | | | | | | |
| 60 | eb | | | | • | | | • | | | | | | |
| 20 | b | 2 | • | | | • | • | • | • | | | • | | |

Notes: 1) Service Area, Gas; 2) Service Area, Gas, Food

| Exit | | * | W | S | K | T | Am | FJ | Lo | Pe | Pi | Sp | TA | Wi |
|---|---|---|---|---|---|---|---|---|---|---|---|---|---|---|
| 289 | b | | n | | | | | | | | | | | |
| 283 | b | | | | | | • | | | | | | | |
| 236 | b | | | | | | | • | | | | | | |
| 233 | b | | | | s | | | | | | | | | |
| 230 | b | | s+ | s | | | | | | | | | | |
| 228 | b | | | | s | | | | | | | | | |
| 196 | b | | s | | | | | | | | | | | |
| 166 | b | 1 | s+ | | | | | | | | | | | |
| 137 | b | 2 | | | | | • | • | • | | | | | |
| 126 | b | | n | | | | | | | | | | | |
| 108 | b | | n | | | | | | | | | | | |
| 80 | b | | s | | | | | | | | | | | |
| 45 | b | | | | | | | | • | | | | | |

Notes: 1) On Oklahoma Hwy 66; 2) Also I-35 / Follows I-35 numbering

240

Interstate 240 in Oklahoma City is 16 miles long. It runs east to west between I-40 and I-44.

| Exit | | * | W | S | K | T | Am | FJ | Lo | Pe | Pi | Sp | TA | Wi |
|---|---|---|---|---|---|---|---|---|---|---|---|---|---|---|
| 1c | b | | n | | | | | | | | | | | |

# Oregon

**Rest Area Usage:** There is a 12 hour stay limit and overnight parking is permitted. Camping is not allowed. **Road Conditions:** 800-977-6368 or 503-588-2941 (general) **State Police:** *General*, 503-378-3720; *Emergency*, 911 **Tourism Contact:** Oregon Tourism Commission, 775 Summer St NE, Salem OR 97310. *Phone*: 800-547-7842 or 503-986-0000. *Internet*: www.traveloregon.com

Interstate 5 runs north to south for 308 miles from the Washington state line to the California state line.

N ↕ S

| Mile Marker | ↗ | * | Info | Arrow | Trees | Restrooms | Phone | Picnic | Vending | Building | Pets | Handicap | Camera | Truck |
|---|---|---|---|---|---|---|---|---|---|---|---|---|---|---|
| 307 | b | | • | | | • | • | | | | | • | | |
| 281 | b | | | • | | • | • | • | • | | • | • | | |
| 240 | b | | | • | | • | • | • | • | | • | • | | |
| 206 | b | | | • | | • | • | • | • | | • | • | | |
| 178 | b | | | • | | • | • | • | • | | • | • | | |
| 144 | sb | | | • | | • | • | • | | | • | • | | |
| 143 | nb | | | • | | • | • | • | | | • | • | | |
| 112 | b | 1 | | • | | • | • | • | • | | • | • | | |
| 82 | b | | | • | | • | • | • | | | • | • | | |
| 63 | b | 2 | | • | | • | • | • | • | | • | • | | |
| 45 | b | 3 | | • | | • | • | • | | | • | • | | |
| 22 | sb | | | • | | • | • | • | • | | • | • | | |
| 14 | b | | • | | | • | • | • | • | | | • | | |
| 9 | nb | | | | | | | | | | | | | • |
| 6 | nb | | | | | | | | | | | | | • |

Notes: 1) Vending Machines nb only; 2) Vending Machines sb only; 3) West at exit to Rest Area / Valley of the Rogue State Park

N ↕ S

| Exit | ↗ | * | W | S | K | T | Am | FJ | Lo | Pe | Pi | Sp | TA | Wi |
|---|---|---|---|---|---|---|---|---|---|---|---|---|---|---|
| 308 | b | | | | w | w | | | | | | | | |
| 307 | b | | | | | | • | | | | | | | |
| 289 | b | | | | w | | | | | | | | | |
| 278 | b | | | | | | | | | | | | • | |
| 271 | b | | e | | | | | | | | | | | |
| 263 | b | | | | | | | | | | • | | | |

| Exit | | * | W | S | K | T | Am | FJ | Lo | Pe | Pi | Sp | TA | Wi |
|---|---|---|---|---|---|---|---|---|---|---|---|---|---|---|
| 256 | b | | | | | e | | | | | | | | |
| 253 | b | | | | w | | | | | | | | | |
| 234 | b | | | | w | | | | | | | | | |
| 199 | b | | | | | | | | | | | | • | |
| 195ab | b | | | | | e | | | | | | | | |
| 174 | b | | e | | | | | | | | | | | |
| 148 | b | | | | | | | | | | • | | | |
| 127 | b | | w | | w | | | | | | | | | |
| 55 | b | | w | | | | | | | | | | | |
| 33 | b | | | | | | | | | | • | | | |
| 30 | b | | e+ | | | w | | | | | | | | |
| 27 | b | | | | w | | | | | | | | | |
| 24 | b | | | | | | | | | • | | | | |
| 21 | b | | w | | | | | | | | | | | |

82

Interstate 82 in Oregon is a short 11-mile route running from the Washington state line to I-84 exit 179.

| Mile Marker | | * | | | | | | | | | | | | |
|---|---|---|---|---|---|---|---|---|---|---|---|---|---|---|
| 1 | b | | • | | | • | • | | | | | • | | |

84

I-84 runs east to west for approximately 378 miles from the Idaho state line to I-5 in Portland.

| Mile Marker | | * | | | | | | | | | | | | |
|---|---|---|---|---|---|---|---|---|---|---|---|---|---|---|
| 377 | wb | | • | | | • | • | • | • | | • | • | | |
| 335 | b | | | • | | • | • | • | • | | • | • | | |
| 295 | b | | | • | | • | • | • | • | | • | • | | |
| 269 | b | | | • | | • | • | • | • | • | • | • | | |
| 254 | b | | | | • | | | | | | | | • | |
| 228 | b | | | • | | • | • | • | • | • | • | • | | |
| 223 | wb | | | | • | | | | | | | | • | |
| 222 | wb | | | | | | | | | | | | | • |
| 221 | eb | | | | • | | | | | | | | • | |
| 220 | wb | | | | | | | | | | | | | • |
| 187 | b | | | • | | • | • | • | • | | • | • | | |
| 160 | b | | | • | | • | • | • | • | | • | • | | |
| 136 | wb | | | | • | | | • | | | | | • | |

| Mile Marker | | * | | | | | | | | | | | | |
|---|---|---|---|---|---|---|---|---|---|---|---|---|---|---|
| 112 | b | | | | • | | | | | | | | | |
| 73 | b | 1 | | • | | • | • | • | | • | • | • | | |
| 66 | wb | 2 | | • | | • | | • | | | | | | |
| 61 | wb | | | | • | | | | | | | | | |
| 58 | eb | | | | • | | | | | | | | • | |
| 53 | eb | 3 | | • | | • | • | • | | | | | | |
| 49 | eb | | | | • | | | | | | | | | |
| 23 | wb | | | | • | | | | | | | | • | |

Notes: 1) RV dump eb / camping in Memaloose State Park; 2) Koberg Beach State Park; 3) Starvation Creek State Park

| Exit | | * | W | S | K | T | Am | FJ | Lo | Pe | Pi | Sp | TA | Wi |
|---|---|---|---|---|---|---|---|---|---|---|---|---|---|---|
| 376 | b | | n | | n | | | | | | • | | | |
| 304 | b | | | | | | • | | | | | | | |
| 265 | b | | | | | | | • | | | | | | |
| 261 | b | | n | | | | | | | | | | | |
| 209 | b | | n | | | | | | | | | | | |
| 188 | b | | | | | | | | | | • | | | |
| 104 | b | | | | | | | | | | • | | | |
| 83 | b | | | | s | | | | | | | | | |
| 62 | b | | s | | | | | | | | | | | |
| 17 | b | | | | | | | • | | | | | • | |
| 16 | b | | n | | | | | | | | | | | |

205

Interstate 205 is a 37-mile route in Oregon and Washington. It forms an open loop around the Portland area. See Washington for that state's part of the Interstate.

| Mile Marker | | * | | | | | | | | | | | | |
|---|---|---|---|---|---|---|---|---|---|---|---|---|---|---|
| 7 | nb | | | | • | | | | | | | | • | |

| Exit | | * | W | S | K | T | Am | FJ | Lo | Pe | Pi | Sp | TA | Wi |
|---|---|---|---|---|---|---|---|---|---|---|---|---|---|---|
| 19 | b | | w | | | | | | | | | | | |
| 14 | b | | | | | w | | | | | | | | |
| 13 | b | | | | w | | | | | | | | | |

## Pennsylvania

**Rest Area Usage:** There is a 2 hour stay limit unless otherwise posted. No camping or overnight parking is permitted. **Road Conditions:** 888-783-6783 (general) **State Police:** *General*, 717-783-5599; *Emergency*, 911 **Tourism Contact:** Pennsylvania Center for Travel, Tourism, & Film Promotion, 404 Forum Bldg, Harrisburg PA 17120. *Phone*: 800-847-4872. *Internet*: www.experiencepa.com

I-70 runs east to west for about 173 miles from the Maryland state line to the West Virginia state line. Portions are also shared with I-76, I-79, and the Pennsylvania Turnpike.

E ↕ W

| Mile Marker | ↗ | * | [?] | [↗] | [tree] | [restrooms] | [phone] | [picnic] | [vending] | [RV] | [pet] | [handicap] | [camera] | [icon] |
|---|---|---|---|---|---|---|---|---|---|---|---|---|---|---|
| 173 | wb | | • | | | • | • | • | • | | • | • | | |
| 156 | eb | | | • | | • | • | • | • | | • | • | | |
| 150 | wb | 2 | | | • | | | | | | | | | |
| 148 | b | 1 | | • | | • | • | • | | | | • | | |
| 142 | wb | 2 | | | • | | | | | | | | | |
| 112 | b | 1 | | • | | • | • | • | | | | • | | |
| 78 | wb | 1 | | • | | • | • | • | | | | • | | |
| 5 | eb | | • | | | • | • | • | • | | • | • | | |

Notes: 1) Service Area, Gas, Food / Also I-76 and PA Tpk / Follows I-76 numbering; 2) Also I-76 and PA Tpk / Follows I-76 numbering

E ↕ W

| Exit | ↗ | * | W | S | K | T | Am | FJ | Lo | Pe | Pi | Sp | TA | Wi |
|---|---|---|---|---|---|---|---|---|---|---|---|---|---|---|
| 161 | b | 1 | | | | | | | | • | | | • | |
| 110 | b | 1 | n+ | | | | | | | | | | | |
| 43ab | b | | s | | s | | | | | | | | | |
| 32 | b | | | | | | | | | | • | | | |
| 19ab | b | 2 | n | n | s | n | | | | | | | | |
| 6 | b | | | | | | | | | • | | | | |

Notes: 1) Shared with I-76/PA Tpk / Follows I-76 numbering; 2) Shared with I-79

Interstate 76 runs east to west for about 350 miles from the New Jersey state line to the Ohio state line. Nearly all of I-76 is also the Pennsylvania Turnpike. A 33-mile portion of the Turnpike is also I-276. Part of the Interstate is also shared with I-70.

| Mile Marker | | * | ? | | | | | | | | | | | |
|---|---|---|---|---|---|---|---|---|---|---|---|---|---|---|
| 352 | b | 1 | • | • | | • | • | • | • | • | | • | | |
| 328 | wb | 2 | | • | | • | • | • | | | | • | | |
| 325 | eb | 3 | | • | | • | • | • | | • | | • | | |
| 305 | wb | 3 | | • | | • | • | • | | | | • | | |
| 290 | eb | 3 | | • | | • | • | • | | | | • | | |
| 259 | wb | 3 | | • | | • | • | • | | • | | • | | |
| 250 | eb | 3 | | • | | • | • | • | | | | • | | |
| 219 | eb | 3 | | • | | • | • | • | | | | • | | |
| 203 | wb | 3 | | • | | • | • | • | | | | • | | |
| 172 | b | 3 | | • | | • | • | • | | • | | • | | |
| 150 | wb | 4 | | | • | | | | | | | | | |
| 148 | b | 5 | | • | | • | • | • | | | | • | | |
| 142 | wb | 4 | | | • | | | | | | | | | |
| 112 | b | 5 | | • | | • | • | • | | | | • | | |
| 78 | wb | 5 | | • | | • | • | • | | | | • | | |
| 75 | eb | 3 | | • | | • | • | • | | | | • | | |
| 61 | eb | | | | • | | | | | | | | | |
| 49 | eb | 3 | | • | | • | • | • | | | | • | | |
| 41 | eb | | | | • | | | | | | | | | |
| 23 | eb | | | | • | | | | | | | | | |
| 22 | eb | 3 | • | | | • | • | • | • | | | • | | |
| 17 | eb | | | | • | | | | | | | | | |
| 13 | eb | | | | • | | | | | | | | | |
| 6 | eb | | | | • | | | | | | | | | |
| 2 | eb | | | | • | | | | | | | | | |

Notes: 1) Welcome Center wb, Rest Area eb / Service Area, Gas, Food / Also I-276 / Follows Tpk numbering; 2) Service Area, Gas, Food / Also I-276 / Follows Tpk numbering; 3) Service Area, Gas, Food; 4) Also I-70; 5) Service Area, Gas, Food / Also I-70

| Exit | | * | W | S | K | T | Am | FJ | Lo | Pe | Pi | Sp | TA | Wi |
|---|---|---|---|---|---|---|---|---|---|---|---|---|---|---|
| 351 | b | 1 | | | | n | | | | | | | | |
| 343 | b | 1 | | n+ | | | | | | | | | | |
| 226 | b | | | | | | • | • | | • | • | | | |
| 161 | b | 2 | | | | | | | | • | | | • | |
| 110 | b | 2 | n+ | | | | | | | | | | | |
| 39 | b | | n | | | | | | | | | | | |
| 28 | b | | n | | | | | | | | | | | |

Notes: 1) Shared with I-276; 2) Shared with I-70

I-78 is approximately 77 miles long. It runs east to west from the New Jersey state line to I-81 east of Harrisburg.

E ↕ W

| Mile Marker | ⤢ | * | | | | | | | | | | | | |
|---|---|---|---|---|---|---|---|---|---|---|---|---|---|---|
| 76 | wb | | • | | | • | • | • | • | | • | • | | |

| Exit | ⤢ | * | W | S | K | T | Am | FJ | Lo | Pe | Pi | Sp | TA | Wi |
|---|---|---|---|---|---|---|---|---|---|---|---|---|---|---|
| 10 | b | | | | | | • | | | | | | | |

Interstate 79 runs north to south for 183 miles from Erie to the West Virginia state line. A small segment is shared with I-70.

N ↕ S

| Mile Marker | ⤢ | * | | | | | | | | | | | | |
|---|---|---|---|---|---|---|---|---|---|---|---|---|---|---|
| 163 | b | | | • | | • | • | • | • | | • | • | | |
| 135 | b | | | • | | • | • | • | • | | • | • | | |
| 110 | sb | | | • | | • | • | • | • | | • | • | | |
| 107 | nb | | | • | | • | • | • | • | | • | • | | |
| 81 | b | | | | • | | • | • | | | | | | |
| 50 | b | | | • | | • | • | • | • | | • | • | | |
| 31 | sb | | | | • | | | | | | | | | |
| 6 | nb | | • | | | • | • | • | • | | • | • | | |

N ↕ S

| Exit | ⤢ | * | W | S | K | T | Am | FJ | Lo | Pe | Pi | Sp | TA | Wi |
|---|---|---|---|---|---|---|---|---|---|---|---|---|---|---|
| 182 | b | | | | w | | | | | | | | | |
| 147ab | b | | w | | w | | | | | | | | | |
| 78 | b | | w | | | | | | | | | | | |
| 55 | b | | | | e+ | | | | | | | | | |
| 19ab | b | 1 | e | e | w | e | | | | | | | | |

Notes: 1) Shared with I-70 / Follows I-70 numbering

Interstate 80 runs east to west for 311 miles from the New Jersey state line to the Ohio state line.

| Mile Marker | ⤢ | * | | | | | | | | | | | | |
|---|---|---|---|---|---|---|---|---|---|---|---|---|---|---|
| 310 | b | 1 | • | • | | • | • | • | • | | • | • | | |
| 295 | eb | | | • | | • | • | • | • | | • | • | | |

| | Mile Marker | ⤢ | * | ? (Information) | ↗ (Rest Area) | Scenic/Trees | Restrooms | Phone | Picnic Tables | Vending | Food | Pet Area | Handicap Access | Camera | RV Dump |
|---|---|---|---|---|---|---|---|---|---|---|---|---|---|---|---|
| E | 270 | eb | | | • | | • | • | • | • | | • | • | | |
| ↕ | 246 | b | | | • | | • | • | • | • | | • | • | | |
| W | 219 | b | | | • | | • | • | • | • | | • | • | | |
| | 194 | b | | | • | | • | • | • | • | | • | • | | |
| | 146 | b | | | • | | • | • | • | • | | • | • | | |
| | 87 | b | | | • | | • | • | • | • | | • | • | | |
| | 56 | b | | | | • | | | | | | | | | |
| | 30 | b | | | • | | • | • | • | • | | • | • | | |
| | 1 | eb | | • | | | • | • | • | • | | • | • | | |

Notes: 1) South at exit to Welcome Center and Rest Area

| | Exit | ⤢ | * | W | S | K | T | Am | FJ | Lo | Pe | Pi | Sp | TA | Wi |
|---|---|---|---|---|---|---|---|---|---|---|---|---|---|---|---|
| E | 308 | b | | n+ | | n+ | | | | | | | | | |
| ↕ | 302 | b | | | | | | • | | | | | | | |
| W | 256 | b | | | | | | | | | | • | | | |
| | 241ab | b | | s+ | | | | | | | | | | | |
| | 232 | b | | | | | | | | | | | | • | |
| | 215 | b | | | | | | | | | • | | | | |
| | 178 | b | | n+ | | n+ | | | | | | | | | |
| | 173 | b | | | | | | | | | | • | | • | |
| | 158 | b | | | | | | | | | | | | • | |
| | 120 | b | | s | | | | | | | | | | | |
| | 101 | b | | s+ | | s+ | | | | | | | | | |
| | 97 | b | | | | | | | | | | • | | | |
| | 78 | b | | | | | | | | | | | | • | |
| | 62 | b | | n | | n | | | | | | | | | |
| | 29 | b | | | | | | | | | | | | • | |

## 81

Interstate 81 runs north to south 233 miles from the New York state line to the Maryland state line.

| | Mile Marker | ⤢ | * | ? (Information) | ↗ (Rest Area) | Scenic/Trees | Restrooms | Phone | Picnic Tables | Vending | Food | Pet Area | Handicap Access | Camera | RV Dump |
|---|---|---|---|---|---|---|---|---|---|---|---|---|---|---|---|
| N | 209 | sb | | • | | | • | • | • | • | | • | • | | |
| ↕ | 203 | nb | | | • | | • | • | • | • | | • | • | | |
| S | 157 | sb | | | • | | • | • | • | • | | • | • | | |
| | 156 | nb | | | • | | • | • | • | • | | • | • | | |
| | 135 | nb | | | | • | | | | | | | | • | |

| | Mile Marker | ⤢ | * | ? | ↗ | Rest area | Restrooms | Phone | Picnic | Vending | RV | Pets | Handicapped | Camera | Trucks |
|---|---|---|---|---|---|---|---|---|---|---|---|---|---|---|---|
| N | 132 | b | | | | • | | | | | | | | | |
| ↕ | 79 | b | | | • | | • | • | • | • | | • | • | | |
| | 38 | b | | | • | | • | • | • | • | | • | • | | |
| S | 2 | nb | | • | | | • | • | • | • | | • | • | | |

| | Exit | ⤢ | * | W | S | K | T | Am | FJ | Lo | Pe | Pi | Sp | TA | Wi |
|---|---|---|---|---|---|---|---|---|---|---|---|---|---|---|---|
| | 219 | b | | | | | | | • | | | | | | |
| | 191ab | b | | e | | e | | | | | | | | | |
| | 190 | b | | | e | | | | | | | | | | |
| | 178 | b | | | | | | | | | • | | | | |
| | 175ab | b | | w | | | | | | | | • | | | |
| | 168 | b | | | | e | | | | | | | | | |
| N | 165ab | b | | | | w | | | | | | | | | |
| ↕ | 124ab | b | | | | e | | | | | | | | | |
| | 100 | b | | | | | | • | | | | | | | |
| S | 77 | b | | | | | | | | | | • | | • | |
| | 72 | b | | | | e | | | | | | | | | |
| | 65 | b | | | | e+ | | | | | | | | | |
| | 52 | b | | | | | | • | • | | • | • | | | |
| | 48 | b | | | | w+ | | | | | | | | | |
| | 45 | b | | | | e | | | | | | | | | |
| | 14 | b | | | | w | | | | | | | | | |
| | 5 | b | | | | | | | | | | | | • | |

83

Interstate 83 is 51 miles long. It runs north to south from I-81 in Harrisburg to the Maryland state line.

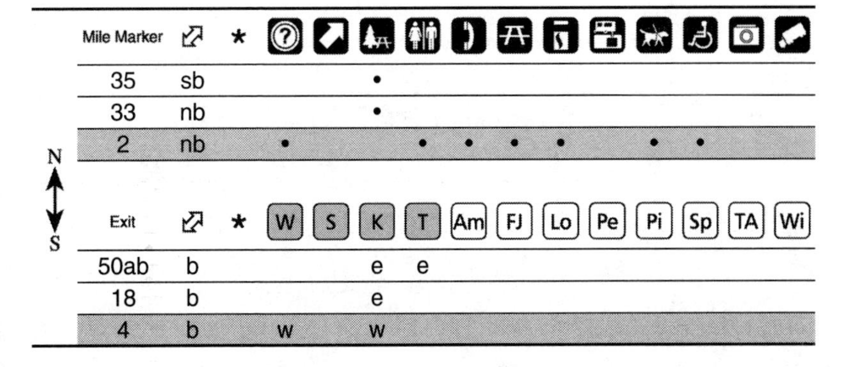

| | Mile Marker | ⤢ | * | ? | ↗ | Rest area | Restrooms | Phone | Picnic | Vending | RV | Pets | Handicapped | Camera | Trucks |
|---|---|---|---|---|---|---|---|---|---|---|---|---|---|---|---|
| | 35 | sb | | | | • | | | | | | | | | |
| | 33 | nb | | | | • | | | | | | | | | |
| N | 2 | nb | | • | | | • | • | • | • | | • | • | | |

| | Exit | ⤢ | * | W | S | K | T | Am | FJ | Lo | Pe | Pi | Sp | TA | Wi |
|---|---|---|---|---|---|---|---|---|---|---|---|---|---|---|---|
| ↕ | 50ab | b | | | | e | e | | | | | | | | |
| S | 18 | b | | | | e | | | | | | | | | |
| | 4 | b | | w | | w | | | | | | | | | |

Interstate 84 runs east to west for 54 miles from the New York state line to I-81 in Scranton.

| Mile Marker | ⤢ | * | [info] | [welcome] | [picnic area] | [restrooms] | [phone] | [picnic table] | [vending] | [RV] | [pet area] | [handicap] | [security] | [truck] |
|---|---|---|---|---|---|---|---|---|---|---|---|---|---|---|
| 53 | b | 1 | • | | | • | • | • | • | | • | • | | |
| 26 | b | | | • | | • | • | • | • | | • | • | | |

Notes: 1) North at exit to Welcome Center

| Exit | ⤢ | * | W | S | K | T | Am | FJ | Lo | Pe | Pi | Sp | TA | Wi |
|---|---|---|---|---|---|---|---|---|---|---|---|---|---|---|
| 53 | b | | s | | s | | | | | | | | | |
| 17 | b | | | | | | • | | | | | | | |

Interstate 90 runs east to west for 46 miles from the New York state line to the Ohio state line.

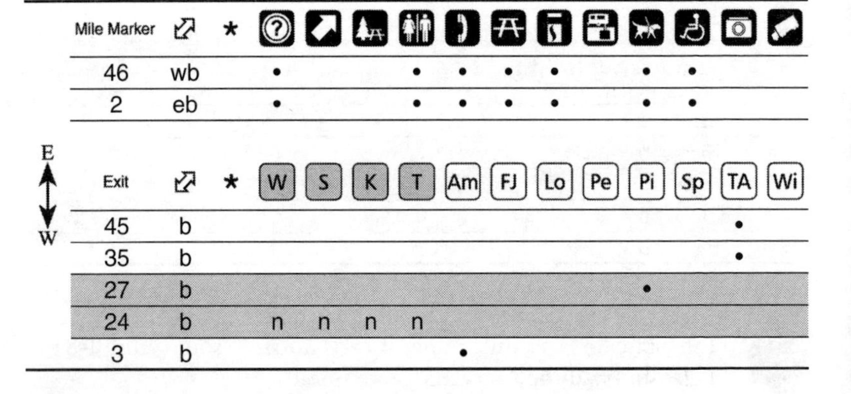

| Mile Marker | ⤢ | * | [info] | [welcome] | [picnic area] | [restrooms] | [phone] | [picnic table] | [vending] | [RV] | [pet area] | [handicap] | [security] | [truck] |
|---|---|---|---|---|---|---|---|---|---|---|---|---|---|---|
| 46 | wb | | • | | | • | • | • | • | | • | • | | |
| 2 | eb | | • | | | • | • | • | • | | • | • | | |

E ↕ W

| Exit | ⤢ | * | W | S | K | T | Am | FJ | Lo | Pe | Pi | Sp | TA | Wi |
|---|---|---|---|---|---|---|---|---|---|---|---|---|---|---|
| 45 | b | | | | | | | | | | | | • | |
| 35 | b | | | | | | | | | | | | • | |
| 27 | b | | | | | | | | | | • | | | |
| 24 | b | | n | n | n | n | | | | | | | | |
| 3 | b | | | | | | • | | | | | | | |

Interstate 95 runs north to south for 51 miles from the New Jersey state line to the Delaware state line.

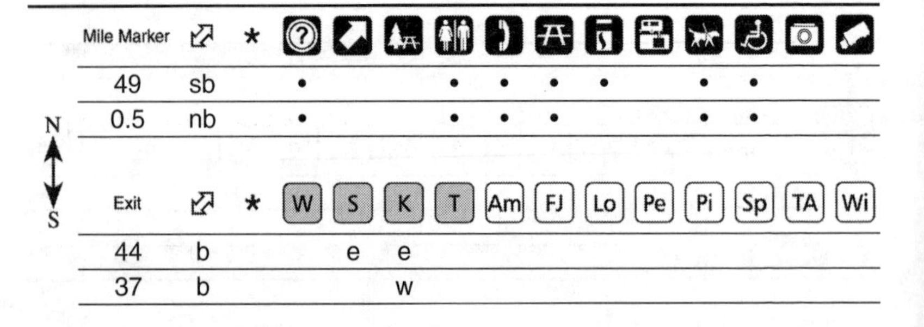

| Mile Marker | ⤢ | * | [info] | [welcome] | [picnic area] | [restrooms] | [phone] | [picnic table] | [vending] | [RV] | [pet area] | [handicap] | [security] | [truck] |
|---|---|---|---|---|---|---|---|---|---|---|---|---|---|---|
| 49 | sb | | • | | | • | • | • | • | | • | • | | |
| 0.5 | nb | | • | | | • | • | • | | | • | • | | |

N ↕ S

| Exit | ⤢ | * | W | S | K | T | Am | FJ | Lo | Pe | Pi | Sp | TA | Wi |
|---|---|---|---|---|---|---|---|---|---|---|---|---|---|---|
| 44 | b | | | e | e | | | | | | | | | |
| 37 | b | | | | w | | | | | | | | | |

| Exit | | * | W | S | K | T | Am | FJ | Lo | Pe | Pi | Sp | TA | Wi |
|---|---|---|---|---|---|---|---|---|---|---|---|---|---|---|
| 35 | b | | w+ | | | | | | | | | | | |
| 32 | b | | | | w | | | | | | | | | |
| 20 | b | | e | | | | | | | | | | | |
| 19 | b | | | | w | | | | | | | | | |
| 8 | b | 1 | w | | | | | | | | | | | |
| 6 | b | 2 | e | | | | | | | | | | | |

Notes: 1) On US 13 / Same as exit 6; 2) On US 13 / Same as exit 8

Interstate 99 is 53 miles long. It runs north to south between Bald Eagle and I-70/I-76/PA Turnpike near Bedford.

| Exit | | * | W | S | K | T | Am | FJ | Lo | Pe | Pi | Sp | TA | Wi |
|---|---|---|---|---|---|---|---|---|---|---|---|---|---|---|
| 31 | b | | e | e | w | e | | | | | | | | |

Interstate 276 near Philadelphia is about 33 miles long. It runs east to west from the New Jersey state line to I-76. It is also part of the Pennsylvania Turnpike.

| Exit | | * | W | S | K | T | Am | FJ | Lo | Pe | Pi | Sp | TA | Wi |
|---|---|---|---|---|---|---|---|---|---|---|---|---|---|---|
| 351 | b | 1 | | | | n | | | | | | | | |
| 343 | b | 1 | | n+ | | | | | | | | | | |

Notes: 1) Also Pennsylvania Turnpike

I-279 in Pittsburgh is nearly 20 miles long. It runs through downtown Pittsburgh, connecting I-79 exit 59ab with I-79 exit 72.

| Exit | | * | W | S | K | T | Am | FJ | Lo | Pe | Pi | Sp | TA | Wi |
|---|---|---|---|---|---|---|---|---|---|---|---|---|---|---|
| 4ab | b | | | | w | | | | | | | | | |

Interstate 376 in Pittsburgh is 15 miles long. It runs east to west connecting I-76/PA Turnpike with I-279.

| Exit | | * | W | S | K | T | Am | FJ | Lo | Pe | Pi | Sp | TA | Wi |
|---|---|---|---|---|---|---|---|---|---|---|---|---|---|---|
| 7 | b | | | | s | | | | | | | | | |

## Rhode Island

**Rest Area Usage:** There is no limit to length of stay and overnight parking is permitted. No camping is allowed. **Road Conditions:** No central phone number. *Internet*: www.dot.state.ri.us **State Police:** *General*, 401-444-1000; *Emergency*, 911 **Tourism Contact:** Rhode Island Travel & Tourism Division, 1 W Exchange St, Providence RI 02903. *Phone*: 888-886-9463 or 401-222-2601. *Internet*: www.visitrhodeisland.com

Interstate 95 runs north to south for 43 miles from the Massachusetts state line to the Connecticut state line. Exit numbers are based on the consecutive numbering system.

| Mile Marker | | * | | | | | | | | | | | | |
|---|---|---|---|---|---|---|---|---|---|---|---|---|---|---|
| 10 | nb | | | | • | | • | | | | | | | |
| 6 | nb | | • | | | • | • | • | • | | • | • | | |

Interstate 295 is a 27-mile open loop route around Providence. This portion is 23 miles long. It runs from I-95 exit 11 to the Massachusetts state line. See Massachusetts for that portion of the Interstate. Exit numbers are based on the consecutive numbering system.

| Exit | | * | W | S | K | T | Am | FJ | Lo | Pe | Pi | Sp | TA | Wi |
|---|---|---|---|---|---|---|---|---|---|---|---|---|---|---|
| 4 | b | | e | | | | | | | | | | | |
| 2 | b | | w | w | | | | | | | | | | |

# South Carolina

**Rest Area Usage:** There is no limit to length of stay, however, no camping or overnight parking is permitted. **Road Conditions:** No central phone number. *Internet*: www.dot.state.sc.us **State Police:** *General*, 803-896-7920; *Emergency*, 911 **Tourism Contact:** South Carolina Department of Parks, Recreation & Tourism, 1205 Pendleton St, Columbia SC 29201. *Phone*: 800-346-3634 or 803-734-1700. *Internet*: www.travelsc.com

## 20

Interstate 20 runs east to west for 142 miles from I-95 near Florence to the Georgia state line.

| Mile Marker | [Direction] | * | [?] | [Arrow] | [Trees] | [Restrooms] | [Phone] | [Picnic table] | [Vending] | [Food] | [Pets] | [Handicapped] | [Camera] | [RV] |
|---|---|---|---|---|---|---|---|---|---|---|---|---|---|---|
| 129 | b | | | | • | | | | | | | | | |
| 93 | b | | | • | | • | • | • | • | | • | • | | |
| 48 | b | | | | • | | | • | | | | | | |
| 20 | b | | | | • | | | | | | | | | |
| 0.5 | eb | | • | | | • | • | • | • | | • | • | | |

| Exit | [Direction] | * | W | S | K | T | Am | FJ | Lo | Pe | Pi | Sp | TA | Wi |
|---|---|---|---|---|---|---|---|---|---|---|---|---|---|---|
| 92 | b | | | | | | | | | | • | | | |
| 74 | b | | | | s | | | | | | | | | |
| 70 | b | | | | | | | • | | | | | | |
| 5 | b | | | | | | | | | | | • | | |

## 26

Interstate 26 is an east-west route that is 221 miles long. It runs from US 17 in Charleston to the North Carolina state line.

| Mile Marker | [Direction] | * | [?] | [Arrow] | [Trees] | [Restrooms] | [Phone] | [Picnic table] | [Vending] | [Food] | [Pets] | [Handicapped] | [Camera] | [RV] |
|---|---|---|---|---|---|---|---|---|---|---|---|---|---|---|
| 204 | eb | | | • | | • | • | • | • | | • | • | | |
| 202 | wb | | | • | | • | • | • | • | | • | • | | |
| 152 | wb | | | • | | • | • | • | • | | • | • | | |
| 150 | eb | | | • | | • | • | • | • | | • | • | | |
| 123 | b | | | • | | • | • | • | • | | • | • | | |
| 88 | wb | | | | • | | | | | | | | | |
| 84 | eb | | | | • | | | | | | | | | |
| 63 | b | | | • | | • | • | • | • | | • | • | | |

E ↕ W

| Mile Marker | | * | ? | | | | | | | | | | | |
|---|---|---|---|---|---|---|---|---|---|---|---|---|---|---|
| 43 | b | | | | • | | | • | | | | | | |
| 9 | b | | | | • | | | | | | | | | |
| 3 | eb | | • | | | • | • | • | • | | • | • | | |

| Exit | | * | W | S | K | T | Am | FJ | Lo | Pe | Pi | Sp | TA | Wi |
|---|---|---|---|---|---|---|---|---|---|---|---|---|---|---|
| 211ab | b | 1 | n | n | | | • | | | | | | | |
| 209 | b | | n | | | | | | | | | | | |
| 199ab | b | | s | | | | | | | | • | | | |
| 159 | b | | | | | | | | | | • | | | |
| 145 | b | | | | | | | | | | | • | | |
| 115 | b | | | | | | | | | | • | | | |
| 111ab | b | | n | | | | | | | | | | | |
| 108 | b | | | | n | | | | | | | | | |
| 104 | b | | | | | | | | | | | • | | |
| 103 | b | | s | s | | s | | | | | | | | |
| 76 | b | | s+ | | | | | | | | | | | |
| 52 | b | | | | | | | | | | • | | | |
| 21ab | b | | s | s | n | | | | | | | | | |

Notes: 1) Discount stores on US 52

Interstate 77 runs north to south for 91 miles from the North Carolina state line to I-26 in Columbia.

N ↕ S

| Mile Marker | | * | ? | | | | | | | | | | | |
|---|---|---|---|---|---|---|---|---|---|---|---|---|---|---|
| 89 | sb | | • | | | • | • | • | • | | • | • | | |
| 66 | b | | | • | | • | • | • | • | | • | • | | |

| Exit | | * | W | S | K | T | Am | FJ | Lo | Pe | Pi | Sp | TA | Wi |
|---|---|---|---|---|---|---|---|---|---|---|---|---|---|---|
| 82ab | b | | | | w | | | | | | | | | |
| 79 | b | | e | | | | | | | | | | | |
| 12 | b | | w | w | | | | | | | | | | |
| 9ab | b | | e | | | w | | | | | | | | |

Interstate 85 runs north to south for 106 miles from the North Carolina state line to the Georgia state line.

| N↕S | Mile Marker | ↗ | * | | | | | | | | | | | | |
|---|---|---|---|---|---|---|---|---|---|---|---|---|---|---|---|
| | 103 | sb | | • | | | • | • | • | • | | • | • | | |
| | 89 | b | | | • | | • | • | • | • | | • | • | | |
| | 23 | sb | | | • | | • | • | • | • | | • | • | | |
| | 18 | nb | | | • | | • | • | • | • | | • | • | | |
| | 0.5 | nb | | • | | | • | • | • | • | | • | • | | |

| N↕S | Exit | ↗ | * | W | S | K | T | Am | FJ | Lo | Pe | Pi | Sp | TA | Wi |
|---|---|---|---|---|---|---|---|---|---|---|---|---|---|---|---|
| | 102 | b | | | | | | | • | | | | | | |
| | 100 | b | | | | | | | | | | • | | | |
| | 92 | b | | e | | | | | | | | | | | |
| | 90 | b | | | | | | | | | | | | | • |
| | 63 | b | | | | | | | | | | • | | • | |
| | 51 | b | | e | | | w | | | | | | | | |
| | 48ab | b | | | w | | | | | | | | • | | |
| | 35 | b | | | | | | | | | | • | | | |
| | 27 | b | | | | | | • | | | | | | | |
| | 21 | b | | e+ | e+ | | | | | | | | | | |
| | 11 | b | | | | | | | | | | | • | | |
| | 4 | b | | | | | | | | | | | • | | |

95

Interstate 95 runs north to south for 198 miles from the North Carolina state line to the Georgia state line.

| N↕S | Mile Marker | ↗ | * | | | | | | | | | | | | |
|---|---|---|---|---|---|---|---|---|---|---|---|---|---|---|---|
| | 196 | sb | | • | | | • | • | • | • | | • | • | | |
| | 172 | b | | | • | | • | • | • | • | | • | • | | |
| | 139 | b | | | • | | • | • | • | • | | • | • | | |
| | 99 | b | 1 | • | • | | • | • | • | • | | • | • | | |
| | 74 | b | | | | • | | | | | | | | | |
| | 47 | b | | | • | | • | • | • | • | | • | • | | |
| | 17 | b | | | | • | | | | | | | | | |
| | 4 | nb | | • | | | • | • | • | • | | • | • | | |

Notes: 1) Welcome Center sb, Rest Area nb

| Exit | ↗ | * | W | S | K | T | Am | FJ | Lo | Pe | Pi | Sp | TA | Wi |
|---|---|---|---|---|---|---|---|---|---|---|---|---|---|---|
| 193 | b | | e | | | | | | | | | | | |
| 181 | b | | | | | | | • | | | | | | |

| | Exit | ↗ | * | W | S | K | T | Am | FJ | Lo | Pe | Pi | Sp | TA | Wi |
|---|---|---|---|---|---|---|---|---|---|---|---|---|---|---|---|
| N | 170 | b | | | | | | | | | | • | | | |
| ↕ | 169 | b | | | | | | | | | • | | | | |
| S | 164 | b | | | | | | | | | | • | | | • |
| | 160a | b | | e | e+ | e+ | | | | | | | | | |
| | 119 | b | | e+ | | | | | | | | | | • | |
| | 57 | b | | e | | e | | | | | | | | | |
| | 8 | b | | e+ | | | | | | | | | | | |
| | 5 | b | | | | | | | | | | | • | | |

Interstate 385 is 42 miles long. It runs north to south, connecting US 276 in Greenville to I-26 near Clinton.

| | Mile Marker | ↗ | * | | | | | | | | | | | | |
|---|---|---|---|---|---|---|---|---|---|---|---|---|---|---|---|
| N ↕ S | 6 | b | | | • | | • | • | • | • | | • | • | | |

| | Exit | ↗ | * | W | S | K | T | Am | FJ | Lo | Pe | Pi | Sp | TA | Wi |
|---|---|---|---|---|---|---|---|---|---|---|---|---|---|---|---|
| N ↕ S | 37 | b | | | | | w | | | | | | | | |
| | 35 | b | | e | | | | | | | | | | | |
| | 27 | b | | w | | | | | | | | | | | |

Interstate 526 is 19 miles long. It forms an open loop around Charleston.

| Exit | ↗ | * | W | S | K | T | Am | FJ | Lo | Pe | Pi | Sp | TA | Wi |
|---|---|---|---|---|---|---|---|---|---|---|---|---|---|---|
| 32 | b | | s | | s | | | | | | | | | |
| 11ab | b | | w | | | | | | | | | | | |

## South Dakota

**Rest Area Usage:** There is a 4 hour stay limit, no camping or overnight parking is permitted. **Road Conditions:** 605-367-5707 or 605-773-7515 (weather) **State Police:** General, 605-773-3105; Emergency, 911 **Tourism Contact:** South Dakota Department of Tourism, 711 E Wells Ave, Pierre SD 57501. Phone: 800-732-5682. Internet: www.travelsd.com

Interstate 29 runs north to south for 253 miles from the North Dakota state line to the Iowa state line.

| Mile Marker | ↗ | * | ? | | | | | | | | | | | |
|---|---|---|---|---|---|---|---|---|---|---|---|---|---|---|
| 251 | sb | | • | | | • | • | • | | | • | • | | |
| 213 | b | | | • | | • | • | • | | | • | • | | |
| 161 | b | | | • | | • | • | • | • | | • | • | | |
| 121 | b | | | • | | • | • | • | • | | • | • | | |
| 103 | b | | | | • | | | | | | | | | |
| 40 | b | | | | • | | | | | | | | | |
| 26 | b | | • | • | | • | • | • | | | • | • | | |

| Exit | ↗ | * | W | S | K | T | Am | FJ | Lo | Pe | Pi | Sp | TA | Wi |
|---|---|---|---|---|---|---|---|---|---|---|---|---|---|---|
| 177 | b | | w+ | | w+ | w+ | | | | | | | | |
| 132 | b | | w | | w | | | | | | | | | |
| 79 | b | | | | e | | | | | | | | | |
| 78 | b | | | e | | | | | | | | | | |
| 77 | b | | e | e | | e | | | | | | | | |

90

Interstate 90 runs east to west for 413 miles from the Minnesota state line to the Wyoming state line.

| Mile Marker | ↗ | * | ? | | | | | | | | | | | |
|---|---|---|---|---|---|---|---|---|---|---|---|---|---|---|
| 412 | b | 1 | • | • | | • | • | • | | • | • | • | | |
| 363 | b | | | • | | • | • | • | • | • | • | • | | |
| 337 | b | | | | • | | | | | | | | | |
| 302 | wb | | | • | | • | • | • | | • | | • | | |
| 301 | eb | | | • | | • | • | • | | • | | • | | |
| 293 | b | | | | • | | | | | | | | | |
| 264 | b | | | • | | • | • | • | | • | | • | • | |
| 221 | wb | | | • | | • | • | • | | • | • | • | | |
| 218 | eb | | | • | | • | • | • | | • | • | • | | |
| 194 | b | | | | • | | | | | | | | | |
| 188 | b | | | | • | | | | | | | | | |
| 167 | wb | | | • | | • | • | • | | • | • | • | | |
| 165 | eb | | | • | | • | • | • | | • | • | • | | |
| 138 | wb | | | | • | • | | | | | | | • | |
| 129 | eb | | | | • | | | | | | | | • | |
| 100 | b | | | • | | • | • | • | • | • | • | • | | |
| 69 | b | | | | • | | | | | | | | | |

| Mile Marker | [arrow] | * | [info] | [welcome] | [trees] | [restrooms] | [phone] | [picnic] | [vending] | [icon] | [pets] | [handicap] | [icon] | [RV dump] |
|---|---|---|---|---|---|---|---|---|---|---|---|---|---|---|
| 42 | b | | | • | | • | • | • | • | • | • | • | | |
| 1 | eb | | • | | | • | • | • | | • | • | • | | |

Notes: 1) Welcome Center wb, Rest Area eb / RV Dump wb only

| Exit | [arrow] | * | W | S | K | T | Am | FJ | Lo | Pe | Pi | Sp | TA | Wi |
|---|---|---|---|---|---|---|---|---|---|---|---|---|---|---|
| 399 | b | | | | | | | | | | • | | | |
| 353 | b | | | | | | | | | | | | • | |
| 332 | b | | s | | n | | • | | | | | | | |
| 66 | b | | | | | | | • | | | | | | |
| 61 | b | | | | | | | • | | | | | | |
| 60 | b | | | | s+ | | | | | | | | | |
| 59 | b | | s | s | | | | | | | | | | |
| 58 | b | | | | | n | | | | | | | | |
| 55 | b | | | | | | • | | | | | | | |
| 14 | b | | | | s | | | | | | | | | |
| 10 | b | | s | | | | | | | | | | | |

Interstate 229 in Sioux Falls is 11 miles long. It connects I-29 with I-90.

| Exit | [arrow] | * | W | S | K | T | Am | FJ | Lo | Pe | Pi | Sp | TA | Wi |
|---|---|---|---|---|---|---|---|---|---|---|---|---|---|---|
| 6 | b | | | | e | | | | | | | | | |
| 3 | b | | | | w+ | | | | | | | | | |

## Tennessee

**Rest Area Usage:** There is a 2 hour stay limit, no camping or overnight parking is permitted. **Road Conditions:** 800-342-3258 (weather), 800-858-6349 (construction) **State Police:** *General*, 615-251-5175; *Emergency*, 911 **Tourism Contact:** Tennessee Department of Tourist Development, 320 Sixth Ave N, 5th Fl, Nashville TN 37243. *Phone*: 800-462-8366 or 615-741-2159. *Internet*: www.tnvacation.com

I-24 runs east to west for approximately 185 miles from the Kentucky state line to I-75 in Chattanooga. Portions are shared with I-40 and I-65.

| Mile Marker | ↗ | * | | | | | | | | | | | | |
|---|---|---|---|---|---|---|---|---|---|---|---|---|---|---|
| 172 | eb | | • | | | • | • | • | • | | • | • | | |
| 160 | b | 1 | • | • | | • | • | • | • | | • | • | | |
| 137 | eb | 2 | | | | | | | | | | | | • |
| 136 | eb | 2 | | | | | | | | | | | | • |
| 133 | b | | | • | | • | • | • | • | | • | • | | |
| 119 | b | 3 | | | • | | | | | | | | | |
| 0.5 | eb | | • | | | • | • | • | • | | • | • | | |

Notes: 1) Welcome Center wb, Rest Area eb; 2) Ramp exit on the left; 3) Trucks only

| Exit | ↗ | * | W | S | K | T | Am | FJ | Lo | Pe | Pi | Sp | TA | Wi |
|---|---|---|---|---|---|---|---|---|---|---|---|---|---|---|
| 184 | b | | | | s | | | | | | | | | |
| 152 | b | | n | | | | | | | | | | | |
| 114 | b | | n | | | | | | | | | | | |
| 78 | b | | n | s | | n | | | | | | | | |
| 64 | b | | | | | | | | | | • | | | |
| 62 | b | | | | | | | | | | | | • | |
| 60 | b | | | | | s | | | | | | | | |
| 56 | b | | | n | | | | | | | | | | |
| 85 | b | 1 | | | | | | | | | | | • | |
| 87 | b | 1 | | | | | | | | | • | | | |
| 4 | b | | s | s | s | s | | | | | | | | |

Notes: 1) Also I-65 / Follows I-65 numbering

**40**

I-40 runs east to west for about 455 miles from the North Carolina state line to the Arkansas state line. Portions are also shared with I-24 and I-75.

| Mile Marker | ↗ | * | | | | | | | | | | | | |
|---|---|---|---|---|---|---|---|---|---|---|---|---|---|---|
| 446 | wb | 1 | • | | | • | • | • | • | | • | • | | |
| 425 | wb | | | • | | • | • | • | • | | • | • | | |
| 420 | eb | | | • | | • | • | • | • | | • | • | | |
| 363 | wb | | | | • | | • | | | | | | | |
| 362 | eb | | | | • | | • | | | | | | | |
| 340 | wb | | | • | | • | • | • | • | | • | • | | |
| 336 | eb | | | • | | • | • | • | • | | • | • | | |
| 306 | wb | | | | • | | | | | | | | | |
| 305 | eb | | | | • | | | | | | | | | |
| 267 | b | | • | | | • | • | • | • | | • | • | | |

| | Mile Marker | ↗ | * | | | | | | | | | | | | |
|---|---|---|---|---|---|---|---|---|---|---|---|---|---|---|---|
| E ↕ W | 252 | b | | | | • | | | • | | | | | | |
| | 228 | wb | | | | • | | | | | | | | | |
| | 226 | eb | | | | • | | | | | | | | | |
| | 170 | b | | | • | | • | • | • | • | | • | • | | |
| | 130 | b | | | • | | • | • | • | • | | • | • | | |
| | 103 | eb | | | | • | | • | | | | | | | |
| | 102 | wb | | | | • | | | | | | | | | |
| | 73 | b | | | • | | • | • | • | • | | • | • | | |

Notes: 1) No trucks

| | Exit | ↗ | * | W | S | K | T | Am | FJ | Lo | Pe | Pi | Sp | TA | Wi |
|---|---|---|---|---|---|---|---|---|---|---|---|---|---|---|---|
| E ↕ W | 435 | b | | s | | | | | | | | | | | |
| | 417 | b | | | | | | | | | | • | | | |
| | 398 | b | | | | | | | | | | • | | | |
| | 394 | b | | | | n | | | | | | | | | |
| | 380 | b | 1 | | | s | | | | | | | | | |
| | 379 | b | 1 | n | n | | | | | | | | | | |
| | 374 | b | 1 | s | | | s | | | | | • | | • | |
| | 369 | b | 1 | | | | | | • | | • | | | • | |
| | 347 | b | | s+ | | | | | | | | | | | |
| | 317 | b | | s | | | | | | | | | | | |
| | 287 | b | | n | | n | | | | | | • | | | |
| | 238 | b | | n | | | | | | | | | | | • |
| | 216 | b | | | | n | | | | | | | | | |
| | 201ab | b | | n | | | | | | | | | | | |
| E ↕ W | 199 | b | | | s | | | | | | | | | | |
| | 188 | b | | | | | | | | | • | | | | |
| | 182 | b | | | | | | | • | | | | | | |
| | 172 | b | | | | | | | | | | | | | • |
| | 143 | b | | | | | | | | | | • | | | |
| | 87 | b | | | | | | | | • | | | | | |
| | 80ab | b | | n | n | s | | | | | | | | | |
| | 68 | b | | | | | | | | | | | | • | |
| | 18 | b | | n | n | | | | | | | | | | |
| | 16ab | b | | | | | n | | | | | | | | |
| | 12 | b | | s | | | | | | | | | | | |
| | 12a | b | | | s | s | | | | | | | | | |

Notes: 1) Shared with I-75

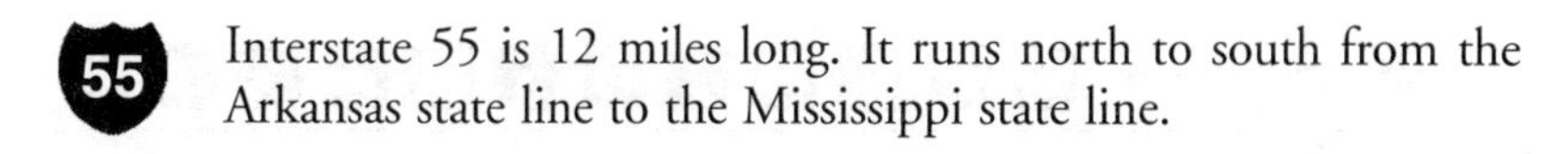

Interstate 55 is 12 miles long. It runs north to south from the Arkansas state line to the Mississippi state line.

| Mile Marker | | * | | | | | | | | | | | | |
|---|---|---|---|---|---|---|---|---|---|---|---|---|---|---|
| 3 | nb | | • | | | • | • | • | • | | • | • | | |

**65**

Interstate 65 runs north to south for 122 miles from the Kentucky state line to the Alabama state line. Part of it is shared with I-24 and I-40.

| Mile Marker | | * | | | | | | | | | | | | |
|---|---|---|---|---|---|---|---|---|---|---|---|---|---|---|
| 121 | sb | | • | | | • | • | • | • | | • | • | | |
| 48 | nb | | | | • | | | | | | | | | |
| 25 | sb | | | | • | | | | | | | | | |
| 24 | nb | | | | • | | | | | | | | | |
| 3 | nb | | • | | | • | • | • | • | | • | • | | |

| Exit | | * | W | S | K | T | Am | FJ | Lo | Pe | Pi | Sp | TA | Wi |
|---|---|---|---|---|---|---|---|---|---|---|---|---|---|---|
| 97 | b | | | | e | | | | | | | | | |
| 96 | b | | e | e | | e | | | | | | | | |
| 90ab | b | | | e | | | | | | | | | | |
| 87 | b | 1 | | | | | | | | | • | | | |
| 85 | b | 1 | | | | | | | | | | | • | |
| 69 | b | | | | | w | | | | | | | | |
| 65 | b | | w | | w | | | | | | | | | |
| 61 | b | | | | | | | | | | | | • | |

Notes 1) Shared with I-24

**75**

Interstate 75 runs north to south for 162 miles from the Kentucky state line to the Georgia state line. Portions are shared with I-640 and I-40.

| Mile Marker | | * | | | | | | | | | | | | |
|---|---|---|---|---|---|---|---|---|---|---|---|---|---|---|
| 161 | sb | | • | | | • | • | • | • | | • | • | | |
| 147 | sb | | | | • | | | | | | | | | |
| 45 | b | | | • | | • | • | • | • | | • | • | | |
| 23 | nb | | | | • | | | | | | | | | |
| 16 | sb | | | | • | | | | | | | | • | |

| Mile Marker | ↗ | * | Info | Direction | Park/Trees | Restrooms | Phone | Picnic | Vending | RV | Pets | Handicap | Camera | Truck |
|---|---|---|---|---|---|---|---|---|---|---|---|---|---|---|
| 13 | sb | | | | • | | • | | | | | | | |
| 0.5 | nb | | • | | | • | • | • | • | | • | • | | |

| Exit | ↗ | * | W | S | K | T | Am | FJ | Lo | Pe | Pi | Sp | TA | Wi |
|---|---|---|---|---|---|---|---|---|---|---|---|---|---|---|
| 141 | b | | | | | | | | | | • | | | |
| 3b | b | 1 | | | w | | | | | | | | | |
| 380 | b | 2 | | | e | | | | | | | | | |
| 379 | b | 2 | w | w | | | | | | | | | | |
| 374 | b | 2 | e | | | e | | | | | • | | • | |
| 369 | b | 2 | | | | | | • | | • | | | • | |
| 27 | b | | e+ | | e+ | | | | | | | | | |
| 5 | b | | e | | e | | | | | | | | | |

Notes: 1) Also I-640 / Follows I-640 numbering; 2) Also I-40 / Follows I-40 numbering

**81** Interstate 81 runs north to south for 76 miles from the Virginia state line to I-40 near Dandridge.

| Mile Marker | ↗ | * | Info | Direction | Park/Trees | Restrooms | Phone | Picnic | Vending | RV | Pets | Handicap | Camera | Truck |
|---|---|---|---|---|---|---|---|---|---|---|---|---|---|---|
| 75 | sb | | • | | | • | • | • | • | | • | • | | |
| 41 | sb | | | • | | • | • | • | • | | • | • | | |
| 38 | nb | | | • | | • | • | • | • | | • | • | | |
| 2 | sb | | | • | | • | • | • | | | • | • | | |

| Exit | ↗ | * | W | S | K | T | Am | FJ | Lo | Pe | Pi | Sp | TA | Wi |
|---|---|---|---|---|---|---|---|---|---|---|---|---|---|---|
| 63 | b | | | w | | | | | | | | | | |
| 36 | b | | | | | | • | | | | • | | | |
| 4 | b | | | | | | | | | | | | | • |

**155** Interstate 155 is 16 miles long. It runs east to west between Dyersburg and the Arkansas state line.

| Mile Marker | ↗ | * | Info | Direction | Park/Trees | Restrooms | Phone | Picnic | Vending | RV | Pets | Handicap | Camera | Truck |
|---|---|---|---|---|---|---|---|---|---|---|---|---|---|---|
| 9 | nb | | • | | | • | • | • | • | | • | • | | |

Interstate 240 is 19 miles long. It forms a partial loop around Memphis.

| Exit | ⤢ | * | W | S | K | T | Am | FJ | Lo | Pe | Pi | Sp | TA | Wi |
|---|---|---|---|---|---|---|---|---|---|---|---|---|---|---|
| 20ab | b | | | n | | | | | | | | | | |
| 17 | b | | s | | | | | | | | | | | |

Interstate 640 is 7 miles long. It forms a partial loop around Knoxville. Part of it is shared with I-75.

| Exit | ⤢ | * | W | S | K | T | Am | FJ | Lo | Pe | Pi | Sp | TA | Wi |
|---|---|---|---|---|---|---|---|---|---|---|---|---|---|---|
| 8 | b | | n | n | | | | | | | | | | |
| 6 | b | | | | s | n | | | | | | | | |
| 3b | b | 1 | | | n | | | | | | | | | |

Notes: 1) Shared with I-75

## Texas

**Rest Area Usage:** There is a 24 hour stay limit, overnight parking is permitted. No camping is allowed. **Road Conditions:** 800-452-9292 (general) **State Police:** *General*, 512-424-2000; *Emergency*, 800-525-5555 **Tourism Contact:** Texas Department of Economic Development, Tourism Division, PO Box 12728, Austin TX 78711. *Phone*: 800-888-8839. *Internet*: www.traveltex.com

Interstate 10 runs east to west for 881 miles from the Louisiana state line to the New Mexico state line. Part of it is shared with I-35.

E ↕ W

| Mile Marker | ⤢ | * | | | | | | | | | | | | |
|---|---|---|---|---|---|---|---|---|---|---|---|---|---|---|
| 879 | wb | | • | | | • | • | • | | | • | • | | |
| 866 | b | | | • | | • | | • | • | | | • | | |
| 837 | b | | | | • | | | • | | | | • | | |
| 789 | b | | | • | | • | • | • | | | • | • | | |
| 730 | b | | | | • | | | • | | | | | | |
| 701 | wb | | | | • | | | • | | | | | | |
| 692 | b | | | • | | • | • | • | • | | • | • | | |
| 657 | b | | | | • | | | • | | | | | | |

| Mile Marker | [icon] | * | [icon] | [icon] | [icon] | [icon] | [icon] | [icon] | [icon] | [icon] | [icon] | [icon] | [icon] | [icon] |
|---|---|---|---|---|---|---|---|---|---|---|---|---|---|---|
| 621 | b | | | • | | • | • | • | • | | • | • | | |
| 590 | b | | | • | | • | • | • | | | • | • | | |
| 531 | wb | | | | • | | | • | | | | | | |
| 529 | eb | | | | • | | | • | | | | | | |
| 514 | b | | | • | | • | • | • | • | | • | • | | |
| 503 | b | | | | • | | | | | | | | • | |
| 497 | b | | | | • | | | • | | | | | | |
| 461 | eb | | | | • | | | • | | | | | | |
| 459 | wb | | | | • | | | • | | | | | | |
| 423 | b | | | | • | | | | | | | | | |
| 394 | b | | | • | | • | • | • | | • | • | • | | |
| 349 | wb | | | | • | | | | | | | | | |
| 346 | eb | | | | • | | | | | | | | | |
| 308 | b | | | • | | • | • | • | | | • | • | | |
| 279 | eb | | | | • | | | • | | | | | | |
| 273 | wb | | | | • | | | • | | | | | | |
| 233 | b | | | • | | • | • | • | | | • | • | | |
| 185 | b | | | | • | | | • | | | | | | |
| 144 | b | | | • | | • | | • | | | • | • | | |
| 136 | wb | | | | • | | | • | | | | | • | |
| 99 | b | | | | • | | | • | | | | | | |
| 98 | eb | | | | • | | | • | | | | | | |
| 77 | wb | 1 | | | • | | | | | | | | | |
| 51 | b | | | • | | • | | • | | | • | • | | |
| 1 | eb | | • | | | • | • | • | | | • | • | | |

Notes: 1) Truck parking area

| Exit | [icon] | * | W | S | K | T | Am | FJ | Lo | Pe | Pi | Sp | TA | Wi |
|---|---|---|---|---|---|---|---|---|---|---|---|---|---|---|
| 873 | b | | | | | | | • | | | | | | • |
| 861a | b | | s | | | | | | | | | | | |
| 851 | b | | | s | | | | | | | | | | |
| 848 | b | | | | | | | | | • | | | | |
| 789 | b | | | | | | | | | | • | | • | |
| 780 | b | | s | s | | | | | | | | | | |
| 778a | b | | | | | n | | | | | | | | |
| 758a | b | | | | | s | | | | | | | | |
| 757 | b | | n | n | | | | | | | | | | |
| 751 | b | | | n | | | | | | | | | | |
| 747 | b | | n | | | s | | | | | | | | |

| Exit | ↗ | * | W | S | K | T | Am | FJ | Lo | Pe | Pi | Sp | TA | Wi |
|---|---|---|---|---|---|---|---|---|---|---|---|---|---|---|
| 732 | b | | | | | | • | | | | | | | |
| 720 | b | | s | | | | | | | | | | | |
| 696 | b | | n | | | | | | | | | | | |
| 632 | b | | | | | | | | • | | | | | |
| 583 | b | | | | | | | • | | | | | • | |
| 582 | b | | | | | | | | | • | • | | | |
| 155b | b | 1 | | | s | | | | | | | | | |
| 558 | b | | s | s | | n | | | | | | | | |
| 540 | b | | n | | | | | | | | | | | |
| 505 | b | | s+ | | | | | | | | | | | |
| 372 | b | | | | | | • | | | | | | | |
| 257 | b | | s | | | | | | | | | | | |
| 140 | b | | | | | | | | • | | • | | | |
| 37 | b | | | | | | • | | • | • | | | | |
| 32 | b | | n+ | | | | | | | | | | | |
| 30 | b | | | n | | | | | | | | | | |
| 28b | b | | n | | | | | | | | | | | |
| 28a | b | | | | n | | | | | | | | | |
| 26 | b | | n | n | | | | | | | | | | |
| 24b | b | | | | | n | | | | | | | | |
| 13ab | b | | | | n | n | | | | | | | | |
| 11 | b | | n | s | | | | | | | | | | |
| 2 | b | | | | | | | | | • | | | | |
| 0 | b | | | | | | | • | | | | | | • |

Notes: 1) Shared with I-35 / Follows I-35 numbering

Interstate 20 runs east to west for 636 miles from the Louisiana state line to I-10 near Kent.

| Mile Marker | ↗ | * | ? | | | | | | | | | | | |
|---|---|---|---|---|---|---|---|---|---|---|---|---|---|---|
| 635 | b | 1 | • | | • | • | • | • | | | • | • | | |
| 608 | b | | | • | | • | • | • | • | | | • | | |
| 574 | b | | | | • | | | • | | | | • | | |
| 538 | b | | | • | | • | • | • | • | • | • | • | | |
| 511 | b | | | • | | • | • | • | • | | • | • | | |
| 390 | b | | | • | | • | • | • | • | | • | • | | |
| 363 | eb | | | | • | | | • | | | | | | |
| 362 | wb | | | | • | | | • | | | | | | |
| 329 | wb | | | | • | | | • | | | | • | | |

| Mile Marker | ↗ | * | [information icon] | [arrow icon] | [trees/picnic icon] | [restrooms icon] | [phone icon] | [picnic table icon] | [vending icon] | [food icon] | [pet icon] | [handicap icon] | [icon] | [icon] |
|---|---|---|---|---|---|---|---|---|---|---|---|---|---|---|
| 327 | eb | | | | • | | | • | | | | • | | |
| 296 | b | | | • | | • | • | • | | | • | • | | |
| 257 | b | | | • | | • | • | • | • | | • | • | | |
| 229 | wb | | | | • | | | • | | | | • | | |
| 228 | eb | | | | • | | | • | | | | • | | |
| 204 | wb | | | • | | • | • | • | | | • | • | | |
| 191 | eb | | | • | | • | • | • | | | • | • | | |
| 168 | b | | | | • | | | • | | | | | | |
| 103 | eb | | | | • | | | | | | | | | |
| 69 | b | | | • | | • | • | • | | | • | • | | |
| 25 | b | | | | • | | | • | | | | • | | |

Notes: 1) Welcome Center wb, Roadside Turnout eb (no facilities)

| Exit | ↗ | * | W | S | K | T | Am | FJ | Lo | Pe | Pi | Sp | TA | Wi |
|---|---|---|---|---|---|---|---|---|---|---|---|---|---|---|
| 540 | b | | | | | | | | • | | | | | |
| 503 | b | | | | | | • | | | | | | | |
| 472 | b | | | | | | | • | | | | | • | |
| 470 | b | | | | | | | | | | • | | | • |
| 466 | b | | | | | | | | • | | | | | |
| 465 | b | | | s | | | | | | | | | | |
| 463 | b | | s | | s | s | | | | | | | | |
| 456 | b | | | | | n | | | | | | | | |
| 449 | b | | s | | s | n | | | | | | | | |
| 439 | b | | | s | | | | | | | | | | |
| 431 | b | | | | | s | | | | | | | | |
| 410 | b | | | | | | | | • | | | | | |
| 409 | b | | | | | | | | | • | | | | |
| 408 | b | | n | | | | | | | | | | | |
| 406 | b | | | | | | | | | | • | | | |
| 349 | b | | | | | | | | • | | | | | |
| 343 | b | | n | | | | | | | | | | | |
| 277 | b | | | | | | | • | | | | | | |
| 244 | b | | | | s | | | | | | | | | |
| 242 | b | | | | | | | | | | | | • | |
| 177 | b | | | | | | • | | | | | | | |
| 121 | b | 1 | n+ | n+ | | | | | | | | | | |
| 42 | b | | n | | | | | • | | | | | | |

Notes: 1) On TX 191

I-27 runs north to south for 124 miles from Amarillo to Lubbock.

N ↕ S

| Mile Marker | ⤢ | * | | | | | | | | | | | | |
|---|---|---|---|---|---|---|---|---|---|---|---|---|---|---|
| 97 | b | | | | • | | | | | | | | | |
| 70 | b | | | | • | | | | | | | | | |
| 29 | b | | | • | | • | • | • | | | • | • | | |

| Exit | ⤢ | * | W | S | K | T | Am | FJ | Lo | Pe | Pi | Sp | TA | Wi |
|---|---|---|---|---|---|---|---|---|---|---|---|---|---|---|
| 116 | b | | | | | | | | • | | | | | |
| 74 | b | | | | | | • | | | | | | | |
| 49 | b | | w | | | | | | | | | | | |
| 1c | b | | | | | | • | | | | | | | |

30

Interstate 30 runs east to west for 224 miles from the Arkansas state line to I-20, west of Fort Worth.

E ↕ W

| Mile Marker | ⤢ | * | | | | | | | | | | | | |
|---|---|---|---|---|---|---|---|---|---|---|---|---|---|---|
| 223 | wb | | • | | | • | • | • | • | | • | • | | |
| 191 | b | | | • | | • | • | • | • | | • | • | | |
| 144 | b | | | • | | • | • | • | • | | • | • | | |

| Exit | ⤢ | * | W | S | K | T | Am | FJ | Lo | Pe | Pi | Sp | TA | Wi |
|---|---|---|---|---|---|---|---|---|---|---|---|---|---|---|
| 223ab | b | | s | | s | | | | | | | | | |
| 220b | b | | | n | | s | | | | | | | | |
| 220a | b | | s | | | | | | | | | | | |
| 201 | b | | s | | | | | | | | | | | |
| 147 | b | | | | | | | | • | | | | | |
| 124 | b | | s | | | | | | | | | | | |
| 122 | b | | | | | | | | | | • | | | |
| 93ab | b | | s | | | | | | | | | | | |
| 70 | b | | | | | | | | • | | | | | |
| 68 | b | | | | | | | | | | | | • | |
| 67b | b | | n | | | s | | | | | | | | |
| 59 | b | | s | | n | | | | | | | | | |
| 54 | b | | | | | | | | | | | | • | |
| 52a | b | | s | s | | | | | | | | | | |
| 30 | b | | | | s | | | | | | | | | |
| 24 | b | | n | n | | s | | | | | | | | |
| 7ab | b | | n | n | | s | | | | | | | | |

Interstate 35 runs north to south for 504 miles from the Oklahoma state line to Laredo. I-35 splits into I-35E and I-35W near Hillsboro and comes together again in Denton.

| Mile Marker | | * | | | | | | | | | | | | |
|---|---|---|---|---|---|---|---|---|---|---|---|---|---|---|
| 503 | b | | | | • | | | | | | | | | |
| 502 | sb | | • | | | • | • | • | | | | • | | |
| 492 | sb | | | | • | | | • | | | | | | |
| 490 | nb | | | | • | | | • | | | | | | |
| 393 | b | 1 | | • | | • | • | • | • | | • | • | | |
| 345 | b | | | | • | | | • | | | | | | |
| 318 | b | | | | • | | | • | | | | | | |
| 311 | b | | | | • | | | • | | | | • | | |
| 281 | b | | | • | | • | • | • | • | | • | • | | |
| 256 | sb | | | • | | • | • | • | • | | • | • | | |
| 255 | nb | | | • | | • | • | • | • | | • | • | | |
| 211 | b | | | • | | • | • | • | • | | • | • | | |
| 180 | b | | | • | | • | • | • | • | • | • | • | | |
| 129 | b | | | • | | • | • | • | • | | • | • | | |
| 93 | b | | | | • | | | • | | | | • | | |
| 59 | b | | | | • | | | • | | | | • | | |
| 18 | b | | • | | | • | • | • | • | | • | • | | |
| 15 | sb | | | | • | | | • | | | | | | |

Notes: 1) I-35E

| Exit | | * | W | S | K | T | Am | FJ | Lo | Pe | Pi | Sp | TA | Wi |
|---|---|---|---|---|---|---|---|---|---|---|---|---|---|---|
| 500 | b | | | | | | • | | | | | | | |
| 498 | b | | e | | | | | | | | | | | |
| 473 | b | | | | | | | | • | | | | | |
| 471 | b | | | | | | | | | | | | • | |
| 469 | b | | | | e | | | | | | | | | |
| 464 | b | 1 | e | | | | | | | | | | | |
| 452 | b | 1 | w | w | | | | | | | | | | |
| 448ab | b | 1 | | | | w | | | | | | | | |
| 436 | b | 1 | | w | | | | | | | | | | |
| 421b | b | 1 | | w | | | | | | | | | | |
| 421a | b | 1 | | | e | | | | | | | | | |
| 415 | b | 1 | | | w | | | | | | | | | |
| 414 | b | 1 | e | | | | | | | | | | | |
| 368a | b | | w | | | | | | • | | | | | |
| 339 | b | | e | | | | | | | | | | | |

| Exit | ↗ | * | W | S | K | T | Am | FJ | Lo | Pe | Pi | Sp | TA | Wi |
|---|---|---|---|---|---|---|---|---|---|---|---|---|---|---|
| 338a | nb | | | e | | | | | | | | | | |
| 337 | b | | | e | | | | | | | | | | |
| 331 | b | | | | | | | • | | | | | | |
| 330 | b | | w+ | | w+ | | | | | | | | | |
| 328 | b | | | | | | | | | | | | | • |
| 306 | b | | | | | | | | • | | | | | |
| 304 | b | | | w | | | | | | | | | | |
| 299 | b | | | | e | | | | | | | | | |
| 261 | b | | e | | | | | | | | | | | |
| 250 | b | | e | | | e | | | | | | | | |
| 240a | b | | e | | | | | | | | | | | |
| 239 | b | | e | | | | | | | | | | | |
| 229 | b | | e | e | | | | | | | | | | |
| 228 | b | | | | | e | | | | | | | | |
| 205 | b | | e | | | w | | | | | | | | |
| 193 | b | | | | | | • | | | | | | | |
| 189 | b | | | | e | | | | | | | | | |
| 186 | b | | e | | | w | | | | | | | | |
| 170 | b | | | w | | | | | | | | | | |
| 169 | b | | | | w | | | | | | | | | |
| 165 | b | 2 | e | | | e | | | | | | | | |
| 155b | b | 3 | | | e | | | | | | | | | |
| 150b | b | | e+ | w | | w | | | | | | | | |
| 144 | b | | | | | | | | • | | | | | |
| 39 | sb | | | | | | | | • | | | | | |
| 38 | nb | | | | | | | | • | | | | | |
| 13 | b | | | | | | | | | | • | | | |
| 4 | b | | | | | e | | | | | | | | |
| 3b | b | | w | | | | | | | | | | | |
| 3a | b | | | w | e | | | | | | | | | |

Notes: 1) I-35E; 2) Shared with I-410; 3) Shared with I-10

Interstate 35W runs north to south for 85 miles. It splits from I-35 near Hillsboro and rejoins I-35 in Denton.

| Mile Marker | ↗ | * | ? | | | | | | | | | | | |
|---|---|---|---|---|---|---|---|---|---|---|---|---|---|---|
| 76 | b | | | | • | | | • | | | | | | |
| 33 | sb | | | • | | • | • | • | | | | • | | |
| 31 | nb | | | • | | • | • | • | | | | • | | |

| Mile Marker | | * | ? | | | | | | | | | | | |
|---|---|---|---|---|---|---|---|---|---|---|---|---|---|---|
| 8 | b | 1 | | | • | | | • | | | | | | |
| 7 | b | 2 | | | • | | | • | | | | | | |

Notes: 1) West at exit to parking area; 2) East at exit to parking area

N ↕ S

| Exit | | * | W | S | K | T | Am | FJ | Lo | Pe | Pi | Sp | TA | Wi |
|---|---|---|---|---|---|---|---|---|---|---|---|---|---|---|
| 65 | b | | | | | | | | | | | | | • |
| 45 | b | | | e | | | | | | | | | | |
| 42 | b | | w+ | | | | | | | | | | | |
| 40 | b | | | | | | | | • | | | | | |
| 38 | b | | | | w | | | | | | | | | |

## 37

I-37 runs north to south for 143 miles from Corpus Christi to I-35 in San Antonio.

N ↕ S

| Mile Marker | | * | ? | | | | | | | | | | | |
|---|---|---|---|---|---|---|---|---|---|---|---|---|---|---|
| 112 | b | | | | • | | | • | | | | • | | |
| 82 | sb | | | • | | • | • | • | | | | • | | |
| 78 | nb | | | • | | • | • | • | | | | • | | |
| 56 | sb | | | | • | | | | | | | | | |
| 44 | sb | | | | • | | | | | | | | | |
| 42 | nb | | | | • | | | | | | | | | |
| 19 | b | | | • | | • | • | • | • | | • | • | | |

| Exit | | * | W | S | K | T | Am | FJ | Lo | Pe | Pi | Sp | TA | Wi |
|---|---|---|---|---|---|---|---|---|---|---|---|---|---|---|
| 135 | b | | | | w | | | | | | | | | |
| 14 | b | | w | | | | | | | | | | | |
| 4a | b | 1 | w+ | | | | | | | | | | | |

Notes: 1) On TX 358

## 40

Interstate 40 runs east to west for 177 miles from the Oklahoma state line to the New Mexico state line.

| Mile Marker | | * | ? | | | | | | | | | | | |
|---|---|---|---|---|---|---|---|---|---|---|---|---|---|---|
| 175 | wb | | | | • | | | • | | | | | | |
| 173 | eb | | | | • | | | • | | | | | | |
| 150 | wb | | | • | | • | | • | | | • | • | | |

| Mile Marker | | * | | | | | | | | | | | | |
|---|---|---|---|---|---|---|---|---|---|---|---|---|---|---|
| 149 | eb | | | • | | • | | • | | | • | • | | |
| 131 | wb | | | | • | | | • | | | | | | |
| 129 | eb | | | | • | | | • | | | | | | |
| 108 | wb | | | | • | | | | | | | | | |
| 106 | eb | | | | • | | | • | | | | | | |
| 86 | b | | | • | | • | • | • | | | • | • | | |
| 76 | b | | • | | | • | • | • | | | | • | | |
| 55 | wb | | | | • | | | | | | | | | |
| 53 | eb | | | | • | | | | | | | | | |
| 32 | b | | | | • | | | • | | | | | | |
| 13 | b | | | | • | | | • | | | | | | |

| Exit | | * | W | S | K | T | Am | FJ | Lo | Pe | Pi | Sp | TA | Wi |
|---|---|---|---|---|---|---|---|---|---|---|---|---|---|---|
| 96 | b | | | | | | | | • | | | | | |
| 81 | b | | | | | | | | | | | | • | |
| 77 | b | | | | | | • | | | | • | | | |
| 76 | b | | | | | | | • | | | | | | |
| 75 | b | | | | | | | | | • | | | | • |
| 74 | b | | | | | | | | • | | | | • | |
| 72b | b | | s | | | | | | | | | | | |
| 71 | b | | | s | | | | | | | | | | |
| 68b | b | | | | s | | | | | | | | | |
| 64 | b | | | | s | s | | | | | | | | |
| 60 | b | | | | | | | | • | | | | | |

44

Interstate 44 is an east/west route that is 15 miles long in Texas. It travels from the Oklahoma state line to Wichita Falls.

| Mile Marker | | * | | | | | | | | | | | | |
|---|---|---|---|---|---|---|---|---|---|---|---|---|---|---|
| 9 | b | | | • | | • | • | • | | | • | • | | |
| 1 | b | 1 | • | | | • | • | • | | | | • | | |

Notes: 1) North at exit 1C to Welcome Center

| Exit | | * | W | S | K | T | Am | FJ | Lo | Pe | Pi | Sp | TA | Wi |
|---|---|---|---|---|---|---|---|---|---|---|---|---|---|---|
| 13 | b | | n | | | | | | | | | | | |
| 3c | b | | n | | | | | | | | | | | |

Interstate 45 runs north to south for about 286 miles from Dallas to TX Highway 87 in Galveston.

| Mile Marker | ↗ | * | | | | | | | | | | | | |
|---|---|---|---|---|---|---|---|---|---|---|---|---|---|---|
| 217 | b | | | • | | • | • | • | • | | • | • | | |
| 187 | b | | | | • | | | • | | | | | | |
| 160 | sb | | | | • | | | • | | | | • | | |
| 155 | nb | | | | • | | | • | | | | • | | |
| 126 | sb | | | • | | • | • | • | • | | • | • | | |
| 124 | nb | | | • | | • | • | • | • | | • | • | | |
| 105 | b | | | | • | | | • | | | | | | |
| 101 | nb | | | • | | • | • | • | • | | • | • | | |

| Exit | ↗ | * | W | S | K | T | Am | FJ | Lo | Pe | Pi | Sp | TA | Wi |
|---|---|---|---|---|---|---|---|---|---|---|---|---|---|---|
| 251 | b | | w | | | | | | | | | | | |
| 198 | b | | | | | | | | • | | | | | |
| 118 | b | | | | | | • | | | | • | | | |
| 116 | b | | w | | | | | | | | | | | |
| 88 | b | | w | w | | | | | | | | | | |
| 87 | b | | | | | w | | | | | | | | |
| 84 | b | | | | w | | | | | | | | | |
| 77 | b | | | | | w | | | | | | | | |
| 73 | b | | w | | | | | | | | | | | |
| 68 | b | | e | | | | | | | | | | | |
| 64 | b | | | e | | | | • | | | | | | |
| 61 | b | | | | | w | | | | | | | | |
| 60a | b | | w | | | | | | | | | | | |
| 59 | b | | w | | w | | | | | | | | | |
| 50 | b | | | | | | | | | | • | | | |
| 41b | b | | | | w | | | | | | | | | |
| 34 | b | | | | | w | | | | | | | | |
| 33 | b | | w | w | | | | | | | | | | |
| 27 | b | | | e | | | | | | | | | | |
| 26 | b | | | | e | w | | | | | | | | |
| 25 | b | | w | | e | | | | | | | | | |
| 15 | b | | e | e | | | | | | | | | | |
| 1a | b | | w+ | | w+ | | | | | | | | | |

410

Interstate 410 is a 53-mile loop around San Antonio. Part of it is also shared with I-35. Exit numbers increase in a clockwise direction.

| Exit | ↗ | * | W | S | K | T | Am | FJ | Lo | Pe | Pi | Sp | TA | Wi |
|---|---|---|---|---|---|---|---|---|---|---|---|---|---|---|
| 165 | b | 1 | e | | | e | | | | | | | | |
| 21 | b | | s | | | | | | | | | | | |
| 17 | b | | | | | n | | | | | | | | |
| 15 | b | | | | n | | | | | | | | | |
| 14 | b | | w | w | | | | | | | | | | |
| 9ab | b | | w | | | | | | | | | | | |
| 7 | b | | | | w | w | | | | | | | | |

Notes: 1) Shared with I-35 / Follows I-35 numbering

I-610 is a 38-mile loop around Houston. Exit numbering begins at Knight Road in southern Houston and increases in a clockwise direction.

| Exit | ↗ | * | W | S | K | T | Am | FJ | Lo | Pe | Pi | Sp | TA | Wi |
|---|---|---|---|---|---|---|---|---|---|---|---|---|---|---|
| 9a | b | | | | | e | | | | | | | | |
| 4b | b | | s | | | | | | | | | | | |
| 1ab | b | | | s | | | | | | | | | | |

Interstate 635 is a 37-mile route in Dallas. Exit numbering begins in Balch Springs and increases in a counter-clockwise direction.

| Exit | ↗ | * | W | S | K | T | Am | FJ | Lo | Pe | Pi | Sp | TA | Wi |
|---|---|---|---|---|---|---|---|---|---|---|---|---|---|---|
| 31 | b | | n | n | | s | | | | | | | | |
| 23 | b | | n | | | | | | | | | | | |
| 22a | b | | | | | n | | | | | | | | |
| 13 | b | | | w | | | | | | | | | | |
| 12 | b | | e | | | | | | | | | | | |
| 7 | b | | | | | e | | | | | | | | |
| 2 | b | | w | | | | | | | | | | | |
| 1b | b | | | | w | | | | | | | | | |

Interstate 820 is a 35-mile route in Fort Worth. Exit numbering begins in Benbrook and increases in a clockwise direction.

| Exit | ↗ | * | W | S | K | T | Am | FJ | Lo | Pe | Pi | Sp | TA | Wi |
|---|---|---|---|---|---|---|---|---|---|---|---|---|---|---|
| 24a | b | | | w | | | | | | | | | | |
| 23 | b | | | | e | | | | | | | | | |
| 20b | b | | n | | | | | | | | | | | |
| 10ab | b | | w | | | | | | | | | | | |

# Utah

**Rest Area Usage:** There is no limit to length of stay and overnight parking is permitted. Camping is not allowed. **Road Conditions:** 801-964-6000 or 800-492-2400 (weather) **State Police:** *General*, 801-965-4379; *Emergency*, 911 **Tourism Contact:** Utah Travel Council, Council Hall - Capitol Hill, 300 N State St, Salt Lake City UT 84114. *Phone*: 800-882-4386 or 801-538-1030. *Internet*: www.utah.com

**15** Interstate 15 runs north to south for about 403 miles from the Idaho state line to the Arizona state line. Parts are shared with I-80 and I-84.

| Mile Marker | | * | | | | | | | | | | | | |
|---|---|---|---|---|---|---|---|---|---|---|---|---|---|---|
| 370 | sb | | • | | | • | • | • | • | | • | • | | |
| 363 | nb | | | • | | • | • | • | • | | • | • | | |
| 329 | b | | | | • | | | | | | | | | |
| 153 | sb | | | | • | | | | | | | | • | |
| 151 | nb | | | | • | | | | | | | | • | |
| 137 | sb | | | • | | • | | • | • | | • | • | | |
| 126 | nb | | | • | | • | | • | • | | • | • | | |
| 88 | b | | | • | | • | • | • | | | • | • | | |
| 44 | b | | | • | | • | • | • | | | • | • | | |
| 2 | nb | | • | | | • | • | • | | | • | • | | |

| Exit | | * | W | S | K | T | Am | FJ | Lo | Pe | Pi | Sp | TA | Wi |
|---|---|---|---|---|---|---|---|---|---|---|---|---|---|---|
| 364 | b | 1 | e | | | | | • | | | | | | |
| 360 | b | 1 | | | | | | • | | | | | | |
| 346 | b | 1 | | | | | | • | | | | | | |
| 344ab | b | 1 | | e+ | e+ | | | | | | | | | |
| 342 | b | | e | | | e | | | | | | | | |
| 335 | b | | | | | e | | | | | | | | |
| 334 | b | | w | w | | | | | | | | | | |
| 322 | b | | | | | e | | | | | | | | |
| 318 | b | | | | e | | | | | | | | | |
| 308 | b | 2 | | | | | | • | | | | | | |
| 306 | b | | w | | | | | | | | | | | |
| 297 | b | | e | | | e | | | | | | | | |

| Exit | ↗ | * | W | S | K | T | Am | FJ | Lo | Pe | Pi | Sp | TA | Wi |
|---|---|---|---|---|---|---|---|---|---|---|---|---|---|---|
| 281 | b | | | | e | | | | | | | | | |
| 279 | b | | e | | | | | | | | | | | |
| 272 | b | | e | | | | | | | | | | | |
| 266 | b | | | e | e | | | | | | | | | |
| 265 | b | | | | | | | • | | | | | | |
| 263 | b | | e | | | | | | | | | | | |
| 261 | b | | | | e | | | | | | | | | |
| 260 | b | | | | e | | | | | | | | | |
| 254 | b | | | | | | | • | | | | | | |
| 222 | b | | | | | | • | • | | | | | | |
| 78 | b | | | | | | | | | | | | • | |
| 57 | b | | e+ | | e+ | | | | | | | | | |
| 39 | b | | | | | | | | | | • | | | |
| 10 | b | | e | | | | | | | | | | | |
| 4 | b | | | | | | | • | | | | | | |

N ↕ S

Notes: 1) Shared with I-84; 2) Shared with I-80

70

Interstate 70 runs east to west for 232 miles from the Colorado state line to I-15 exit 132 near Beaver.

| Mile Marker | ↗ | * | ? | ↗ | | | | | | | | | | |
|---|---|---|---|---|---|---|---|---|---|---|---|---|---|---|
| 226 | wb | | | | • | • | | • | | | | • | • | |
| 188 | wb | | • | | | • | • | • | | | | • | | |
| 178 | eb | | | • | | • | | • | | | | • | • | |
| 144 | wb | | | • | | • | | | | | | • | • | |
| 141 | eb | | | | | | | | | | | | | • |
| 140 | b | | | • | | • | | | | | | • | • | |
| 139 | eb | | | | | | | | | | | | | • |
| 120 | b | | | • | | • | | | | | | • | | |
| 114 | b | | | • | | • | | | | | | • | | |
| 102 | b | | | • | | • | | | | | | • | • | |
| 84 | b | | | • | | • | | | | | • | • | | |
| 16 | eb | | | | | | | | | | | | | • |

E ↕ W

| Exit | ↗ | * | W | S | K | T | Am | FJ | Lo | Pe | Pi | Sp | TA | Wi |
|---|---|---|---|---|---|---|---|---|---|---|---|---|---|---|
| 162 | b | | | | | | • | | | | | | | |
| 40 | b | | | | | | | • | | | | | | |
| 37 | b | | | | s+ | | | | | | | | | |

Interstate 80 runs east to west for 197 miles from the Wyoming state line to the Nevada state line. Part of it is also I-15.

| | Mile Marker | [b/eb/wb] | * | [info] | [arrow] | [trees] | [restrooms] | [phone] | [picnic] | [vending] | [map] | [pets] | [handicap] | [camera] | [truck] |
|---|---|---|---|---|---|---|---|---|---|---|---|---|---|---|---|
| | 170 | b | 1 | • | • | | • | • | • | • | | • | • | | |
| | 166 | b | | | | • | | | | | | | | • | |
| E | 147 | wb | | | • | | • | • | • | • | | • | • | | |
| ↕ | 144 | eb | | | | • | | | | | | | | • | |
| ↕ | 136 | wb | | | | | | | | | | | | | • |
| W | 101 | wb | | | | • | | | | | | | | • | |
| | 54 | b | | | • | | • | • | • | • | | • | • | | |
| | 10 | b | | | • | | • | • | • | • | | • | • | | |

Notes: 1) Welcome Center wb, Rest Area eb

| Exit | [b/eb/wb] | * | W | S | K | T | Am | FJ | Lo | Pe | Pi | Sp | TA | Wi |
|---|---|---|---|---|---|---|---|---|---|---|---|---|---|---|
| 145 | b | | s | | | | | | | | | | | |
| 308 | b | 1 | | | | | | • | | | | | | |
| 99 | b | | | | | | | • | | | | | • | |

Notes: 1) Also I-15 / Follows I-15 numbering

Interstate 84 runs east to west for about 120 miles from I-80 near Coalville to the Idaho state line. Portions are shared with I-15.

| | Mile Marker | [b/eb/wb] | * | [info] | [arrow] | [trees] | [restrooms] | [phone] | [picnic] | [vending] | [map] | [pets] | [handicap] | [camera] | [truck] |
|---|---|---|---|---|---|---|---|---|---|---|---|---|---|---|---|
| | 111 | b | | | | • | | | | | | | | • | |
| E | 94 | wb | | | • | | • | | • | | | • | • | | |
| ↕ | 91 | eb | | | • | | • | | • | | | • | • | | |
| W | 363 | wb | 1 | | • | | • | • | • | • | | • | • | | |
| | 370 | eb | 1 | | • | | • | • | • | • | | • | • | | |

Notes: 1) Shared with I-15 / Follows I-15 numbering

| | Exit | [b/eb/wb] | * | W | S | K | T | Am | FJ | Lo | Pe | Pi | Sp | TA | Wi |
|---|---|---|---|---|---|---|---|---|---|---|---|---|---|---|---|
| | 81 | b | | n | | | n | | | | | | | | |
| E | 364 | b | 1 | n | | | | | • | | | | | | |
| ↕ | 360 | b | 1 | | | | | | • | | | | | | |
| ↕ | 346 | b | 1 | | | | | | • | | | | | | |
| W | 344ab | b | 1 | | n+ | n+ | | | | | | | | | |
| | 7 | b | | | | | | | • | | | | | | |

Notes: 1) Also I-15 / Follows I-15 numbering

Interstate 215 is 29 miles long. It forms a partial loop around Salt Lake City. Exit numbers increase in a clockwise direction.

| Exit | ↗ | * | W | S | K | T | Am | FJ | Lo | Pe | Pi | Sp | TA | Wi |
|---|---|---|---|---|---|---|---|---|---|---|---|---|---|---|
| 28 | b | | | | | | | • | | | | | | |
| 13 | b | | e | | | | | | | | | | | |
| 10 | b | | | e | | | | | | | | | | |
| 9 | b | | w | | | | | | | | | | | |

## Vermont

**Rest Area Usage:** There is no limit to length of stay, however, no camping or overnight parking is permitted. **Road Conditions:** 800-429-7623 (weather) **State Police:** General, 802-244-8775; Emergency, 911 **Tourism Contact:** Vermont Department of Tourism, 6 Baldwin St, Drawer 33, Montpelier VT 05633. Phone: 800-837-6668. Internet: www.1-800-vermont.com

I-89 runs north to south for 130 miles from the United States/ Canada border to the New Hampshire state line. Exit numbers are based on the consecutive numbering system.

| Mile Marker | ↗ | * | Information | Welcome Center | Scenic/Park | Restrooms | Phone | Picnic Tables | Vending | Food | Pet Area | Handicap Access | TV/Weather | RV Dump |
|---|---|---|---|---|---|---|---|---|---|---|---|---|---|---|
| 129 | sb | | | • | | • | • | • | | | • | | | |
| 111 | b | | | • | | • | • | • | • | | • | • | | |
| 82 | b | | | • | | • | • | • | • | | • | • | | |
| 67 | sb | | | | • | | | | | | | | | |
| 66 | nb | | | | • | | | | | | | | | |
| 34 | b | | | • | | • | • | • | | | | • | | |
| 9 | b | | | • | | • | • | • | • | | | | | |

| Exit | ↗ | * | W | S | K | T | Am | FJ | Lo | Pe | Pi | Sp | TA | Wi |
|---|---|---|---|---|---|---|---|---|---|---|---|---|---|---|
| 13 | b | 1 | | | w+ | | | | | | | | | |
| 12 | b | | e | | | | | | | | | | | |
| 7 | b | | e | | | | | | | | | | | |

Notes: 1) On US 7

I-91 runs north to south for 178 miles from the United States/ Canada border to the Massachusetts state line. Exit numbers are based on the consecutive numbering system.

| Mile Marker | | * | | | | | | | | | | | | |
|---|---|---|---|---|---|---|---|---|---|---|---|---|---|---|
| 176 | sb | | • | | | • | • | • | | | • | • | | |
| 167 | b | | | | • | | | • | | | | | | |
| 154 | nb | | | | • | | | | | | | | | |
| 143 | nb | | | | • | | | | | | | | • | |
| 141 | sb | | | • | | • | • | • | • | | | • | | |
| 122 | nb | | | | • | | | | | | | | • | |
| 115 | sb | | | | • | | | | | | | | | |
| 114 | nb | | | | • | | | | | | | | | |
| 100 | b | 1 | | • | • | • | • | • | | | • | • | | |
| 68 | b | | | • | | • | • | • | • | | • | • | | |
| 39 | b | | | | • | | | • | | | | | | |
| 24 | b | | | | • | | | • | | | | | | |
| 20 | nb | | | | • | | | | | | | | | |
| 6 | nb | | • | | | • | • | • | • | | • | • | | |

Notes: 1) Rest Area nb, Roadside Turnout sb (no facilities)

Interstate 93 in Vermont is 11 miles long. It runs between I-91 and the New Hampshire state line. Exit numbers are based on the consecutive numbering system.

| Mile Marker | | * | | | | | | | | | | | | |
|---|---|---|---|---|---|---|---|---|---|---|---|---|---|---|
| 1 | nb | | • | | | • | • | • | • | | • | • | | |

## Virginia

**Rest Area Usage:** There is a 2 hour stay limit unless otherwise posted. No camping or overnight parking is permitted. **Road Conditions:** 800-367-7623 (weather) **State Police:** *General*, 804-674-2000; *Emergency*, 804-553-3444 **Tourism Contact:** Virginia Tourism Corp, 901 E Byrd St, Richmond VA 23219. *Phone*: 800-932-5827 or 804-786-4484. *Internet*: www.virginia.org

Interstate 64 runs east to west for 299 miles from I-264 in Chesapeake to the West Virginia state line. Part of it is shared with I-81.

| | Mile Marker | | * | | | | | | | | | | | | |
|---|---|---|---|---|---|---|---|---|---|---|---|---|---|---|---|
| E ↕ W | 213 | b | 1 | • | • | | • | • | • | • | | • | • | | |
| | 169 | eb | | | • | | • | • | • | • | | • | • | | |
| | 168 | wb | | | • | | • | • | • | • | | • | • | | |
| | 113 | wb | | | • | | • | • | • | • | | • | • | | |
| | 105 | eb | | | • | | • | • | • | • | | • | • | | |
| | 104 | eb | | | | • | | | | | | | | • | |
| | 100 | eb | | | | • | | | | | | | | • | |
| | 199 | wb | 2 | | • | | • | • | • | • | | • | • | | |
| | 2 | eb | 3 | • | | | • | • | • | • | | • | • | | |

Notes: 1) Welcome Center eb, Rest Area wb; 2) Also I-81 / Follows I-81 numbering; 3) No trucks

| | Exit | | * | W | S | K | T | Am | FJ | Lo | Pe | Pi | Sp | TA | Wi |
|---|---|---|---|---|---|---|---|---|---|---|---|---|---|---|---|
| E ↕ W | 290ab | b | | s | s | | | | | | | | | | |
| | 289ab | b | | | | n | s | | | | | | | | |
| | 286ab | b | | | | s | | | | | | | | | |
| | 281 | b | | | | | s | | | | | | | | |
| | 279 | b | | | | n | | | | | | | | | |
| | 263ab | b | | n | | | n | | | | | | | | |
| | 256ab | b | | | | n | | | | | | | | | |
| | 255ab | b | | n | n | | s | | | | | | | | |
| | 195 | b | | | | n+ | | | | | | | | | |
| | 183 | b | | | | n | | | | | | | | | |
| | 180 | b | 1 | | n | | | | | | | | | | |
| | 178ab | b | | s+ | | | s+ | | | | | | | | |
| | 213 | b | 2 | | | | | | | | | • | | | |
| | 205 | b | 2 | | | | | • | | | | | | | |
| | 55 | b | | n | | | | | | | | | | | |
| | 16 | b | | | | s | | | | | | | | | |
| | 14 | b | | s | | | | | | | | | | | |

Notes: 1) On Broad St; 2) Also I-81 / Follows I-81 numbering

Interstate 66 runs east to west for 77 miles from Washington, D.C. to I-81 exit 300 near Strasburg.

| Mile Marker | ↗ | * | ? | ↗ | Trees | Restrooms | Phone | Picnic | Vending | RV | Pet | Handicap | Camera | Truck |
|---|---|---|---|---|---|---|---|---|---|---|---|---|---|---|
| 48 | b | 1 | • | • | | • | • | • | | | • | • | | |

Notes: 1) Welcome Center wb, Rest Area eb

| Exit | ↗ | * | W | S | K | T | Am | FJ | Lo | Pe | Pi | Sp | TA | Wi |
|---|---|---|---|---|---|---|---|---|---|---|---|---|---|---|
| 55 | b | | n | | | | | | | | | | | |
| 47ab | b | | s | | s | | | | | | | | | |

77

Interstate 77 runs north to south for 67 miles from the West Virginia state line to the North Carolina state line. Part of it is also I-81.

| Mile Marker | ↗ | * | ? | ↗ | Trees | Restrooms | Phone | Picnic | Vending | RV | Pet | Handicap | Camera | Truck |
|---|---|---|---|---|---|---|---|---|---|---|---|---|---|---|
| 61 | sb | | • | | | • | • | • | • | | • | • | | |
| 59 | nb | | | • | | • | • | • | • | | • | • | | |
| 56 | nb | | | | | | | | | | | | | • |
| 6 | sb | | | | | | | | | | | | | • |
| 4 | sb | | | | | | | | | | | | | • |
| 3 | sb | | | | | | | | | | | | | • |
| 1 | nb | | • | | | • | • | • | • | | • | • | | |

N ↕ S

| Exit | ↗ | * | W | S | K | T | Am | FJ | Lo | Pe | Pi | Sp | TA | Wi |
|---|---|---|---|---|---|---|---|---|---|---|---|---|---|---|
| 80 | b | 1 | | | | | | • | | | | | | |
| 77 | b | 1 | | | | | | • | | | | | | |
| 41 | b | | | | | | | | | | | | • | |

Notes: 1) Also I-81 / Follows I-81 numbering

I-81 runs north to south for 325 miles from the West Virginia state line to the Tennessee state line. Portions are shared with I-64 and I-77.

| Mile Marker | ↗ | * | ? | ↗ | Trees | Restrooms | Phone | Picnic | Vending | RV | Pet | Handicap | Camera | Truck |
|---|---|---|---|---|---|---|---|---|---|---|---|---|---|---|
| 320 | sb | | • | | | • | • | • | • | | • | • | | |
| 262 | b | | | • | | • | • | • | • | | • | • | | |
| 232 | b | | | • | | • | • | • | • | | • | • | | |
| 199 | sb | 1 | | • | | • | • | • | • | | • | • | | |
| 158 | sb | | | • | | • | • | • | • | | • | • | | |
| 129 | nb | | | • | | • | • | • | • | | • | • | | |
| 108 | b | | | • | | • | • | • | • | | • | • | | |

N ↕ S

| | Mile Marker | ⇗ | * | [?] | [arrow] | [trees] | [restrooms] | [phone] | [picnic table] | [vending] | [icon] | [pet] | [handicap] | [icon] | [icon] |
|---|---|---|---|---|---|---|---|---|---|---|---|---|---|---|---|
| N | 61 | nb | 2 | | • | | • | • | • | • | | • | • | | |
| ↕ | 53 | sb | | | • | | • | • | • | • | | • | • | | |
| | 13 | nb | 3 | | • | | • | • | • | • | | • | • | | |
| S | 1 | nb | 2 | • | | | • | • | • | • | | • | • | | |

Notes: 1) Also I-64; 2) No trucks; 3) Truckers only

| | Exit | ⇗ | * | W | S | K | T | Am | FJ | Lo | Pe | Pi | Sp | TA | Wi |
|---|---|---|---|---|---|---|---|---|---|---|---|---|---|---|---|
| | 323 | b | | | | | | | • | | | | | | |
| | 313 | b | | w | | w | w | | | | | | | | |
| | 291 | b | | | | | | • | | | | | | | |
| N | 283 | b | | w | | | | | | | | | | | |
| ↕ | 247 | b | | e | | e | | | | | | | | | |
| | 222 | b | | w | | | | | | | | | | | |
| S | 213 | b | 1 | | | | | | | | | • | | | |
| | 205 | b | 1 | | | | | • | | | | | | | |
| | 150 | b | | | | | | | | | | • | | • | |
| | 143 | b | | e+ | | | e+ | | | | | | | | |
| | 137 | b | | e | | | | | | | | | | | |
| | 84 | b | | | | | | | | • | | | | | |
| N | 80 | b | 2 | | | | | | • | | | | | | |
| ↕ | 77 | b | 2 | | | | | | • | | | | | | |
| | 72 | b | 3 | | | | | | | | | | | • | |
| S | 47 | b | | w | | w | | | | | | | | | |
| | 29 | b | | | | | | | | | • | | | | |
| | 17 | b | | | | w | | | | | | | | | |
| | 7 | b | | w | | | | | | | | | | | |
| | 1 | b | | e+ | | | | | | | | | | | |

Notes: 1) Also I-64; 2) Also I-77; 3) Off I-77 Exit #41

**85** Interstate 85 is 69 miles long. It runs north to south from I-95 in Petersburg to the North Carolina state line.

| | Mile Marker | ⇗ | * | [?] | [arrow] | [trees] | [restrooms] | [phone] | [picnic table] | [vending] | [icon] | [pet] | [handicap] | [icon] | [icon] |
|---|---|---|---|---|---|---|---|---|---|---|---|---|---|---|---|
| | 55 | b | | | • | | • | • | • | • | | • | • | | |
| N | 32 | b | | | • | | • | • | • | • | | • | • | | |
| ↕ | .5 | nb | | • | | | • | • | • | • | | • | • | | |

| | Exit | ⇗ | * | W | S | K | T | Am | FJ | Lo | Pe | Pi | Sp | TA | Wi |
|---|---|---|---|---|---|---|---|---|---|---|---|---|---|---|---|
| S | 12 | b | | e | | | | | | | | | | | |

Interstate 95 runs north to south for 179 miles from the Maryland state line to the North Carolina state line.

| Mile Marker | ↗ | * | ? | | | | | | | | | | | |
|---|---|---|---|---|---|---|---|---|---|---|---|---|---|---|
| 155 | b | 1 | | • | | • | • | • | • | | • | • | | |
| 154 | b | 2 | | • | | • | • | • | • | | • | • | | |
| 131 | sb | | • | | | • | • | • | • | | • | • | | |
| 107 | b | | | • | | • | • | • | • | | • | • | | |
| 37 | nb | | | • | | • | • | • | • | | • | • | | |
| 1 | nb | 1 | • | | | • | • | • | • | | • | • | | |

Notes: 1) No trucks; 2) Truckers only

| Exit | ↗ | * | W | S | K | T | Am | FJ | Lo | Pe | Pi | Sp | TA | Wi |
|---|---|---|---|---|---|---|---|---|---|---|---|---|---|---|
| 169ab | b | | | | w | | | | | | | | | |
| 160ab | b | | | | e | | | | | | | | | |
| 158ab | b | | | | | w | | | | | | | | |
| 156 | b | | | | w | | | | | | | | | |
| 143ab | b | | w | | | | | | | | | | | |
| 130ab | b | | w | | w | w | | | | | | | | |
| 104 | b | | | | | | | • | | • | • | | | |
| 98 | b | | | | | | • | | | | | | | |
| 92 | b | | | | | | | | | | | | • | |
| 89 | b | | | | | | | | | | | | • | |
| 86 | b | | | | | w | | | | | | | | |
| 83ab | b | | w | | | | | | | | | | | |
| 61ab | b | | | | w | w | | | | | | | | |
| 54 | b | | e | e | e | e | | | | | | | | |
| 47 | b | | w | | | | | | | | | | | |
| 11 | b | | e | | | | | | | | | | | |

Interstate 295 in the Richmond area is 53 miles long. It connects I-64 with I-95 near Petersburg.

| Exit | ↗ | * | W | S | K | T | Am | FJ | Lo | Pe | Pi | Sp | TA | Wi |
|---|---|---|---|---|---|---|---|---|---|---|---|---|---|---|
| 43 | b | | s+ | | | | | | | | | | | |
| 37ab | b | | e+ | | | | | | | | | | | |

## Washington

**Rest Area Usage:** There is an 8 hour stay limit and overnight parking is permitted. No camping is allowed. **Road Conditions:** 800-695-7623 (weather) **State Police:** *General*, 360-753-6540; *Emergency*, 911 **Tourism Contact:** Washington State Tourism, PO Box 42500, Olympia WA 98504. *Phone*: 800-544-1800. *Internet*: www.experiencewashington.com

I-5 runs north to south for 277 miles from the United States/ Canada border to the Oregon state line.

N ↕ S

| Mile Marker | | * | | | | | | | | | | | | |
|---|---|---|---|---|---|---|---|---|---|---|---|---|---|---|
| 269 | sb | | • | | | • | • | • | • | | • | • | | |
| 267 | nb | | | • | | • | • | • | • | | • | • | | |
| 238 | b | | | • | | • | • | • | | | • | • | | |
| 207 | b | | | • | | • | • | • | • | • | • | • | | |
| 188 | sb | | | • | | • | • | • | • | • | | • | | |
| 140 | nb | | | • | | • | • | • | • | • | | • | | |
| 93 | sb | | | • | | • | • | • | • | | • | • | | |
| 90 | nb | | | • | | • | • | • | • | | • | • | | |
| 54 | b | | | • | | • | • | • | | | • | • | | |
| 12 | sb | | | • | | • | • | • | • | • | • | • | | |
| 11 | nb | | | • | | • | • | • | • | • | • | • | | |

N ↕ S

| Exit | | * | W | S | K | T | Am | FJ | Lo | Pe | Pi | Sp | TA | Wi |
|---|---|---|---|---|---|---|---|---|---|---|---|---|---|---|
| 256b | b | | | | | e | | | | | | | | |
| 256a | b | | e | | | e | | | | | | | | |
| 255 | b | | | | e | | | | | | | | | |
| 230 | b | | | | | e | | | | | | | | |
| 229 | b | | | | e | | | | | | | | | |
| 227 | b | | e | | | | | | | | | | | |
| 200 | b | | w | | | | | | | | | | | |
| 189 | b | 1 | | | w+ | | | | | | | | | |
| 183 | b | | e | | | | | | | | | | | |
| 182 | b | | | | | w | | | | | | | | |
| 174 | b | 2 | | w+ | w+ | | | | | | | | | |
| 173 | b | | | | | e | | | | | | | | |
| 154b | b | | | | | e | | | | | | | | |

N ↕ S

| Exit | ⤢ | * | W | S | K | T | Am | FJ | Lo | Pe | Pi | Sp | TA | Wi |
|---|---|---|---|---|---|---|---|---|---|---|---|---|---|---|
| 143 | b | | w | | w | w | | | | | | | | |
| 142 | b | | | | | | | • | | | | | | |
| 136ab | b | | | e | | | | • | | | | | | |
| 109 | b | | | | w | | | | | | | | | |
| 108 | b | | | | w | e | | | | | | | | |
| 79 | b | | w | | w | | | | | | | | | |
| 39 | b | | | | | w | | | | | | | | |
| 5 | b | | w | | | | | | | | | | | |

Notes: 1) On Evergreen Way; 2) On WA Hwy 99

**82** Interstate 82 runs east to west for 133 miles from the Oregon state line to I-90 exit 110 near Ellensburg.

E ↕ W

| Mile Marker | ⤢ | * | | | | | | | | | | | | |
|---|---|---|---|---|---|---|---|---|---|---|---|---|---|---|
| 80 | b | 1 | | • | | • | • | • | | • | | • | | |
| 24 | eb | | | • | | • | • | • | | • | • | • | | |
| 22 | wb | | | • | | • | • | • | | • | • | • | | |
| 8 | b | | | | • | | | | | | | | • | |

Notes: 1) South at exit to Rest Area

| Exit | ⤢ | * | W | S | K | T | Am | FJ | Lo | Pe | Pi | Sp | TA | Wi |
|---|---|---|---|---|---|---|---|---|---|---|---|---|---|---|
| 69 | b | | n | | | | | | | | | | | |
| 34 | b | | | | n | | | | | | | | | |
| 33 | b | | n | | | s | | | | | | | | |

**90** Interstate 90 runs east to west for about 300 miles from the Idaho state line to I-5 in Seattle.

E ↕ W

| Mile Marker | ⤢ | * | | | | | | | | | | | | |
|---|---|---|---|---|---|---|---|---|---|---|---|---|---|---|
| 299 | wb | | | • | | • | • | • | | | • | • | | |
| 242 | b | 1 | | • | | • | • | • | • | • | • | • | | |
| 199 | b | 2 | | • | | • | • | • | • | • | • | • | | |
| 162 | wb | | | • | | • | • | • | | • | • | • | | |
| 161 | eb | | | • | | • | • | • | | • | • | • | | |
| 139 | b | | | | • | | | | | | | | • | |
| 126 | b | | | • | | • | • | • | • | | • | • | | |
| 89 | b | | | • | | • | • | • | • | • | • | • | | |

Notes: 1) RV dump eb only; 2) RV dump wb only

E ↕ W

| Exit | ↗ | * | W | S | K | T | Am | FJ | Lo | Pe | Pi | Sp | TA | Wi |
|---|---|---|---|---|---|---|---|---|---|---|---|---|---|---|
| 291 | b | | s | | | | | | | | | | | |
| 286 | b | | | | | | | • | | | | | | |
| 285 | b | | | | n | | | | | | | | | |
| 276 | b | | | | | | | • | | | | | | |
| 109 | b | | | | | | | • | | | | | | |
| 106 | b | | | | | | | | | | • | | | |
| 34 | b | | | | | | • | | | | | | | |
| 15 | b | | | | | s | | | | | | | | |

I-182 is 15 miles long. It runs east to west from US 12 in Pasco to I-82.

| Exit | ↗ | * | W | S | K | T | Am | FJ | Lo | Pe | Pi | Sp | TA | Wi |
|---|---|---|---|---|---|---|---|---|---|---|---|---|---|---|
| 12a | b | | | | s | | | | | | | | | |
| 3 | b | | n | | | | | | | | | | | |

Interstate 205 is a 37-mile route in Oregon and Washington. It forms an open loop around the Portland area. See Oregon for that state's part of the Interstate.

| Exit | ↗ | * | W | S | K | T | Am | FJ | Lo | Pe | Pi | Sp | TA | Wi |
|---|---|---|---|---|---|---|---|---|---|---|---|---|---|---|
| 30 | b | | | | | w | | | | | | | | |
| 28 | b | | w | | | | | | | | | | | |

Interstate 405 is 30 miles long. It forms a partial loop around Seattle.

| Exit | ↗ | * | W | S | K | T | Am | FJ | Lo | Pe | Pi | Sp | TA | Wi |
|---|---|---|---|---|---|---|---|---|---|---|---|---|---|---|
| 10 | b | 1 | | | | e+ | | | | | | | | |
| 2 | b | | w | | | | | | | | | | | |
| 1 | b | | | | | e | | | | | | | | |

Notes: 1) On Factoria Blvd

# West Virginia

**Rest Area Usage:** There is no limit to length of stay, however, no camping or overnight parking is permitted. **Road Conditions:** 877-982-7623 (weather) **State Police:** *General*, 304-746-2100; *Emergency*, 911 **Tourism Contact:** West Virginia Division of Tourism, 2101 Washington St E, Charleston WV 25305. *Phone*: 800-225-5982 or 304-558-2200. *Internet*: www.callwva.com

Interstate 64 runs east to west for 189 miles from the Virginia state line to the Kentucky state line. Portions are shared with I-77 and the West Virginia Turnpike.

| Mile Marker | ↗ | * | [?] | [arrow] | [tree] | [restrooms] | [phone] | [picnic] | [vending] | [RV] | [pets] | [handicap] | [camera] | [truck] |
|---|---|---|---|---|---|---|---|---|---|---|---|---|---|---|
| 179 | wb | | • | | | • | • | • | | | • | • | | |
| 147 | wb | | | | | | | | | | | | | • |
| 137 | eb | | | | | | | | | | | | | • |
| 136 | eb | | | | | | | | | | | | | • |
| 45 | b | 1 | | • | | • | • | • | • | | | • | | |
| 69 | eb | 2 | | • | | • | • | • | • | | • | • | | |
| 72 | wb | 1 | | • | | • | • | • | • | | | • | | |
| 35 | b | | | • | | • | • | • | • | • | • | • | | |
| 10 | eb | | • | | | • | • | • | • | | • | • | | |

Notes: 1) Service Area, Gas, Food / Also I-77 / Follows I-77 numbering; 2) Shared with I-77 / Follows I-77 numbering

| Exit | ↗ | * | W | S | K | T | Am | FJ | Lo | Pe | Pi | Sp | TA | Wi |
|---|---|---|---|---|---|---|---|---|---|---|---|---|---|---|
| 169 | b | | s | | | | | | | | | | | |
| 95 | b | 1 | | | n | | | | | | | | | |
| 48 | b | 2 | n+ | | n+ | | | | | | | | | |
| 56 | b | | | | n | | | | | | | | | |
| 47ab | b | | s | | | | | | | | | | | |
| 45 | b | | | | | | | | | | • | | | |
| 39 | b | | | | s | | | | | | | | • | |
| 15 | b | | s | | | | | | | | | | | |

Notes: 1) Also I-77 / Follows I-77 numbering; 2) Also I-77 / Follows I-77 numbering / On US 19

Interstate 68 is 32 miles long. It runs east to west from the Maryland state line to I-79 exit 148 near Morgantown.

| Mile Marker | ↗ | * | ? | ↗ | Trees | Restrooms | Phone | Picnic | Vending | RV | Pets | Handicap | Camera | Truck |
|---|---|---|---|---|---|---|---|---|---|---|---|---|---|---|
| 31 | wb | | • | | | • | • | • | • | | • | • | | |
| 17 | eb | | | | | | | | | | | | | • |
| 12 | wb | | | | | | | | | | | | | • |

Interstate 70 runs east to west for 14 miles from the Pennsylvania state line to the Ohio state line.

| Mile Marker | ↗ | * | ? | ↗ | Trees | Restrooms | Phone | Picnic | Vending | RV | Pets | Handicap | Camera | Truck |
|---|---|---|---|---|---|---|---|---|---|---|---|---|---|---|
| 13 | wb | | • | | | • | • | • | • | • | • | • | | |

E ↕ W

| Exit | ↗ | * | W | S | K | T | Am | FJ | Lo | Pe | Pi | Sp | TA | Wi |
|---|---|---|---|---|---|---|---|---|---|---|---|---|---|---|
| 11 | b | | | | | | • | | | | | | • | |

I-77 runs north to south for 187 miles from the Ohio state line to the Virginia state line. Portions are also I-64 and the West Virginia Turnpike.

N ↕ S

| Mile Marker | ↗ | * | ? | ↗ | Trees | Restrooms | Phone | Picnic | Vending | RV | Pets | Handicap | Camera | Truck |
|---|---|---|---|---|---|---|---|---|---|---|---|---|---|---|
| 166 | b | 1 | • | • | | • | • | • | • | • | • | • | | |
| 72 | nb | 2 | | • | | • | • | • | • | | | • | | |
| 69 | sb | 3 | | • | | • | • | • | • | | • | • | | |
| 45 | b | 2 | | • | | • | • | • | • | | | • | | |
| 18 | sb | | | | • | | | | | | | | • | |
| 17 | nb | 4 | | • | | • | • | • | • | | | • | • | |
| 9 | b | | • | | | • | • | • | • | | • | • | | |

Notes: 1) Welcome Center sb, Rest Area nb; 2) Service Area, Gas, Food / Also I-64; 3) Also I-64; 4) Service Area, Gas, Food

N ↕ S

| Exit | ↗ | * | W | S | K | T | Am | FJ | Lo | Pe | Pi | Sp | TA | Wi |
|---|---|---|---|---|---|---|---|---|---|---|---|---|---|---|
| 138 | b | | e | | | | | | | | | | | |
| 95 | b | 1 | | | e | | | | | | | | | |
| 48 | b | 2 | e+ | | e+ | | | | | | | | | |
| 9 | b | | e | | w | | | | | | | | | |

Notes: 1) Also I-64; 2) Also I-64 / On US 19

Interstate 79 runs north to south for 161 miles from the Pennsylvania state line to I-77 exit 104 near Charleston.

| Mile Marker | | * | | | | | | | | | | | | |
|---|---|---|---|---|---|---|---|---|---|---|---|---|---|---|
| 159 | sb | | • | | | • | • | • | • | • | • | • | | |
| 123 | b | | | • | | • | • | • | • | • | • | • | | |
| 85 | b | | | • | | • | • | • | • | • | • | • | | |
| 49 | b | | | • | | • | • | • | • | • | • | • | | |

| Exit | | * | W | S | K | T | Am | FJ | Lo | Pe | Pi | Sp | TA | Wi |
|---|---|---|---|---|---|---|---|---|---|---|---|---|---|---|
| 152 | b | | | | w | | | | | | | | | |
| 132 | b | | e | e | | | | | | | | | | |
| 119 | b | | | | e | | | | | | | | | |
| 117 | b | | e | | | | | | | | | | | |
| 99 | b | | e | | | | | | | | | | | |
| 9 | b | | | | w | | | | | | | | | |

Interstate 81 runs north to south for 26 miles from the Maryland state line to the Virginia state line.

| Mile Marker | | * | | | | | | | | | | | | |
|---|---|---|---|---|---|---|---|---|---|---|---|---|---|---|
| 25 | sb | | • | | | • | • | • | | | • | • | | |
| 2 | nb | | • | | | • | • | • | • | | • | • | | |

| Exit | | * | W | S | K | T | Am | FJ | Lo | Pe | Pi | Sp | TA | Wi |
|---|---|---|---|---|---|---|---|---|---|---|---|---|---|---|
| 20 | b | | | | | | | | | | | | • | |
| 13 | b | | e | | | | | | | | | | | |

## Wisconsin

**Rest Area Usage:** There is no limit to length of stay, however, no camping or overnight parking is permitted. **Road Conditions:** 800-762-3947 (general) **State Police:** *General*, 608-266-3212; *Emergency*, 911 **Tourism Contact:** Wisconsin Department of Tourism & Travel Information, PO Box 7606, Madison WI 53707. *Phone*: 800-432-8747. *Internet*: www.travelwisconsin.com

I-39 is about 205 miles long. It runs north to south from US 51 in Merrill to the Illinois state line. Part of it is also shared with I-90 and I-94.

| Mile Marker | | * | ? | | | | | | | | | | | |
|---|---|---|---|---|---|---|---|---|---|---|---|---|---|---|
| 183 | sb | | | | • | • | | • | | | | | | |
| 178 | nb | | | | • | • | | • | | | | | | |
| 120 | sb | | | • | | • | • | • | • | | • | • | | |
| 118 | nb | | | • | | • | • | • | • | • | • | • | | |
| 113 | b | 1 | | • | | • | • | • | • | • | • | • | | |
| 168 | sb | 2 | | • | | • | • | • | • | | • | • | | |
| 187 | nb | 2 | • | | | • | • | • | • | | • | • | | |

Notes: 1) Also I-90 and I-94 / Follows I-90 numbering; 2) Also I-90 / Follows I-90 numbering

| Exit | | * | W | S | K | T | Am | FJ | Lo | Pe | Pi | Sp | TA | Wi |
|---|---|---|---|---|---|---|---|---|---|---|---|---|---|---|
| 208 | b | | w | | | | | | | | | | | |
| 191 | b | | | | w | | | | | | | | | |
| 188 | b | | e | e | | | | | | | | | | |
| 161 | b | | | | w | | | | | | | | | |
| 158 | b | | e | | | e | | | | | | | | |
| 92 | b | | e | | e | | | | | | | | | |
| 135a | b | 1 | | | w | | | | | | | | | |
| 132 | b | 1 | | | | | | | | | | | • | |
| 160 | b | 2 | | | | | • | | | | | | | |
| 171bc | b | 2 | w | | w | w | | | | | | | • | |
| 185 | b | 2 | w | | | | | | | | • | | | |

Notes: 1) Also I-90 and I-94 / Follows I-90 numbering; 2) Also I-90 / Follows I-90 numbering

Interstate 43 runs north to south for 192 miles from US 41 in Green Bay to I-90/I-39 in Beloit. Portions of it is shared with I-94 and I-894.

| Mile Marker | | * | ? | | | | | | | | | | | |
|---|---|---|---|---|---|---|---|---|---|---|---|---|---|---|
| 168 | b | | | • | | • | • | • | • | • | • | • | | |
| 32 | b | 1 | | • | | • | • | • | • | • | • | • | | |

Notes: 1) RV dump nb only

N ↕ S

| Exit | ⤢ | * | W | S | K | T | Am | FJ | Lo | Pe | Pi | Sp | TA | Wi |
|---|---|---|---|---|---|---|---|---|---|---|---|---|---|---|
| 183 | b | | w+ | | w+ | | | | | | | | | |
| 149 | b | | e | | | | | | | | | | | |
| 126 | b | | e | | | | | | | | | | | |
| 123 | b | | | | e+ | | | | | | | | | |
| 96 | b | | e | | | | | | | | | | | |
| 92 | b | | | | | w | | | | | | | | |
| 76 | b | | e | | | | | | | | | | | |
| 314a | sb | 1 | | | e | e | | | | | | | | |
| 9ab | b | 2 | | | e | e | | | | | | | | |
| 60 | b | | w | | | | | | | | | | | |
| 43 | b | | w | | | | | | | | | | | |
| 21 | b | | | | w | | | | | | | | | |
| 1ab | b | | w | | | | | | | | | | | |

Notes: 1) Also I-94 / Follows I-94 numbering; 2) Also I-894 / Follows I-894 numbering

Interstate 90 runs east to west for 188 miles from the Illinois state line to the Minnesota state line. Parts of it are shared with I-39 and I-94.

E ↕ W

| Mile Marker | ⤢ | * | | | | | | | | | | | | |
|---|---|---|---|---|---|---|---|---|---|---|---|---|---|---|
| 187 | wb | 1 | • | | | • | • | • | • | | • | • | | |
| 168 | eb | 1 | | • | | • | • | • | • | | • | • | | |
| 113 | b | 2 | | • | | • | • | • | • | • | • | • | | |
| 75 | wb | 3 | | • | | • | • | • | • | | • | • | | |
| 74 | eb | 3 | | • | | • | • | • | • | | • | • | | |
| 22 | wb | | | • | | • | • | • | • | | • | • | | |
| 20 | eb | | | • | | • | • | • | • | | • | • | | |
| 1 | eb | | • | | | • | • | • | • | • | • | • | | |

Notes: 1) Also I-39; 2) Also I-39 and I-94; 3) Also I-94

E ↕ W

| Exit | ⤢ | * | W | S | K | T | Am | FJ | Lo | Pe | Pi | Sp | TA | Wi |
|---|---|---|---|---|---|---|---|---|---|---|---|---|---|---|
| 185 | b | 1 | s | | | | | | | | • | | | |
| 171bc | b | 1 | s | | s | s | | | | | | | • | |
| 160 | b | 1 | | | | | • | | | | | | | |
| 135a | b | 2 | | | s | | | | | | | | | |
| 132 | b | 2 | | | | | | | | | | | • | |
| 108 | b | 3 | | | | | | | | • | | | | |
| 69 | b | 3 | | | s | | | | | | • | | | |

| Exit | ↗ | * | W | S | K | T | Am | FJ | Lo | Pe | Pi | Sp | TA | Wi |
|---|---|---|---|---|---|---|---|---|---|---|---|---|---|---|
| 55 | b | 3 | | | | s | | | | | | | | |
| 25 | b | | n | | | | | | | | | | | |
| 5 | b | | | | | s | | | | | | | | |
| 4 | b | | s | s | | | | | | | | | | |

Notes: 1) Also I-39; 2) Also I-94 and I-39; 3) Also I-94

I-94 runs east to west for about 350 miles from the Illinois state line to the Minnesota state line. Portions are shared with I-39, I-43, and I-90.

| Mile Marker | ↗ | * | | | | | | | | | | | | |
|---|---|---|---|---|---|---|---|---|---|---|---|---|---|---|
| 347 | b | 1 | • | | | • | • | • | • | | • | • | | |
| 264 | wb | | | • | | • | • | • | • | | • | • | | |
| 261 | eb | | | • | | • | • | • | • | | • | • | | |
| 113 | b | 2 | | • | | • | • | • | • | • | • | • | | |
| 75 | wb | 3 | | • | | • | • | • | • | | • | • | | |
| 74 | eb | 3 | | • | | • | • | • | • | | • | • | | |
| 124 | eb | | | • | | • | • | • | • | | • | • | | |
| 122 | wb | | | • | | • | • | • | • | | • | • | • | |
| 43 | b | | | • | | • | • | • | • | | • | • | | |
| 2 | b | | • | | | • | • | • | • | | • | • | | |

Notes: 1) North at exit to Welcome Center; 2) Also I-39 and I-90 / Follows I-90 numbering; 3) Also I-90 / Follows I-90 numbering

| Exit | ↗ | * | W | S | K | T | Am | FJ | Lo | Pe | Pi | Sp | TA | Wi |
|---|---|---|---|---|---|---|---|---|---|---|---|---|---|---|
| 333 | b | | | | | | | | | • | | | | |
| 329 | b | | | | | | | | | | • | | | |
| 322 | b | | | | | | | | | | • | | | |
| 319 | b | | s | s | | | | | | | | | | |
| 314a | sb | 1 | | | n | n | | | | | | | | |
| 297 | b | | | s | n+ | s | | | | | | | | |
| 295 | b | | s | | | | | | | | | | | |
| 287 | b | | s | | | s | | | | | | | | |
| 282 | b | | | | n | | | | | | | | | |
| 135a | b | 2 | | | s | | | | | | | | | |
| 132 | b | 2 | | | | | | | | | | | • | |
| 108 | b | 3 | | | | | | | | • | | | | |
| 69 | b | 3 | | | s | | | | | | • | | | |

E ↕ W

| Exit | ↗ | * | W | S | K | T | Am | FJ | Lo | Pe | Pi | Sp | TA | Wi |
|---|---|---|---|---|---|---|---|---|---|---|---|---|---|---|
| 55 | b | 3 | | | | s | | | | | | | | |
| 143 | b | | s | | | | | | | | | | | |
| 116 | b | | s | | | | | • | | | | | | |
| 88 | b | | | | | | • | | | | | • | | |
| 70 | b | | n | n | | n | | | | | | | | |
| 41 | b | | n | | s | | | | | | | | | |
| 4 | b | | | | | | | | | | | | • | |
| 2 | b | | s | | s | n | | | | | | | | |

Notes: 1) Also I-43; 2) Also I-90 and I-39 / Follows I-90 numbering; 3) Also I-90 / Follows I-90 numbering

## Wyoming

**Rest Area Usage:** There is no limit to length of stay, however, no camping or overnight parking is permitted. **Road Conditions:** 888-996-7623 or 307-772-0824 (general) **State Police:** *General*, 307-777-4305; *Emergency*, 911 **Tourism Contact:** Wyoming Division of Tourism, I-25 at College Dr, Cheyenne WY 82002. *Phone*: 800-225-5996. *Internet*: www.wyomingtourism.org

Interstate 25 runs north to south for 300 miles from I-90 in Buffalo to the Colorado state line.

N ↕ S

| Mile Marker | ↗ | * | [?] | [↗] | [tree] | [restrooms] | [phone] | [picnic table] | [icon] | [icon] | [pet] | [handicapped] | [icon] | [icon] |
|---|---|---|---|---|---|---|---|---|---|---|---|---|---|---|
| 274 | b | | | | • | | | | | | | | | |
| 254 | b | 1 | | • | | • | • | • | | | • | • | | |
| 219 | b | | | | • | | | | | | | | | |
| 175 | sb | | | | • | | | | | | | | | |
| 171 | nb | | | | • | | | | | | | | | |
| 153 | b | | | | • | | | | | | | | | |
| 129 | b | | | | • | | | | | | | | | |
| 126 | b | 2 | | • | | • | • | • | | • | • | • | | |
| 91 | b | | | • | | • | | • | | | • | • | | |
| 67 | nb | | | | • | | | | | | | | | |
| 65 | b | | | | • | | | | | | | | | |
| 54 | b | 2 | | • | | • | • | • | | • | • | • | | |
| 7 | b | 3 | • | | | • | • | • | | • | • | • | | |

Notes: 1) West at exit to Rest Area; 2) East at exit to Rest Area; 3) West at exit to Welcome Center

| Exit | ↗ | * | W | S | K | T | Am | FJ | Lo | Pe | Pi | Sp | TA | Wi |
|---|---|---|---|---|---|---|---|---|---|---|---|---|---|---|
| 185 | b | | w | w | w | w | | • | | | | | | |
| 7 | b | | | | | | | • | | | | | | |

**80** Interstate 80 runs east to west for about 403 miles from the Nebraska state line to the Utah state line.

| Mile Marker | ↗ | * | [?] | [↗] | [trees] | [restrooms] | [phone] | [picnic table] | [vending] | [icon] | [pet] | [handicap] | [icon] | [icon] |
|---|---|---|---|---|---|---|---|---|---|---|---|---|---|---|
| 401 | b | 1 | • | | | • | • | • | • | | • | • | | |
| 343 | b | | | | • | | | | | | | | | |
| 341 | b | | | | • | | | | | | | | | |
| 333 | b | | | | • | | | | | | | | | |
| 323 | b | 2 | | • | | • | • | • | | | • | • | | |
| 307 | b | | | | • | | | | | | | | | |
| 267 | b | 3 | | • | | • | • | • | | | • | • | | |
| 262 | b | | | | • | | | | | | | | | |
| 228 | b | 2 | | • | | • | • | • | | | • | • | | |
| 190 | wb | | | | • | | | | | | | | | |
| 189 | eb | | | | • | | | • | | | | | | |
| 144 | b | | | • | | • | • | • | | | • | • | | |
| 143 | b | | | | • | | | | | | | | | |
| 135 | b | | | | • | | | | | | | | | |
| 71 | b | | | | • | | | | | | | | | |
| 60 | b | | | | • | | | | | | | | | |
| 54 | eb | | | | • | | | | | | | | | |
| 49 | wb | | | | • | | | | | | | | | |
| 41 | b | 3 | | • | | • | • | • | | | • | • | | |
| 33 | eb | | | | • | | | | | | | | | |
| 27 | b | | | | • | | | | | | | | | |
| 14 | b | | | | • | | | | | | | | | |
| 6 | b | 1 | • | | | • | • | • | • | • | • | • | | |

Notes: 1) South at exit to Welcome Center; 2) North at exit to Rest Area; 3) South at exit to Rest Area

| Exit | ↗ | * | W | S | K | T | Am | FJ | Lo | Pe | Pi | Sp | TA | Wi |
|---|---|---|---|---|---|---|---|---|---|---|---|---|---|---|
| 377 | b | | | | | | | | | | | | • | |
| 316 | b | | n+ | | | | | | | | | | | |

| Exit | | * | W | S | K | T | Am | FJ | Lo | Pe | Pi | Sp | TA | Wi |
|---|---|---|---|---|---|---|---|---|---|---|---|---|---|---|
| 310 | b | | | | n+ | | | | | | • | | | |
| 214 | b | | | | | | • | | | | | | | |
| 209 | b | | | | | | | • | | | | | | |
| 104 | b | | | | | | | • | | | | | | |
| 102 | b | | s | | n | | | | | | | | | |
| 30 | b | | | | | | | | | | | | • | |
| 10 | b | | | | | | | | | • | | | | |
| 6 | b | | | | | | | | | | • | | | |
| 5 | b | | n | | | | | | | | | | | |
| 3 | b | | | | | | | • | | | | | | |

E ↕ W

Interstate 90 runs east to west for 208 miles from the South Dakota state line to the Montana state line.

| Mile Marker | | * | | | | | | | | | | | | |
|---|---|---|---|---|---|---|---|---|---|---|---|---|---|---|
| 189 | b | 1 | • | | | • | • | • | • | | • | • | | |
| 177 | b | | | | • | | | | | | | | | |
| 171 | b | | | | • | | | | | | | | | |
| 163 | b | | | | • | | | | | | | | | |
| 153 | b | 2 | | • | | • | • | • | | | • | • | | |
| 138 | b | | | | • | | | | | | | | | |
| 110 | b | | | | • | | | | | | | | | |
| 88 | b | 2 | | • | | • | • | • | | | • | • | | |
| 68 | b | | | | • | | | | | | | | | |
| 59 | b | | | | • | | | | | | | | | |
| 39 | wb | | | | • | | | | | | | | • | |
| 31 | eb | | | | • | | | | | | | | | |
| 23 | b | 3 | • | | | • | • | • | | | • | • | | |
| 15 | wb | | | | • | | | | | | | | | |

E ↕ W

Notes: 1) South at exit to Welcome Center; 2) North at exit to Rest Area; 3) North at exit to Welcome Center

| Exit | | * | W | S | K | T | Am | FJ | Lo | Pe | Pi | Sp | TA | Wi |
|---|---|---|---|---|---|---|---|---|---|---|---|---|---|---|
| 126 | b | | s | | s | | | • | | | | | | |
| 25 | b | | s | | | | | | | | | | | |
| 20 | b | | | | s | | | | | | | | | |